NOTES

ON

CENTRAL AMERICA;

PARTICULARLY THE STATES OF

HONDURAS AND SAN SALVADOR:

THEIR GEOGRAPHY, TOPOGRAPHY, CLIMATE, POPULATION, RESOURCES, PRODUCTIONS, etc., etc.,

AND THE PROPOSED

HONDURAS INTER-OCEANIC RAILWAY.

BY E. G. SQUIER,

FORMERLY CHARGÉ D'AFFAIRES OF THE UNITED STATES TO THE REPUBLICS OF CENTRAL AMERICA.

With Original Maps and Illustrations.

NEW YORK:

HARPER & BROTHERS, PUBLISHERS,

FRANKLIN SQUARE.

1855.

TO

CARL RITTER,

GEOGRAPHER,

This Memoir is respectfully Dedicated

BY THE AUTHOR.

CONTENTS.

MAPS AND ILLUSTRATIONS.

GEOGRAPHICAL INTRODUCTION.

In the year 1850, while occupying the position of diplomatic representative of the United States in Central America, it became requisite for me to visit the Bay of Fonseca, which has a commanding geographical position between the states of Nicaragua and San Salvador, on the Pacific Ocean. During my residence at the port of La Union, my attention was arrested by the circumstance that portions of this bay were swept by strong winds from the north, leading me to infer that there must exist an interruption in the great mountain chain of the Cordilleras, which otherwise would interpose an impassable barrier to the winds blowing from that direction. This inference was strengthened on learning that the north winds prevailed only during the period of their continuance on the Atlantic coast, and was confirmed by the additional circumstance that the current of wind reaching the Pacific was only felt over a very narrow space, not exceeding ten miles in breadth. It was with no surprise, therefore, on ascending the volcano of Conchagua, which rises above the port of La Union, that I turned my glass to the northward, and saw that the mountains of Honduras seemed to be completely interrupted in that direction.

Then, this fact only interested me as a remarkable feature in the general physical character of the country; nor was it until the autumn of 1852 that I was led to reflect upon it in connection with the subject of inter-oceanic communications. At this time the practical examination of the Isthmus of Tehuantepec, with reference to the construction of a railway between the seas, had resulted in establishing the fact of the total absence of adequate ports for the purpose upon both oceans. The project of a communication at that point had, moreover, become involved, politically, to such a degree that little hope could be entertained of its successful prosecution until a new and permanent order of things should be established in Mexico, a result which the previous history of that country gave no warrant for anticipating as likely to happen for many years.

The unwilling conviction was consequently forced upon the public mind that, in order to reach California, it would continue to be necessary to follow the tedious and circuitous route by way of the Isthmus of Panama.

It was then that the observations which I had made at La Union induced me to inquire if there might not be a feasible railway route across the continent, terminating on the Bay of Fonseca, in reference to which, and on other grounds, I had ventured the prediction that, "from its position and capacity, it must ultimately become the great emporium of trade and the centre of enterprise upon that side of the continent." I soon found that, as early as 1540, the officers of the Spanish crown had discovered a favorable passage between the seas upon this very line, and that they had founded the city of Comayagua "midway between the oceans" for the purpose of obtaining "an easy communication between the Atlantic and Pacific," by means of which "much sickness, and waste of human life, and many of the fatigues and privations which were experienced in the journey from Nombre de Dios to Panama would be avoided."

On presenting my views upon the subject to a few personal friends and public-spirited gentlemen, it was determined to incur the expense of verifying them by a direct and careful examination of the country in question. I at once proceeded to organize a competent corps of reconnaissance for the purpose, and was fortunate enough to secure the co-operation and assistance of several gentlemen of acknowledged scientific and practical ability. It will not be invidious to mention the names of Lieutenant W. N. JEFFERS, U. S. N., late Assistant Professor of Mathematics in the United States Naval Academy; Dr. S. W. WOODHOUSE, whose qualifications in the field had been fully tested in the Government Expedition to the Colorado of California, under command of Captain Sitgreaves; and Mr. D. C. HITCHCOCK, who accompanied the party as draughtsman.

The expedition sailed from the United States in the month of February, 1853, and in the month of April following commenced its operations in the field, taking the Bay of Fonseca as its point of departure. The accuracy of my previous inferences was speedily and fully verified, as will appear in the pages which follow. A line of observations and barometrical admeasurements was carried completely across the continent by Lieutenant Jeffers. A similar line was carried from Leon de Nicaragua to the city of Comayagua, in Honduras, by Dr. Woodhouse; and another by myself from Comayagua to the town of Santa Rosa, in the extreme western border of Honduras, thence to the city of San Salvador, in the state of the same name, and afterward throughout the length of that state, from Sonsonate to the port of La Union, our point of departure.

It is upon the observations made, and the facts collected in the progress of this reconnaissance, and in conducting the negotiations resulting from it, that the hurried memoir herewith presented is principally founded. And here I am free to say, that it was my original intention to confine it to a simple explanation of the MAP OF HONDURAS AND SAN SALVADOR which accompanies this volume; and I have only been led to give it its present extension and form from the conviction that the public interest in these hitherto little known yet prospectively important states would hardly be satisfied with a mere detail of their physical features and characteristics.

Yet, in attempting to present even these in an intelligible manner, I have been compelled to depend almost entirely upon my own observations. Indeed, the whole undertaking has been, I had almost said, a creation, inasmuch as there are no authorities or accredited sources of information upon which to proceed, or which might serve as a nucleus for an aggregation of facts. The former condition of Central America, under the jealous and exclusive colonial system of Spain, and the distracting and deplorable circumstances under which it has suffered since its independence, have been eminently unfavorable for every kind of local research, whether in the departments of geography or general statistics. Upon all subjects connected with the history, the natural features and resources, climate, population, productions, trade, and resources of the country, there exists a profound and almost universal ignorance. Even the persons supposed to be best informed upon these subjects are seldom able to give any comprehensive series of facts, or of accurate observations bearing upon any one of them, and the inquirer is left to a laborious process of accumulation, which is alike difficult and discouraging. He looks in vain for printed books or public documents to assist him. Of the few which have made their appearance, there nowhere exists a complete collection; and it is equally vain to seek for data among the state and local archives, where, to an original total lack of order, gross neglect and wanton destruction have been superadded, to confound and defeat all investigation.

It might be supposed that, in respect of the general geography of the country at large, or of its various states, it would be easy to obtain some kind of clear and positive information; but, excepting a map of the single state of Guatemala, constructed by Don Alejandro Marure, and entitled "ATLAS GUATEMALTECO, *en ocho Cartas*, *formadas y grabadas en Guatemala, de orden del Gefe del Estado, C. Doctor Mariano Galvez, año* 1832," I am not aware that any map of the whole or of any considerable portion of the country was ever constructed or engraved in all Central America. The few maps, so called, which exist in the archives of some of the states, are hardly a single remove from the rude tracings which the Indian makes on the sand as a guide to his companions on the war-path. I was nevertheless fortunate enough to find, in the possession of a gentleman resident in the city of San Salvador, an unfinished MS. map of Central America, entitled "MAPA DEL REYNO DE GUATEMALA, *año* 1818, *por* COL. LACIERRA, *Ingenero Real.*" This map, so far as it relates to Costa Rica, Nicaragua, and Guatemala, is very full, and, so far as my personal observation goes, generally quite accurate. It has, however, been of but little service to me in the construction of the accompanying map, for the reason that the states of Honduras and San Salvador have been left completely blank, without even an attempt to define their coast-line upon the Pacific. I have only followed it in respect to some of the geographical features of what is called the "Mosquito Shore," where its general accuracy finds confirmation in the accounts which have reached us of that coast. The map of Marure, as I have said, relates exclusively to Guatemala, so that I have derived no assistance in the construction of my own map from native, or what may perhaps be called indigenous, sources.

Humboldt, when attempting to construct a map of New Spain, remarked the entire insufficiency and inaccuracy of all the published maps of that country. Not only were important places wrongly located, but topographical features, chains of mountains, and large rivers were laid down where none existed, while others which really did exist were entirely left out. "Most of the American maps executed in Europe," he observed, "are filled with names which are unknown in the country itself. These errors are perpetuated, and it often becomes exceedingly difficult to conjecture their origin."*

Mexico was comparatively much better known than Central America, and if the early maps of the former country were wrong, those of the latter can only be characterized as geographically absurd. Even in later times, although the coasts have been defined with great accuracy, the interior geography has remained as obscure as it was a hundred years ago. The latest maps, some of which are sufficiently pretentious, are for the most part conjectural, and the

* New Spain, vol. i., p. lxxxv., Introduction.

geographical features which they indicate are wholly inapplicable to the country which they profess to represent. The mention here of an instance, illustrative of the scanty knowledge which the world has hitherto possessed of Central America, may not be inappropriate. Notwithstanding the project of opening a communication between the Atlantic and Pacific Oceans, through Nicaragua, had been discussed for three hundred years, yet, up to the publication of my map of that state in 1851, a chain of high mountains was represented in every engraved map which had fallen under my notice as intervening between Lake Managua and the Pacific. The city of Leon was represented either as situated on a mountain or surrounded by mountains; and in all speculations on the subject of an inter-oceanic canal, a river flowing into the sea at or near the port of Realejo, and called "Rio Tosta," was constantly referred to as probably affording some facilities for the purpose; yet there are no mountains between the northern extremity of Lake Managua and the ocean; the city of Leon stands in the centre of a vast plain; and there is no such stream as the "Rio Tosta" known. And even in the map of Mr. Baily, published in London in 1851, an uninterrupted chain of mountains is represented as extending from Lake Managua to the Gulf of Fonseca, whereas there is no such chain, nor are there any mountains, except a series of volcanic cones, entirely detached from each other, rising in the plain. This error is the more surprising, as Mr. Baily was employed by General Morazan, president of the Old Federation of Central America, to make a reconnaissance of the Isthmus of Nicaragua with reference to the projected ship-canal.

Again: the city of Comayagua, the capital of Honduras, which was a large and flourishing town before Hudson discovered the Bay of New York, seldom varies less than a degree from its true latitude and longitude, and in many maps it still bears the name of Valladolid, which fell into disuse nearly one hundred and fifty years ago! The city of Tegucigalpa, the first in Honduras in point of population, has a position still more variable than Comayagua.

There is another great source of annoyance to travelers in Central America, which is the stereotyped recurrence of the names of places in the maps, which, if they ever existed, are now unknown, or which are mere hamlets, unworthy of a place except in maps of great detail, while really important places do not appear at all. We thus see the town of Tambla, in Honduras, laid down in most maps of the country, while Las Piedras and the Villa de San Antonio, which exist in the same plain, do not appear. Yet Tambla is a petty village of some 200 inhabitants, while Las Piedras has upward of 6000, and San Antonio more than 2500! Again: in the Department of Gracias, in the same state, Guancapla, a collection of a few huts, is conspicuously indicated, while the large and flourishing town of Santa Rosa, containing some 6000 inhabitants, is entirely omitted.

These examples might be multiplied indefinitely; but they are errors consequent on the limited information which the world has hitherto possessed of these countries. Map-makers, destitute of requisite accurate data, have been obliged to copy the works of their predecessors, and thus contribute to the perpetuation of their errors. That they have done this, with little or no care to test the accuracy of what they have copied, can also be excused on the ground that hitherto these countries have not had sufficient interest to make accuracy a matter of any practical importance. Now, however, the case is widely different: not only is the value of Central America, in every point of view, beginning to be appreciated, but the enterprise of our people is setting in that direction in a full and increasing current.

Apart from these strictly geographical errors, there are others in the various maps of Central America which are without apology and excuse; I mean, the servile perpetuation in American maps of the arbitrary political subdivisions of the country, made under English authority, to sustain the pretensions of the British government. This servility on the part of American map-makers shows how little pains they use to verify the facts which they undertake to present, and how profoundly ignorant they have continued to keep themselves of the issue of the scrutiny to which, in Central America, British pretensions have been subjected. Several maps have been published within a year in the United States which are obnoxious to the severest censure on this score.

I have selected, as an illustration of the justice of these censures, and as affording an opportunity of correcting several surprising blunders, a sheet map, entitled "JOHNSTON'S ILLUSTRATED AND EMBELLISHED MAP AND CHART OF THE NEW WORLD. *New York*, 1844." And here I may observe that, although this map, so far as Central America is concerned, both geographically and politically, is full of the most egregious errors, yet it is in no degree more open to criticism than nine tenths of the maps of equal pretensions which have been published in the United States. 1. For the first time in any map, we find Vera Paz laid down as a distinct state. It is now, as it has always been, a department of the province and state of Guatemala. 2. The British establishment of Belize, the boundaries of which are clearly defined by the treaties between England and Spain as extending only from the Rio Jabon to the Rio Hondo, is represented as including more than four times the amount of territory legitimately pertaining to it, and extending from the Rio Hondo down to the Bay of Amatique. No such limits were ever conceded by Spain, nor by the inheritors of her territorial rights in that quarter of the world, nor have they ever been recognized by the United States or any other civilized country. They are impudent pretensions, which map-makers in England, accessory to the schemes of their own government, have adopted without scruple. The representation of the State of Michigan as a part of Canada West could not be more at variance with truth ; and the acceptance of such pretensions in respect to Michigan by American map-makers would not be one whit more absurd than this servility to English authorities in the political divisions of Central America. 3. Honduras, which extends from sea to sea, having a frontage of upward of fifty miles on the Pacific (Gulf of Fonseca), is represented in this map as entirely cut off from that ocean by the states of San Salvador and Nicaragua, which are designated as contiguous ; whereas, as I have said, they are separated by the territories of Honduras. 4. Nearly one third of Central America is assigned to the "Mosquito Shore," which is here represented as a distinct and sovereign state. The term "Mosquito Shore" never had a political sense, but has always been used geographically to designate a portion of the eastern coast of Central America. The Indians known as "Mosquitos" are only a few thousands of miserable savages, who are strictly confined to the coast, and have never had establishments of any kind inland. Essentially fishers, they find a scanty subsistence in the numerous lagoons and creeks near the sea, their only traffic consisting of a few turtle-shells and a little sarsaparilla. Even if these savages were entitled to rank as a nation, they have not, nor could they ever have, the shadow of a pretense of sovereignty over the fractional part of the wide expanse of territory which this map assigns to them. But they have no title of sovereignty over any portion of the country, however small ; they do not claim it for themselves ; it is only set up on their behalf, by Great Britain for sinister purposes, and, so far from being admitted, is positively denied by the United States and every other nation of the globe. The portion of territory assigned by this map to the fictitious Mosquito nationality above the Rio Wanks or Segovia belongs to Honduras; the part below pertains to Nicaragua. 5. The northern boundary of Costa Rica is inaccurate, and not conceded by Nicaragua. But this error may be excused on the ground of conflict of claims between those states. It is, perhaps, not to be expected that a map-maker should have the means of testing the merits of questions of this kind. The true northern boundary line of Costa Rica, as defined in her own Constitution, extends from the lower mouth of the River San Juan to the Rio Salto de Nicoya or Alvarado, falling into the Gulf of Nicoya. Consequently, the territories of Costa Rica do not touch the River San Juan nor Lake Nicaragua, but fall far to the southward of both. The map in question is therefore erroneous in this respect. In short, so far as Central America is concerned, it has no claim to be regarded as an authority. It can serve no purpose except to confuse and mislead.

It may be claimed that the map here alluded to is general in its character, and does not pretend to specific accuracy. Such, however, is not the case with a large map recently published in London, which has very generally been accepted as an authority, namely, "MAP OF CENTRAL AMERICA, *including the States of Guatemala, Honduras, San Salvador, Nicaragua, and Costa Rica, etc., etc., by* JOHN BAILY, ESQ., R. M.—*Trelawney Saunders, London,* 1850

We are not surprised to find embodied in this map all the territorial pretensions and arbitrary political divisions of the country devised and set up by the British government. A few strokes of the colorist's brush have been sufficient to indicate British sovereignty over two thirds of the Department of Vera Paz in Guatemala, to convert the islands belonging to Honduras, in the bay of the same name, into British dependencies, and to carry Mosquito jurisdiction over more than half of the respective states of Honduras and Nicaragua. Nor has it been less potent in settling the question of boundary between Nicaragua and Costa Rica in favor of the latter state, in which, by a singular coincidence, British influence has always predominated! These peculiarities of the map, in view of its origin, can hardly be regarded as surprising. Those who constructed it have probably smiled to know with what ignorant servility it has been copied on this side of the Atlantic.

It may nevertheless be said of this map that it is the nearest approximation to accuracy which has yet been published. Still, in many important geographical as well as political features it is deficient, and in others totally wrong. Leaving out of view both Guatemala and Costa Rica, we find a number of most important errors in the remaining states, which appear all the more surprising, since Mr. Baily not only resided for many years in Central America, but must have traveled over a great part of its territories. Thus, in San Salvador, the great river Lempa is represented as constituting the boundary between that state and Honduras, whereas it flows, for the greater part of its length, through the longitudinal centre of the state, and forms its northern boundary for only a few miles of its course. Again: the upper waters of the Rio Santiago, in the Department of Gracias, Honduras, are represented as describing the segment of a circle from east to west before taking their general course, east by north, to the sea, whereas the very reverse is the fact. As one of the consequences of this error, the town and ruins of Copan are thrown within the territory of Guatemala, although, in fact, they fall considerably within the boundaries of Honduras. The Lake of Yojoa is presented with the extraordinary feature of five distinct outlets! The course of the Rio Humuya is also deflected much too far to the eastward of its course. The rivers Guallambre and Guyape, which, in fact, unite to form the River Patuca or Patook, falling into the Bay of Honduras at Brus or Brewer's Lagoon, are represented as constituting the principal affluents of the great River Wanks or Segovia, entering the Caribbean Sea at Cape Gracias á Dios. This river also, which rises in the Mountains of Chili, around the town of Ocotal or Nueva Segovia, in the Nicaraguan department of the same name, is represented as originating far to the north-east of those mountains, while the upper waters of the Rio Escondido, or Bluefields River, are substituted in place of those of the Rio Wanks. The Rio Goascoran, interlocking its head-waters with those of the Rio Humuya, and flowing southward into the Bay of Fonseca, is entirely omitted. The errors in the positions of places are not less remarkable, but infinitely more numerous. These, however, are not surprising, since most of the towns have necessarily been laid down from the representations of persons who had very imperfect notions of distances and directions.

The distinguished Prussian geographer Berghaus was the first to indicate, with even approximate accuracy, the great physical features of Central America. Instead of admitting a continuous chain of mountains extending through that country from Tehuantepec to Panama, he divided the mountains of Central America into three distinct systems or groups: first, that of Costa Rica, with the volcano of Cartago for a nucleus; second, that of Honduras; and, third, that of Guatemala. Between the first and second intervenes the transverse basin of the Nicaragua lakes, with a minimum altitude of land of one hundred and eighty feet; and between the second and third the plain of Comayagua, with its dependent valleys, having a maximum altitude of but little more than two thousand feet. Under this view, and in all general respects, Berghaus's Map of Central America, published in his "*Physikalischen Atlas*" in 1840, has been, up to within a very recent period, far the best representation of the geography of that country.

In explanation of the map of Honduras and San Salvador which I herewith present to the public, it is proper to say that the leading points upon the line of the proposed railway through Honduras were determined by Lieutenant Jeffers from numerous and careful astronomical observations. They constitute the basis upon which the relations of the places visited by the expedition or its members were calculated. These calculations are entitled to additional confidence from the circumstance that there are, both in Honduras and San Salvador, a number of elevated and commanding mountain and volcanic peaks, which are almost constantly kept in view by the traveler, and which always enable him to determine his position with considerable accuracy. The bearings of these determinate points were never neglected when an opportunity occurred for observing them, and have served a most useful and satisfactory purpose in the construction of this map. It will be remarked that those places, of which the position is regarded as having been fixed with approximate accuracy, are indicated by a light line drawn under them. All other places are inserted on the best information that could be obtained, and in a few instances conjecturally. The course of the Rio Patuca, and the relative positions of the towns situated on its upper waters, are on the authority of a rude map constructed by the mahogany-cutters who are established on the Patuca River and its tributaries. Much of the information embodied in that portion of the map embraced within the boundaries of the Department of Gracias, Honduras, is drawn from a MS. map of that department, constructed in 1838 by Don José Maria Cacho, actual secretary of state of Honduras, and at that period commissioner of the census then ordered by the Congress of the old republic.

I may here observe that little reliance can be placed upon the "Itinerários" which are appended to the various "Calendários" published in Central America in respect of distances. The computations are in leagues, and have been obtained chiefly from the professional *arrieros*, or muleteers of the country, whose estimates of distances are very loose, depending, as they often naïvely confess, "upon the qualities of their mules." I have found that the value of a league, in the comparatively level grounds of San Salvador and in the plains of Honduras, seldom exceeds two English miles; while, in the broken and mountainous districts, it falls below a mile and a half of horizontal distance.

What I have said of the geographical data embraced in this memoir and in the accompanying maps is equally true of the general statistics and facts which are here presented. They have been chiefly obtained from direct observation and laborious personal inquiry, in a detached and often obscure form, and are necessarily imperfect. For instance, the facts relating to population have been collected from an inspection of the parochial registers in some instances, and from tables published irregularly and without digestion in the "Gacetas Officiales" of the respective states. Few, who have not undertaken a similar task, can adequately comprehend how great an amount of labor is requisite to arrive at results under such adverse circumstances, and how unsatisfactory these results will often prove to be, even after every effort has been exhausted to render them complete and accurate. No one can be more sensible of the defects of this memoir, and its deficiencies in respect to several important subjects of inquiry and interest, than myself. Still, I flatter myself that it will prove of value, as constituting a point of departure for other investigators, who, by correcting its errors and gradually supplying its omissions, shall finally complete the design of presenting to the world a full and accurate view of the character, climate, resources, population, and general physical and political condition of the various divisions of Central America; and I am not without the hope that this attempt may have an influence in awakening the attention of the people and governments of that country to the importance of collecting, digesting, and making public the data bearing upon all these subjects.

I am not aware of more than one work which has been printed in Central America that even professed to give a general view of the country, its character, and resources, viz., The History of the Kingdom of Guatemala, by Juarros. This work, however, is chiefly historical, and is little more than a transcript from the municipal and monkish chronicles of Guatemala. Reference is rarely made to the physical features of the country, and even then in an exaggerated and marveling tone, which always denotes the absence of positive knowledge. Such stories as the production of "a plant like a gourd" from sowing the eggs of an insect known as the *Chapulin*, are not too absurd to find a grave relation in the history of Juarros. Yet, strange to say, nearly all that has been written or published in Central America upon the country itself has been a servile repetition, seldom even varying in language, of the statements and speculations of Juarros!

Subsequently to the independence, Don José de la Valle, and after him Don Alejandro Marure, devoted some attention to the study of the country under its physical aspects, and to the collection of facts illustrative of its resources and political condition; but, except a memoir on the proposed ship-canal of Nicaragua, and a brief chronological list of events in the history of Central America, we have nothing on these subjects from the pen of Marure, although it is said that, in common with Valle, he wrote largely upon them all. It only remains to mention the name of Don José Maria Cacho to complete the list of natives of Central America who have done any thing worthy of mention in the department here indicated. His brief notes on the Department of Gracias, in Honduras, possess a real value, and might serve as a model of similar researches to his countrymen.

What little illustration Central America has received has therefore been at the hands of foreigners; but their works have been, for the most part, rapid narrations of travel and adventure, shallow in observation, and inaccurate in their statements. Few of them have been written by persons competent by education, or accustomed by habit to close and accurate research. They are chiefly devoted to superficial views of society, and highly-colored accounts of political incidents and commotions, of which their authors failed to ascertain the origin not less than to detect the significance. From this, perhaps, too sweeping condemnation, I may except the works of Thompson, Henderson, Young, Roberts, Dunn, Baily, and Crowe, which certainly contain many and valuable facts and observations.

Upon a review of the whole subject, I have thought that I might render the public a service in subjoining, in the Appendix to this memoir, a list of the various books and pamphlets bearing directly upon Central America as a whole, or upon its various parts, which have been published since the commencement of this century, and which have fallen under my observation. My object has been to make this list as complete as possible, without regard to the values of the various works themselves. It will be observed that the titles follow each other in chronological order.

NOTES

ON

CENTRAL AMERICA.

CHAPTER I.

GEOGRAPHICAL AND TOPOGRAPHICAL FEATURES OF CENTRAL AMERICA, AND THEIR INFLUENCE ON POPULATION.

CENTRAL AMERICA, in respect of geographical position, almost realizes the ancient idea of the centre of the world. Not only does it connect the two grand divisions of the American continent, the northern and the southern hemispheres, but its ports open to Europe and Africa on the east, and to Polynesia, Asia, and Australia on the west.

Looking at the map, we find, at the Isthmus of Tehuantepec, the Gulf of Mexico approaching to within two hundred miles of the Western Ocean, the waters of the River Coatzacoalcos, which flows into the former, almost interlocking with those of the Chicapa, flowing into the latter. Below this point the continent widens, embracing the high table-lands of Guatemala upon the west, and the broad plains of Tabasco, Chiapa, and Yucatan upon the north and east. The Gulf or Bay of Honduras, however, closes around this section upon the southeast, and again narrows the continent to less than one hundred and fifty miles. The country intervening between this bay and the Pacific is marked by a complete interruption of the Cordilleras, and is traversed by a great transverse valley, running due north and south, through which the large river Ulua finds its way to the Atlantic, and the smaller river Goascoran flows into the Bay of Fonseca, on the Pacific. Still lower down, and passing the grand transverse basin of Nicaragua, is the well-known narrow Isthmus of Panama or Darien, over which the tide of emigration has twice poured its floods, once upon Peru, and again upon the glittering shores of California.

Nor are the topographical characteristics of Central America less remarkable than its geographical features. In its physical aspect and configuration of surface, it has very justly been observed that it is an epitome of all other countries and climates of the globe. High mountain ranges, isolated volcanic peaks, elevated table-lands, deep valleys, broad and fertile plains, and extensive alluvions, are here found grouped together, relieved by large and beautiful lakes and majestic rivers; the whole teeming with animal and vegetable life, and possessing every variety of climate, from torrid heats to the cool and bracing temperature of eternal spring.

The great chain of the Cordilleras here, as in South America, runs nearest to the Pacific coast, but in places it is interrupted, as I have already said, and assumes the form of detached ranges and isolated elevations, groups or knots of hills, between which the streams from the interior high valleys or elevated plains wind their way to the two oceans. As a consequence, the principal alluvions border on the Gulf of Mexico and the Caribbean Sea. Here rains fall, in greater or less abundance, for the entire year; vegetation is rank, and the climate is damp and proportionally insalubrious. The trade winds blow from the northeast; and the moisture with which they are saturated, condensed on the elevated parts of the continent, flows down toward the Atlantic. The Pacific slope is therefore comparatively dry and healthful, as are also the elevated regions of the interior.

Topographically, Central America presents three marked centres of elevation, which have, to a certain degree, fixed its political divisions. The first is the great plain, or broken table-land, in which is situated the city of Guatemala, and which is upward of four thousand feet above the sea. Here the large rivers Usumasinta and Tabasco, flowing northward through Chiapa and Tabasco into the Gulf of Mexico, take their rise. Their sources interlock with those of the Motagua or Gualan, running eastward into the Gulf of Honduras, and with those of the small streams which send their waters westward into the Pacific.

A group of mountains occupies Honduras, presenting an almost mural front toward the Pacific, but shooting out numerous spurs or subordinate branches, like the fingers of an outspread hand, toward the north and east. Between these ranges, and in some cases almost encircled by hills, are several broad valleys or plains of different elevations, in which are gathered the waters of thousands of rivulets and small streams, forming numerous considerable rivers, which radiate north and east into the Caribbean Sea, and south and west into the Southern Ocean. Among the most remarkable are the Chamelicon, the Ulua, Lean, Roman or Tinto, Patuca, Coco (Wanks or Segovia), upon the eastern slope; the Choluteca, Nacaome, Goascoran, San Miguel, and Lempa, upon the western.

Intervening between this and the third great centre of elevation in Costa Rica is the basin of the Nicaraguan lakes, with its verdant slopes and gently undulating plains. The nucleus of the elevation in Costa Rica is the great volcano of Cartago, which towers in its midst. Here the Cordilleras assume their general character of a great, unbroken mountain barrier, but soon subside again in low ridges on the Isthmus of Panama.

Besides the rivers of Central America, the largest of which I have enumerated, there are a number of large and beautiful lakes, viz.: Nicaragua and Managua, in Nicaragua; Yojoa or Taulebé, in Honduras; Guija and Ilopango, in San Salvador; and Golfo Dulce, Peten or Itza, Atitlan, and Amatitlan, in Guatemala. Of these, the Lakes of Nicaragua and Managua are much the largest.

I have said that the ports of Central America open to Europe and Africa on one hand, and to Polynesia, Asia, and Australia on the other. On the Atlantic, Guatemala has Belize, Izabal, and Santo Tomas (the last only of much value); Honduras has Omoa, Puerto Caballos, Puerto Sal, Triunfo de la Cruz, Truxillo, and others; Nicaragua has Gracias á Dios, Bluefields, and San Juan. Costa Rica has no good port on the east, but has several on the west, of which Golfo Dulce, Punta Arenas, and Caldera are the principal. Nicaragua has, upon the Pacific, Culebra, Salinas, San Juan del Sur, and Realejo; Honduras, a cluster in the Bay of Fonseca, viz.: Amapala (a free port), San Lorenzo, and La Paz; San Salvador has La Union, also in the Bay of Fonseca, Jiquilisco or Espiritu Santo, Jaltepec or Concordia, La Libertad, and Acajutla or Sonsonate. The last two can hardly be called ports, being, in fact, only roadsteads. Guatemala has but one port or roadstead, called Iztapa. The best of all these ports on the Atlantic are Santo Tomas, Omoa,

Puerto Caballos, and San Juan del Norte; on the Pacific, Realejo, the free port of Amapala (Island of Tigre), and La Union.

The area of Central America may be calculated, in round numbers, at 155,000 square miles—very nearly equal to that of the New England and the Middle States combined. The population may be estimated at not far from 2,000,000, of which Guatemala has 850,000; San Salvador, 394,000; Honduras, 350,000; Nicaragua, 300,000; and Costa Rica, 125,000.

The geographical and topographical features of all countries have had, and always must have, an important and often a controlling influence upon the character and destiny of their populations. The nature and extent of this influence receives a striking illustration both in the past and the present condition of Central America. At the period of the discovery, it was found in the occupation of two families of men, presenting in respect to each other the strongest points of contrast. Upon the high plateaus of the interior of the country, and upon the Pacific declivity of the continent, where the rains are comparatively light, the country open, and the climate relatively cool and salubrious, were found great and populous nations, far advanced in civilization, and maintaining a systematized religious and civil organization. Upon the Atlantic declivity, on the other hand, among dense forests, nourished by constant rains into rank vigor, on low coasts, where marshes and lagoons, sweltering under a fierce sun, generated deadly miasmatic damps, were found savage tribes of men, without fixed abodes, living upon the natural fruits of the earth, and the precarious supplies of fishing and the chase, without religion, and with scarcely a semblance of social or political establishments.

It is impossible to resist the conviction that the contrasting conditions of these two great families were principally due to the equally contrasting physical conditions of their respective countries. With the primitive dwellers on the Atlantic declivity of Central America, no considerable advance, beyond the rudest habits of life, was possible. He was powerless against the exuberant vitality of savage nature, which even the civilized man, with all the appliances that intelligence has gradually called to his aid, is unable to subdue, and which still retains its ancient dominion over the broad alluvions, both of Central and South America. His means of sustenance were too few and too precarious to admit of his making permanent establishments, which, in turn, would involve an adjustment of the relations of men and the organization of society. He was therefore a hunter from necessity, nomadic in his habits, and obliged to dispute his life with men who, like himself, were scarcely less savage than the beasts of the forests.

Civilization could never have been developed under such adverse conditions. It could only originate where favorable physical circumstances afforded to man some relief from the pressure of immediate and ever-recurring wants—where a genial climate, and an easily-cultivated soil, bountiful in indigenous fruits, would enable him not only to make his permanent abode, but to devote a portion of his time to the improvement of his superior nature.

Such were the circumstances which surrounded the dweller on the high plains of Honduras and Guatemala. There, wide and fertile savannas invited to agriculture, and yielded to the rudest implements of cultivation an ample harvest. The maize, that great support of aboriginal civilization in America, was probably indigenous there, and was thence carried northward over Mexico and the Floridas by the various families who established themselves in those regions, and whose languages and traditions point to the plateaus of Guatemala as their original seat.

The natural conditions which favored the development of mankind in one portion of Central America, and rigidly suppressed it in another, are still active and potential. The Spaniards stopped not to maintain an unequal struggle against savage nature on the Atlantic slope of the continent, but established themselves upon the dryer, more salubrious, and more genial Pacific declivity. The Mosquito Shore still remains the haunt of savages, whom three hundred years of contact with civilization have failed to improve; while the State of San Salvador sustains a population twice as great in proportion to its area as any other equal extent of Spanish America, and relatively as great as that of New England itself.

These natural conditions will continue to foster settlement and population on the one hand, and discourage and oppose it on the other; and not until those portions of Central and South America which are most favored in respect of position and climate are filled to overflowing, and the progress of discovery, both in science and in art, has invested men with augmented ability to combat successfully the diseases and physical difficulties which exist in the valleys of the Amazon and Orinoco, and on the Mosquito Shore, will those regions be subjected to the influences of civilization, or become the seats of any considerable populations.

The natural relations of Central America, as indicated by the physical facts already pointed out, are clearly with the Pacific and the states which now exist or may spring into existence upon that coast. To California and the greater part of Mexico, as also to some of the states of South America, it must come, sooner or later, to sustain a position corresponding with that which the West Indies have held toward the United States and Europe, with the important addition of being an established route of travel, and perhaps ultimately of commerce, between the eastern and western hemispheres. Its destiny is plainly written in the outlines of its coast, and is printed on its surface, not less than demonstrated by its geographical position.

CHAPTER II.

OBSERVATIONS ON THE CLIMATE OF CENTRAL AMERICA IN GENERAL.

THE peculiarities of Central America, in respect of configuration of surface, will explain the almost endless variety of climate to which I have alluded, and which is nowhere more remarkable than in that country. Situated between 8° and 17° north latitude, were it not for these features, the general temperature would be somewhat higher than that of the West Indies. As it is, the climate of the coast is nearly the same with that of the islands alluded to, and exceedingly uniform. It is modified somewhat by the shape and position of the shore, and by the proximity of the mountains, as well as by the prevailing winds. The heat on the Pacific coast is not, however, so oppressive as on the Atlantic; less, perhaps, because of any considerable difference of temperature than on account of the greater dryness and purity of the atmosphere.

In the northern part of the State of Guatemala, in what is called "Los Altos," the Highlands, the average temperature is lower than in any other part of the country. Snow sometimes falls in the vicinity of Quezaltenango, the capital of this department, but soon disappears, as the thermometer seldom remains at the freezing point for any considerable length of time. In the vicinity of the city of Guatemala, the range of the thermometer is from 55° to 80°, averaging about 72° of Fahrenheit. Vera Paz, the northeastern department of Guatemala, and embracing the coast below Yucatan to the Gulf of Dulce, is nearly ten degrees warmer. This coast, from Belize downward to Izabal and Santo Tomas, is hot and unhealthy. The same remark applies, in a less degree, to the northern and eastern coast of Honduras, from Omoa to Cape Gracias á Dios. A favorable circumstance here is the close approach of the mountains to the shore, and the prevalence, for a considerable portion of the year, of cool and bracing winds from the north. The State of San Salvador lies wholly on the Pacific. It is smaller than any of the others, but proportionally better populated. It is less elevated than either Guatemala or Honduras, and its general temperature is probably higher. The heat, however, is never oppressive, except at a few points near the coast, as for instance Sonsonate, San Miguel, and La Union, all of which owe their excessively high temperature to local circumstances. Honduras, as its name implies (being the plural of "*hondura*," depth), has a very diversified surface, and a consequent diversity of temperature. The climate is generally delightful, the average temperature at Tegucigalpa, Comayagua, Juticalpa, and Gracias, the principal towns, being about 74°. The Department of Segovia, in Nicaragua, bordering on Honduras, has a like surface and temperature. The principal part of Nicaragua, however, is widely different in all respects, and has a topography and climate peculiarly its own. The average temperature of the great basin of the lakes is about 79° or 80°: a result due not to its elevation, but to other favorable and modifying causes, which I have fully pointed out in my work on that country. The population of Costa Rica is concentrated on the western or Pacific slope of the volcano of Cartago, and, as a consequence, almost any degree of temperature may be obtained, according to the elevation, from the intense heat of the port of Punta Arenas to the constant spring of San José, or to the autumnal temperature of the belt above the ancient capital of Cartago. The eastern slopes of Costa Rica may be said to be uninhabited, and the coast from Chiriqui Lagoon northward is low and unhealthy. Indeed, the entire Atlantic coast of Central America, from Truxillo downward, embracing the whole of what is called the Mosquito shore, is subject to the same remark. Hence this coast has scarcely any inhabitants, except a few squalid Indians, while the coast of the Pacific is lined with towns, and occupied by a very considerable population.

What are called the "seasons" under the tropics, namely, the wet and dry, are much influenced in their commencement and duration by local causes, so that what is literally true of one place can only be partially so of another. The widest differences are, of course, between the Atlantic and Pacific slopes of the continent. The whole of Central America comes within the zone of the northeast trade winds, which, sweeping across the Atlantic, reach the continent almost saturated with vapor. The portion of moisture of which they are deprived by the Caribbean Islands is probably again nearly, if not quite, made up in their passage over the sea of the same name. These winds are intercepted by the high mountain centres of Guatemala, Honduras, and Costa Rica, and the vapor precipitated from them flows down to the Atlantic, through a multitude of streams and rivers. But the mountains of Central America are not all high enough to entirely intercept the trade winds. They are, moreover, broken through by transverse valleys, like that of the Nicaraguan Lakes, and that of Comayagua in Honduras. As a consequence, the trades, for a great part of the year, blow entirely across the continent, reaching the Pacific slope deprived of their moisture, and cooled by a passage over the elevated region of the interior. Hence result the greater salubrity of that declivity, the comparative coolness and dryness of its climate, and its consequently greater population.

There is, properly speaking, no dry season on the Atlantic littoral of Central America. For about four months of the year, from May to October, the trades are intermittent; consequently, less moisture is precipitated, and this slope has then its nearest approach to what is called the "dry season."

During these months, the trades, as I have just said, being intermittent, the Pacific declivity is subject to winds from the west and southwest, which precipitate their waters against the western slopes of the mountains, and constitute the rainy season. As these Pacific winds are seldom more than exaggerated sea-breezes, and are rarely of more than a few hours' continuance, the rains which follow from them are brief, occurring generally in the afternoon and night. It is rare to witness an entire day of rain, although there are occasionally meteoric combinations which produce what the Spaniards call *Temporales*, or rains of several days' continuance. During a residence of three rainy seasons in Central America, I witnessed but one *Temporal*.

What I have said applies strictly to the respective Atlantic and Pacific coasts. The central plateaus, or high table-lands of the interior, have a climate of their own, subject neither to heavy rains nor excessive droughts. The winds which reach them, as well from the west as the east, are first deprived of the greater part of their moisture, but both bring with them more or less rain. From the circumstance that they lie nearest the Pacific, these plateaus partake most of the climate of that coast, with which their seasons also measurably coincide. The plain of Comayagua, situated in the very centre of Honduras, and equidistant from the two great seas, may be taken as an illustration. More or less rain falls there during every month in the year; but, during the prevalence of the dry season on the Pacific, it is only in the form of showers of brief duration, while during the wet season the rains are comparatively long and heavy. Continuous rains, or *Temporales*, are unknown.

These general remarks will be found supported by the following data, which comprise about all the information that I have been able to collect on this subject from personal observations or from authentic sources:

Costa Rica.—"The climate of Costa Rica is very humid, the rain falling for six months of the year. It is cool and healthy on the Pacific coast; hot, wet, and unhealthy on the Atlantic; cold and salubrious on the table-lands of the interior, where the thermometer ranges from 65° to 75° of Fahr. in the course of the year. It must be observed that the rainy season on the Pacific and in the interior is from April to November; but upon the Atlantic coast this order of things is reversed, and the rainy season is from November to February."*

Nicaragua.—Observations were made, during the progress of the survey for a ship-canal in Nicaragua, in 1850–51, by the gentlemen connected with that en-

* *Bosquejo de la Republica de Costa Rica, etc.*, por Felipe Molina, p. 28. Galindo (*Journal of the Royal Geographical Society of London*, vol. vi., p. 134) observes that the climate of Costa Rica is exceedingly varied, ranging from 50° to 60° of Fahr., according to the elevation.

terprise. These observations were confined to the isthmus which lies between Lake Nicaragua and the Pacific, at a point where the trade winds, sweeping through the valley of the San Juan River, and over Lake Nicaragua, find no high mountains to precipitate their moisture until they reach the volcanic peaks of Ometepec and Madeira. Hence it happens that this Isthmus of Rivas receives a greater amount of rain annually than any other portion of the Pacific coast of Central America.

OBSERVATIONS AT RIVAS, NICARAGUA—1850-51.

Date.	Average. Thermom.	Highest. Thermom.	Lowest. Thermom.	Range.
	° ′	° ′	° ′	° ′
September, 1850	78 12	88	71	17
October, do.	77 0	86	70	16
November, do.	78 42	86	74	12
December, do.	77 11	84	72	12
January, 1851	76 40	87	69	18
February, do.	76 0	84	70	14
March, do.	77 0	84	72	12
April, do.	78 83	88	72	16
May, do.	78 29	91	68	23
June, do.	77 12	88	71	17
July, do.	76 98	86	71	15
August, do.	76 20	86	71	15
Sept. 12th, do.	79 10	86	74	12
Total mean . .	77 42	86 45	71 15	15 30

Here it will be observed that the maximum range was in the month of May, and was 23°. The mean range for the year, however, was only 15°. The heat at no time of the year is as great as it is during the summer months in New York. For June, July, and August of 1850, the mean average range of the thermometer at the town of Lansingburg, New York, was 71° 5′, the mean highest 93° 66′, the mean lowest 47° 33′, and the mean range 46° 33′. At Jamaica, Long

Island, for July and August of the same year, the mean average was 75° 15′, the mean highest 95° 50′, the mean lowest 61° 50′, and the mean range 43° 27′.

In respect of rain, the principal surveyor has given us the result of careful admeasurements made at Rivas for one year, from September 9th, 1850, to September 25th, 1851. The amount was taken in inches and decimals, and is as follows:

		Inches.			Inches.
September,	1850 . .	7.005	April,	1851 . .	0.430
October,	do. . .	17.860	May,	do. . .	9.145
November,	do. . .	1.395	June,	do. . .	14.210
December,	do. . .	3.210	July,	do. . .	22.640
January,	1851 . .	0.380	August,	do. . .	11.810
February,	do. . .	0.000	September,	do. . .	13.240
March,	do. . .	1.410			
Total inches					102.735

For the exact year, from September 9th, 1850, to September 9th, 1851, the amount of rain was 97.71 inches. The whole number of days during which rain fell was 139, and the whole number of dry days was 226. During the six months, from May to October inclusive, distinguished as the wet season, the whole fall was 90.89 inches, and during the remaining six months, distinguished as the dry season, only 6.82 inches.

But these observations, as I have said, were made at Rivas, under the lee of the volcano of Ometepec, where more rain falls than at Granada or Leon, in the northern portion of the state. At Rivas there was but one month, February, in which no rain fell. In 1850, in Leon, no rain fell for three months, from the first of January to the first of April.

The average annual fall of rain and snow in the State of New York, during the ten years preceding 1846, according to the report of the Regents of the University, is 34.14 inches. The greatest fall in any one year during that period was 37.04 inches, and the least, 32.10 inches.

Honduras.—The northern and eastern coast of Honduras has unquestionably a higher temperature than any other portion of the state. It however diminishes rapidly as we penetrate inland. The modifying influence of the neighboring mountains is felt even before the increase in altitude becomes perceptible. Her table-lands have, of course, a climate varying with their height above the sea, and their exposure to the prevailing winds. Consequently, there can be no generalization on the subject of the climate of Honduras, except so far as to say that it has a variety adapted to every caprice, and a temperature suitable for the cultivation of the products of every zone.

Among the data on this subject are the observations made by Mr. Thomas Young, at the mouth of Black River, on the Bay of Honduras, lat. 16° N., long. 85° W., for one year (1840–41?). The subjoined remark accompanies the table:

"The climate here is pretty equable, only varying, throughout the year, from 62° to 86° Fahr., so that nothing need be apprehended from excessive heats, especially as, during the greater part of the year, it is tempered by the grateful sea-breeze, and sometimes by the invigorating dry north wind.

"When the northers terminate, and the sea-breeze again blows, the effect on the human frame, and indeed on every thing around, is plainly perceptible. All nature partakes of its influence, and few can tell the enjoyment expressed by the man who has been crouching round a fire in a cold wet north as he eagerly rushes out to enjoy the health-giving breeze."

SUMMARY OF THERMOMETRICAL OBSERVATIONS

Taken daily at Noon, at the mouth of Black River, Honduras, for one Year (1840–41).

Months.	Average Temperature.	Prevailing Winds.*	Prevailing Weather.
January . .	62° to 66°	Northers.	Wet: sometimes fine by being a dry north.
February .	66° to 70°	"	" " "
March . . .	70° to 74°	Unsettled sea-breezes and northeasters.	Dry.
April	74° to 76°	Northeasters and sea-breezes.	"
May	78°	Strong sea-breezes.	"
June . . .	78° to 82°	" "	"
July	82°	" "	Wet.
August. . .	84° to 86°	Light variable airs or calms.	Dry.
September	84° to 86°	" " "	"
October . .	78°	Sea-breezes, sometimes a light north.	Dry or wet according to wind.
November	72° and less	Northers.	Wet: sometimes fine by being a dry north.
December.	62° to 66°	"	Wet.

Other observations were made, in 1844, on the same coast, a little to the eastward of Black River, in the vicinity of Carataska Lagoon, by a competent Prussian commission, Messrs. Müller, Fellechner, and Hesse. They were carried on from June 13th to August 2d of that year, with the following results:

Observations at Carataska Lagoon from June 13th to August 2d, 1844.

6 o'clock	A.M.,	26°	of Centigrade	= 78.5° of Fahr.
11 "	"	28.4° "	"	= 83.1° " "
3 "	P.M.,	28.5° "	"	= 83.4° " "
7 "	"	27.3° "	"	= 82° " "

This is equal to an average mean of 27.8° of Cent.,

* "At the beginning of October, what are called the *Norths* commence and generally continue, with little variation, till the return of February or March. While these winds last, the mornings and evenings are cold, frequently unpleasantly so; and what in this country is understood by a *wet north*, might perhaps furnish no very imperfect idea of a November day in England. A *dry north*, on the contrary, is beautiful, agreeable, and invigorating."—*Henderson's Honduras*, p. 14.

C

22.24° of Reaum., and 82° of Fahr. During this time the wind blew steadily from the E., E.N.E., or N.E., with the exception of three days (the 22d, 23d, and 24th of June) from the S.W., and one day (July 31st) from the N.W. The extreme range of the thermometer during this period was from the mean minimum of 61° Fahr., July 2d, to the mean maximum of 85° Fahr., July 4th. Captain Haly, for twenty years a resident at Cape Gracias, states that during the coldest months, viz., October, November, and December, the range of the thermometer at that point is from 60° to 65° of Fahr.

At the port of Omoa, also on the same coast, and in the same latitude, but three degrees to the westward of Black River, for one week, from the 5th to the 12th of July, 1853, the thermometer had an average of 85° Fahr. at noon; its greatest range, from six o'clock in the morning to the same hour in the evening, having been from 80° to 87°. During this period, the mornings were generally very pleasant, with showers from nine to twelve. The sea-breeze set in between twelve and one, and from that time until six in the evening it was clear. During the evening and night the land-breeze was accompanied with frequent violent showers.

Proceeding inland to the great transverse plain of Comayagua, elevated 1800 feet above the sea, my observations, made in 1853, gave the following results:

MEAN RANGE OF THERMOMETER AT COMAYAGUA.

Months (1853).	6 A.M.	12 M.	3 P.M.	6 P.M.
April (part) . .	75° 7′	81° 9′	84° 0′	80° 2′
May	75° 5′	81° 2′	80° 3′	78° 5′
June	74° 4′	78° 5′	80° 8′	78° 3′
Average . . .	75° 2′	80° 5′	81° 7′	79° 0′

That is to say, during the above months, the mean

temperature, from six o'clock in the morning until the same hour in the evening, was 79° 1′. The highest or maximum point touched by the thermometer during these months was 88°; the lowest or minimum, 68°; an extreme range of 20°. It may be observed here that, from certain peculiarities of the position of the city of Comayagua, its temperature rules higher than that of any other portion of the valley or plain in which it is situated. The temperature of Las Piedras and of San Antonio, distant about fourteen miles, has a mean of from three to five degrees lower. A little place called "El Sitio," not twenty minutes' ride from Comayagua, and not perceptibly higher, has a mean of at least five degrees less.

It should also be borne in mind that, in the interior, the months of April, May, and June are the hottest of the year, and that for the remaining nine months the temperature is considerably lower. November, December, and January are positively cool, and fires sometimes become necessary for comfort.

My remaining direct observations on the temperature of Honduras were too few and too disconnected to be of much value. The following data, however, may serve to illustrate its variety:

City of Tegucigalpa, 3420 feet elevation, for four days, from April 28 to May 4, 1853, inclusive:

Maximum	85°	Fahr.
Minimum	68°	"
Mean average	77° 5′	"

Guajiquero (Indian town), 5265 feet elevation, May 4, 1853, six o'clock A. M., 56° Fahr.

Intibucat, 4950 feet elevation, July 4, 1853, six o'clock A. M., 56°; eleven o'clock A. M., 62°.

City of Gracias, 2520 feet elevation:

July 6, 1853,	12	M.	78°	Fahr.
" " "	7½	P.M.	75°	"
July 7, "	6	A.M.	72°	"
" " "	9	"	75°	"
" " "	2	P.M.	79°	"
" " "	6	"	76°	"
July 8, "	5	A.M.	70° 5′	"

Sta. Rosa, Department of Gracias, 3400 feet above the sea, for three weeks during the month of July, 1853:

Maximum	75°	Fahr.
Minimum	68°	"
Mean average	71° 15′	"

The plain in which is situated the city of Guatemala is elevated between 3000 and 4000 feet above the sea, and lies within eighty miles of the Pacific. The following data relating to its climate are from the Official Gazette:

From 1st to 7th of September, 1854, the extreme range of thermometer was from 64° to 75° of Fahr.; average mean, 68°. It rained for four days during the week, commencing at two o'clock P.M. The remaining three days were dry. Wind generally from S.W.

From 15th to 21st, extreme range of thermometer, 64° to 72° of Fahr.; mean average for the week, 68°. Wind S.W. Rained every day.

From 21st to 28th, extreme range of thermometer, 63° to 76° of Fahr.; average mean, 69°. Rained five days, commencing at two o'clock P.M. Wind generally S.E., changing once to N.E.

The Gazette calculates the entire fall of water for the rainy season at 108 inches, or 5 inches per week. But I doubt if this be more than an estimate, for there are many reasons for believing that the amount of rain which falls there is considerably less than that on the isthmus between Lake Nicaragua and the Pacific, where, from actual observations, it appears that the fall of rain for 1852 was but 97.7 inches. The average amount of rain which falls in America, under the tropics, is calculated by Professor Johnson, in his Tables, at 113 inches. At some points in Brazil, as, for instance, San Luis de Maranhao, the annual average is 276 inches; and in Guadalupe and some of the Lesser Antilles as high as 292 inches!*

Belize.—The British establishment of Belize, situated near the southern extremity of the peninsula of Yucatan, on the Bay of Honduras, in lat. 17° 39′ N., and long. 88° 12′ W., has a temperature and climate which may be regarded as common to the entire eastern coast of Guatemala and Yucatan, and probably not far different from that of the islands off the same coast in the Bay of Honduras. Observations were made here by Captain George Henderson, commander of the garrison in the year 1806, for seven months, from February to August inclusive, with the following results:†

"FEBRUARY.—Thermometer; morning, 77° Fahr.; noon, 81° Fahr.; prevailing winds, N., E., and E.N.E.; clear days, 15.

"Heavy rain generally during the night; frequent heavy

* Thompson asserts of the general temperature of the city of Guatemala, that "the mean heat, during the day, from the first of January to the first of July, is 75° of Fahr.; at night, 63°. In the summer months the average may be taken at ten degrees higher."—*Narrative of Official Visit*, etc., p. 468.

† "The climate of this part of the American continent is greatly superior to that of most other parts of the same vast portion of the globe, either in higher or lower degrees of latitude. It is equally superior to the climate of the West India islands generally, for persons whose health and constitutions have become impaired from the effects of the latter very frequently acquire a sudden restoration of both after an arrival in Honduras.

"With the exception of a few months of the year, this country is constantly refreshed by regular sea breezes, accompanied by an average of heat that may be taken at the temperature of 80°."—*Henderson's Honduras*, p. 13.

showers during the day. This month being included in what is denoted the *dry season*, the rains that have fallen have been considered unusual.

"MARCH.—Morning, 77°; noon, 81°; 21 clear days; prevailing winds, N., N.E., E.N.E., and S.E.

"The greater part of this month has been dry and pleasant; light dews at night. The sea-breeze, which prevails with great regularity at this season, has been partial and moderate.

"APRIL.—Morning, 80°; noon, 85°; 21 clear days; prevailing winds, S.E., E.S.E., and E.

"The whole of this month has been particularly fine, and the breezes regular and strong. Rains, with loud thunder, frequent during the night, sometimes accompanied with sudden and violent gusts of wind.

"MAY.—Morning, 82°; noon, 85°; 21 clear days; prevailing winds, S. or E.S.E.

"This month has been particularly dry, but exceedingly pleasant from the regularity and strength of the sea-breeze. The conclusion of it, however, being cloudy, and attended with frequent heavy showers, shows the approach of the periodical rains.

"JUNE.—Morning, 81°; noon, 83°; 14 clear days; prevailing winds, E., N.E., and E.N.E.

"The wet season generally commences in the early part of this month, about the 10th, and continues through the remainder of it. This season the rains have set in earlier than common. Thunder at this time is also frequent, and sometimes tremendously violent.

"JULY.—Morning, 81°; noon, 83°; 12 clear days; prevailing winds, N.E., E., and S.E.

"The weather for the greater part of this month has been unsettled and stormy; much vivid lightning, chiefly at night, accompanied with loud thunder.

"AUGUST.—Morning, 81°; noon, 84°; 19 clear days; prevailing winds, N.E., E., and S.E.

"The greater part of this month has been exceedingly close and sultry, with frequent and heavy thunder-storms."

CHAPTER III.

POPULATION—GUATEMALA, SAN SALVADOR, HONDURAS, NICARAGUA, AND COSTA RICA.

THE population of Central America, in the absence of reliable data, can only be calculated approximately. Attempts were made under the crown, and subsequently under the republic, to effect a complete census, but with very unsatisfactory results, since it has always been found that the ignorant masses of the people, and especially the Indians, avoid a census as in some way connected with military conscription or taxation. They have been known to abandon their homes, and hide themselves for weeks in the mountains, to escape the commissioners! Again: the bulk of the Spanish population exists on the Pacific slope of the continent, while on the Atlantic declivity the country is either uninhabited, or sparsely occupied by Indian tribes, of which the number is wholly unknown. A considerable aboriginal population exists in the district of Peten, in the north of Guatemala, and there are several tribes, such as the Xicaques, Payas, Tonglas, Woolwas, Towkas, Ramas, Guatusos, etc., in the Atlantic divisions of Honduras, Nicaragua, and Costa Rica, none of whom have entered, as an element, in any calculation of the absolute population of the country.

The royal census of the Captain-Generalcy of Guatemala (which included not only the five states of Central America, but also the present state of Chiapa, and the district of Soconusco in Mexico), made in 1778, gave an aggregate of 805,339 inhabitants. Under this census Guatemala (exclusive of Chiapa and Soconusco) had 392,272 inhabitants.

San Salvador (including Sonsonate, which is now one of its departments) had 161,954 inhabitants.

The diocese of Comayagua, comprising the Province (now State) of Honduras, had 88,143 inhabitants. Thirteen years subsequently, in 1791, an enumeration was made of the population of the same diocese, by its bishop, which gave 93,500, or an increase of 5,357. But, as I have already said, these returns merit but little confidence, and can not be made the basis of any estimate of the actual population of Central America.

In 1825, the state authorities of Guatemala undertook a census, which resulted in an aggregate of 507,126 inhabitants, being an augmentation, in forty-seven years, of only 114,854. Another attempt was made, by the same authorities, twelve years later, in 1837, which gave a total of 490,787, or less by 16,339 than in 1825! This census was discredited at the time, and Don José de la Valle, a statistician of some eminence, made a calculation that the state then contained 600,000 inhabitants.

A census was ordered by the general government of the Republic of Central America in 1834, but the results were imperfect, and have never been published.

In the absence, then, of direct returns, we must have recourse to other means of calculation. In this we are assisted by partial returns of births and deaths in the various districts of several of the states.

Humboldt deduced, from a careful observation of the laws of population in Mexico, that the proportion of births was as 1 to 17, and of deaths as 1 to 30 of the whole population, and that the proportion of births to deaths in the country at large was as 17 to 10. Now, as Mexico, in general aspect, climate, and other conditions, corresponds very closely with Central America, we might assume that the latter country would show but a slight deviation from the same law.

But the data which we possess go to show that the proportion of births to deaths in Central America is considerably greater than in Mexico. In Costa Rica, according to the tables for 1850, the births were 4767, and the deaths 1786, being a proportion of births to deaths of 47 to 17. Again: in Guatemala, for the year 1852, we have the following returns, exclusive of the district of Peten: births, 38,858; deaths, 21,298, or about 10 deaths to 19 births. In San Salvador we have similar results. In the Department of Sonsonate, for the six months ending December 30th, 1853, the births were 1731, deaths 879, or about 10 deaths to 21 births. In the Department of Cuscatlan, for the three months ending December 30th, 1853, births 505, deaths 104. This department seems to be remarkably salubrious. For the first six months of the year 1849, the births were reported at 1900, and the deaths 403. In the Department of San Salvador, embracing the capital, for the last three months of 1849, births 786, deaths 222. In the Department of La Paz, however, which is comparatively low and unhealthy, this excess of births is not sustained, since, for the last quarter of 1853, we find, births 353, deaths 244. The following statistical tables will serve to verify these results:

GUATEMALA.

Official Statement of Marriages, Births, and Deaths in the State of Guatemala for the Year 1852, exclusive of the District of Peten.

Departments.	Marriages.	Births.	Deaths.	Increase.
* Guatemala	240	3416	1848	1568
Sacatepequez . . .	170	1688	1182	506
Amatitlan	130	1481	1073	408
Escuintla.	135	825	421	404
† Vera Paz	828	4260	1642	2618
Santa Rosa	149	1313	466	847
Jutiapa	113	790	291	499
Chiquimula	562	4155	2127	2028
Izabal.	32	67	85	−18
Chimaltenango . .	330	2550	2192	358
Quezaltenango . .	403	3119	1560	1559
Suchitepequez . .	216	1682	736	946
Totonicapam . . .	905	5307	2896	2411
Sololá.	658	3083	1697	1386
San Marcos	592	2711	1744	867
Huehuetenango. .	373	2411	1338	1073
Total	5836	38858	21298	17478

The unhealthy port of Izabal, or Golfo Dulce, decreased in population 18.

* The births and deaths in the city of Guatemala were, in 1805, according to the *Kalendario* of that year:

Marriages 205
Births 1360
Deaths 1337

In 1823, according to Thompson, who gave 50,000 as the aggregate population, the births and deaths were as follows:

Births 1551
Deaths 729

In 1854, according to official tables:

Marriages 172
Births 1467
Deaths 548

† In 1833, it was calculated by Don José Asmitia, then Secretary of State of Guatemala, that the Department of Vera Paz, exclusive of Peten, contained 60,237 inhabitants. The number of marriages in that year was 645; births, 4048; deaths, 1186.

COSTA RICA.

Official Statement of Marriages, Births, and Deaths in the State of Costa Rica for 1850.

Departments.	Marriages.	Births.	Deaths.	Increase.
San José	178	1492	466	1026
Cartago	165	956	293	663
Heredia	128	911	362	549
Alejuela	131	939	424	515
Guanacaste	62	471	223	248
Total	664	4769	1768	3001

SAN SALVADOR—IMPERFECT.

Departments.	Marriages.	Births.	Deaths.	Increase.
Sonsonate . . (6 months) .	173	1731	879	852
Cuscatlan . . (9 months) .	135	2405	816	1589
San Salvador (3 months) .	98	786	222	564
La Paz . . . . (3 months) .	19	353	244	109
Total	425	5275	2161	3114

SUMMARY.

States.	Births.	Deaths.	Increase.
Guatemala . (1852) . . .	38,856	21,298	17,578
Costa Rica . (1850) . . .	4,769	1,768	3,001
San Salvador (imp.) . . .	5,275	2,161	3,114
Total	48,900	25,227	23,693

It results, therefore, that the proportions of births to deaths in Central America is very nearly as 244 to 126, or about 20 to 10. The State of Honduras, which is generally remarkably salubrious, would probably show about the same proportion with Costa Rica, while Nicaragua, although comparatively low, would not fall much behind Guatemala.

Now, assuming the proportion of births and deaths, as fixed by Humboldt in treating of Mexico, to be in respect to the aggregate population as 1 to 17 of the former, and 1 to 30 of the latter, we deduce $(38,858 \times 17)+(21,298 \times 30) \div 2 = 648,763$ as the population of

Guatemala. There are many reasons for believing, however, that this number falls considerably short of the truth. In Costa Rica, the total population, exclusive of the wild tribes, was put down, under the last census, at 95,000, which, it will be seen by reference to preceding tables, gives a proportion of births 1 to 20, and of deaths 1 to 54, of the entire population.

Señor Barberena, of Guatemala, to whom the returns for that state for 1846 were referred, calculated that the births were in the proportion of 1 to 25 of the total population. The births for the year in which he wrote (1849) being 36,998, he deduced 934,495 as the population of the state. I am, however, inclined to think that this is too high an estimate. If we adopt the ratio of births and deaths in Costa Rica as applicable to Guatemala, we have 1,013,126 as the population of the state—a number clearly too great.

I prefer to estimate the total population of Guatemala for 1852 at 787,000, which gives a proportion of births as 1 to 21, and of deaths as 1 to 38 of the entire population, equivalent to about 850,000 on the first day of January, 1855.

Costa Rica, according to the last census, had 100,174 inhabitants, including 5000 savages, in the proportion of 90,000 whites and Ladinos to 10,000 Indians, as follows:

COSTA RICA.

Departments.	Population.
San José	31,749
Cartago	23,209
Heredia	17,289
Guanacaste	9,112
Alejuela	12,575
Punta Arenas	1,240
Savage Tribes	5,000
Total	100,174

Don Felipe Molina, in his "*Bosquejo de Costa Rica,*" regards this result as short of the truth, and estimates that the actual population of Costa Rica in 1850 was not far from 150,000; but his views upon this point are not sustained by any reliable data. The present population of Costa Rica, under the ratio of increase shown by the returns of 1850, must now (1855) be little short of 125,000.

In respect to Nicaragua, we have the authority of Don Miguel Sarabia, its last governor under the crown, who wrote a memoir on that state in 1823.* He says, "The population at the last *padron* (registry), in the year 1813, gave a total of 149,751 inhabitants. We know this to have been imperfect, having been taken by unskillful persons, and under many difficulties. The population in many sections is dispersed and inaccessible, and an enumeration is associated in the minds of the vulgar with ideas of contributions and personal service. An enumeration made in 1800, although probably not more correct, gave a population of 159,000. It would thus appear that there had been a diminution of numbers; but such is not the fact, as is evident from all concurrent testimony, the growth of the towns, and the circumstance that there have been neither famines, wars, or other causes to produce such a result." Nevertheless, taking the census of 1813 for the basis of his calculation, and estimating the decennial increase at fifteen per cent., he arrives at a total of 174,213 in 1823. But, retaining the same elements of calculation, on the basis of the census of 1800, we would have, in 1823, a population of 212,000.

According to the returns of a census attempted in

* *Bosquejo Politico Estadistico de Nicaragua, formado in el año de* 1823, por Miguel Gonzalez Sarabia, General de Brigada. Guatemala, 1824.

Nicaragua in 1846, the total population of that state, exclusive of the Department of Guanacaste (in dispute with Costa Rica), was 257,000, distributed among five departments, as follows:

NICARAGUA—1846.

Departments.	Population.
Meridional	20,000
Oriental	95,000
Occidental	90,000
Septentrional of Segovia	12,000
" " Matagalpa	40,000
Total	257,000

Assuming these returns to be correct, we may safely estimate the present population of Nicaragua at 300,000.

San Salvador has, relatively to its extent, much the largest population of any of the states of Central America, but we are without complete census returns, except for a single department. In the year 1849, the Department of Cuscatlan had a total of 62,361 inhabitants, distributed in four districts, as follows: District of Suchitoto, 13,234; Cojutepeque, 25,737; Chalatenango, 14,011; Tejutla, 9379 = 62,361. Of these, 16,165 were men, 17,903 women, 15,026 boys, and 13,317 girls. The town of Cojutepeque had 11,072 inhabitants; that of Suchitoto, 6251; Ilobasco, 4259; and Chalatenango, 3052.

Now, by reference to the preceding returns of births and deaths in several of the departments of this state, we find that the quarterly increase in the department of Cuscatlan is 523, in that of Sonsonate 425, in that of San Salvador 564, and in that of La Paz 109, from which we may legitimately infer that San Salvador and Sonsonate have respectively about the same number of inhabitants with Cuscatlan, and that La Paz has about one fourth as many. Of the two remaining departments, San Miguel has probably more than Cuscatlan, and San Vicente two thirds as many. La Paz has also more than might be inferred from the returns of births and deaths for the single quarter of 1852, which may have been exceptional and unfavorable.

Assuming these elements of calculation to be good, and that the population of the Department of Cuscatlan has had a constant annual increase of about 2000, as evinced by the returns of births and deaths, we have the following estimate of the population of the entire state at the commencement of the present year:

SAN SALVADOR—1855.

Departments.	Population.
Cuscatlan	75,000
Sonsonate	75,000
San Salvador	80,000
San Miguel	80,000
La Paz	28,000
San Vicente	56,000
Total	394,000

The data necessary for calculating the population of Honduras are even fewer than we possess concerning the other states of Central America. We have neither absolute returns of population, nor returns of births and deaths. The only facts which bear upon the matter are the bishop's census of the province in 1791, which gave 93,500 as the total population, and the census of the single department of Gracias in 1834, which gave 30,017 inhabitants. We may nevertheless assume for this state a ratio of increase as great as for any other state of Central America, for none has a climate more salubrious. Taking the same ratio of increase with Costa Rica, the Department of

Gracias would now have 50,000 inhabitants, which number, after having traveled over much of the department, I am convinced is not far from the truth. Now, of the remaining departments of Honduras, it is probable that Sta. Barbara and Choluteca about equal Gracias in population, while Tegucigalpa and Comayagua exceed, and Yoro and Olancho fall below it in this respect. Having visited and passed through all of the departments except Yoro and Olancho, I estimate their respective populations as follows, in round numbers, and exclusive of the wild Indian tribes in the eastern section of the state:

HONDURAS—1855.

Departments.	Population.
Sta. Barbara	45,000
Gracias	55,000
Comayagua	70,000
Tegucigalpa	65,000
Choluteca	50,000
Olancho	45,000
Yoro	20,000
Total	350,000

These calculations are all exclusive of the Indians, who are not directly incorporated in the civil organization of the various states, or who fall under the local denomination of "*Tribus Errantes*"—a misapplied designation, since all the Central American Indians are fixed in their habits of life. The nearest approach to a nomad life is found among the mongrel savages called "Moscos" or "Mosquitos," on what is known as the "Mosquito Shore." They are a mixed breed of negroes and Indians, who derive their principal support from the creeks and lagoons on the coast, to which their residence is strictly confined. It is not probable that they number more than 6000. The number of the Xicaques, Payas, Towkas, Woolwas, and Ramas, which intervene between the coast and the Spanish settlements, can not be accurately estimated. The Guatusos, Talamancas, and other tribes in Nicaragua and Costa Rica are also omitted in the above estimates, as are also the Itzaes and affiliated families, Lacandones, Manches, etc., occupying the northern part of the Department of Vera Paz, in Guatemala, and who are supposed to be numerous. Nearly all of these Indians admit a qualified allegiance to the various states within which they fall, but the relationship is scarcely more than nominal. Thus, in 1836, the government of Central America made a kind of treaty with the Manches, in which the Indians acknowledged the sovereignty of the republic, but were to be exempt from the operations of its laws for six years, and, furthermore, were never to be called in question as to their religion, nor disturbed in their practice of polygamy. Wherever the governments assume to exercise jurisdiction, it is through Indian officials, who nevertheless administer affairs after the immemorial manner of the Indians themselves, as in the case of the Nahuals of the Balsam Coast of San Salvador, who live almost within sight of the capital of the state.

The aggregate population of Central America, as deduced from the foregoing data, is as follows:

CENTRAL AMERICA—1855.

States.	Area in Square Miles.	Population.	Number to Square Mile.
Guatemala.	43,380	850,000	20 nearly.
Honduras	39,600	350,000	9
San Salvador . . .	9,594	394,000	41
Nicaragua	49,500	300,000	6
Costa Rica	13,590	125,000	10 nearly.
Total	155,664	2,019,000	13

Scanty as this population seems to be, it is nevertheless, relatively to the area of Central America, much larger than that of any of the Spanish American states. Chili has scarcely two thirds as many inhabitants to the square mile, and Mexico but little more than half as many, as will appear from the subjoined Table, compiled from the latest and most authentic sources.

COMPARATIVE TABLE.

Countries.	Square Miles.	Population.	Number to Square Mile.
Central America . .	155,934	2,019,000	13
Mexico	762,000	7,853,000	10
New Granada	380,000	1,360,000	$3\frac{2}{3}$
Venezuela	410,000	887,100	$2\frac{1}{7}$
Ecuador.	320,000	550,000	$1\frac{3}{4}$
Peru	405,000	1,500,000	$3\frac{1}{2}$
Bolivia	380,000	1,200,000	$3\frac{1}{6}$
Chili	170,000	1,300,000	8
Brazil	2,720,000	4,450,000	2 nearly.

The data bearing upon the proportion of sexes in the aggregate population, although too imperfect to be worth presenting, nevertheless go to show that, as in Mexico, there is a considerable preponderance of females over males. The disproportion between the sexes in births is not so great as in deaths; for while there are nearly as many males born as females, considerably more of the former die annually than of the latter. This is confirmed by general observation, since the fact that there are more old women than old men could scarcely escape the notice of the most careless traveler. This result is not to be ascribed to any supposed exemption of females from fatigue and exposure, as they really perform an equal share of the labor of the country, and, excepting in the towns, are quite as much exposed to influences detrimental to health as the males. They are, however, much less addicted to drunkenness, a vice which, under the tropics, is rapid and certain in its consequences. The returns of the partial census of Nicaragua, in 1846, gave for the Department Occidental (Leon) 25,870 males, and 48,058 females; total, 73,928, or a proportion of almost two females to one male. Assuming that there are no errors in these figures, we can only partially account for the disparity by ascribing it to the wars which afflicted that department for several years previously, and in which its inhabitants maintained an obstinate conflict, single handed, not only against the remaining districts of the state, but against the combined forces of Honduras and San Salvador. The Department of Cuscatlan, in San Salvador, as we have seen, had, in 1849, a population of 16,165 men, and 17,903 women, an excess of 1838 women; while, on the other hand, the boys were 15,026, girls 13,317, or an excess of 1709 boys.*

The relative proportions of whites, mixed (Ladinos), and Indians, in the populations of the various Spanish American states, is a subject of profound interest, and to the modern student will appear of vital consequence in all speculations on the condition, capacities, and destinies of the people of those countries. But here we have also to regret the absence of reliable data; for while it is the concurrent testimony of all intelligent and observing men in Central America that the pure whites are not only relatively but absolutely decreasing in numbers, and that the pure Indians are rapidly increasing, and the Ladinos more and more approximating to the aboriginal type, yet the statistics

* "In Central America, an extraordinary excess is observable in the births of white and Ladina females over those of the males; the former being in the proportion to the latter as six, or at least as five to four. Among the Indians, the births of males and females are about equal."—Col. GALINDO, *Journ. Roy. Geog. Soc. of London*, vol. vi., p. 126.

bearing directly upon the subject are imperfect or wholly wanting. The actual Bishop of Guatemala, Sr. Don Garcia Pelaez, writing in 1841, and proceeding upon the census of 1837 and other data within his reach, estimated the population of Central America, at that time, to be, Spaniards and white Creoles, 89,979; Ladinos, 619,167; Indians, 681,367; total, 1,390,513. This calculation allows one white inhabitant to sixteen mixed and Indian, which proportion, I entertain no doubt, has now decreased to, at most, one of the former to twenty of the latter.

Don Miguel Sarabia, whose memoir on Nicaragua, written in 1823, is elsewhere quoted, estimated the entire population of that province at that period at 174,213, and gave it as his judgment that about two fifths, or 79,680, were Indians, two fifths Ladinos, and less than one fifth whites." The latter he considered as diminishing in numbers, and such, he observes, "*is their general tendency.*"

Colonel Galindo, an intelligent Irishman, in the service of the old Federation of Central America, in a communication to the Royal Geographical Society of London, estimated the entire population of Central America, at the period when he wrote (1837?), at 1,900,000, divided as follows:

States.	Indians.	Ladinos.	Whites.	Totals.
Guatemala . .	450,000	150,000	100,000	700,000
Honduras . . .		240,000	60,000	300,000
San Salvador.	90,000	230,000	80,000	400,000
Nicaragua. . .	120,000	120,000	110,000	350,000
Costa Rica . .	25,000		125,000	150,000
Total . . .	685,000	740,000	475,000	1,900,000

The proportion of whites is largely over-estimated by Galindo. He puts down Honduras as without an Indian population, when there can be little doubt that at least one third, if not one half of its inhabitants, apart from the wild tribes, are of pure Indian stock.

Mr. Thompson, who was British commissioner to the old Federation of Central America in 1823, estimated the relative proportions of the people as follows:

Whites and Creoles	One fifth.
Mixed Classes	Two fifths.
Indians	Two fifths.

He estimated the Europeans, "or perfect whites," at not more than 5000. Mr. Crowe, referring specifically to Guatemala, calculates the proportions as follows:

Indians	Three fifths.
Ladinos	One fourth.
Whites	One fortieth.
Mulattoes	One eightieth.
Negroes	One fiftieth.
Sambos	One one hundredth.

Ladinos, it may be observed, is a term signifying gallant men, and is understood to apply to the descendants of whites and Indians. It is only used in Central America.

The following Table probably exhibits very nearly the exact proportions in Central America, so far as they may be deduced from existing data and from personal observation:*

* The various classes in Mexico were estimated by Mr. Brantz Mayer in 1842 as follows:

Indians	4,000,000
Whites	1,000,000
Negroes	6,000
Mixed	2,009,000
Total	7,015,000

This estimate gives a ratio of whites as one to seven of the entire population. In some of the states the proportion is greater, in others less. In Peru, Humboldt calculated the white population as 12 in 100, or about one to nine.

Whites	100,000
Mixed	800,000
Negroes	10,000
Indians	1,109,000
Total	2,019,000

From the foregoing facts and observations, it may be deduced generally that Central America is relatively the most populous portion of Spanish America; that, while its population is increasing in a constant and rapid ratio, the exotic or European element is not only decreasing relatively, but in fact; and that the direct tendency of things is to its speedy absorption in the indigenous or aboriginal races. In this respect, as indeed in its moral and intellectual condition, Central America, not less than all Spanish America, seems to furnish a striking illustration of the laws which have been established as the results of anthropological inquiries during the past fifty years. Neither the statesman nor political economist can safely overlook or disregard these results, since, by the course of events, and the multiplication of means and facilities of communication, nations and races are more and more brought in contact, and the question of the nature and character of their relationship made of immediate and practical importance.

It may be claimed without hesitation that the wide physical, intellectual, and moral differences which all history and observation have distinguished as existing between the various families of man, can be no longer regarded as the consequences of accident or of circumstances; that is to say, it has come to be understood that their physical, moral, and intellectual traits are radical and permanent, and that there can be no admixture of widely-separated families, or of superior with inferior races, which can be harmonious, or otherwise than disastrous in its consequences. Anthropological science has determined the existence of two laws of vital importance in their application to men and nations:

First. That in all cases where a free amalgamation takes place between two different stocks, unrestrained by what is sometimes called prejudice, but which is, in fact, a natural instinct, the result is the final and absolute absorption of one in the other. This absorption is more rapid as the races or families thus brought in contact approximate in type, and in proportion as one or the other preponderates in numbers; that is to say, Nature perpetuates no human hybrids, as, for instance, a permanent race of mulattoes.

Second. That all violations of the natural distinctions of race, or of those instincts which were designed to perpetuate the superior races in their purity, invariably entail the most deplorable results, affecting the bodies, intellects, and moral perceptions of the nations who are thus blind to the wise designs of Nature, and unmindful of her laws. In other words, the offspring of such combinations or amalgamations are not only generally deficient in physical constitution, in intellect, and in moral restraint, but to a degree which often contrasts unfavorably with any of the original stocks.

In no respect are these deficiencies more obvious than in matters affecting government. We need only point to the anarchical states of Spanish America to verify the truth of the propositions here laid down. In Central and South America, and Mexico, we find a people not only demoralized from the unrestrained association of different races, but also the superior stocks becoming gradually absorbed in the lower, and their institutions disappearing under the relative barbarism of which the latter are the exponents. If existing causes and conditions continue to operate, many years can not pass before some of these countries will have relapsed into a state not far removed from that in which they were found at the period of the conquest.

In Mexico there are less than two millions of whites, or of persons having a preponderance of white blood, out of a population of eight millions; in Central America, less than two hundred thousand out of two millions; and in South America at large, the proportions are nearly the same. It is impossible, while conceding all the influence which can be rationally claimed for other causes, to resist the conviction that the disasters which have befallen those countries are due to a grand practical misconception of the just relations of the races which compose them. The Indian does not possess, still less the South Sea Islander, and least of all the negro, the capacity to comprehend the principles which enter into the higher order of civil and political organizations. His instincts and his habits are inconsistent with their development, and no degree of education can teach him to understand and practice them.

In the Sandwich Islands there are about 60,000 natives still remaining. It may be alleged that they have constituted and sustained a regular government, and have thus evinced the requisite conditions to enter into the great family of nations. But it is notorious that, whatever there exists of government, both in its origin and administration, is the work of foreigners and of white men.

To the Indians upon our southwestern border these remarks are scarcely less applicable. Under no circumstances have the North American Indians exhibited an appreciation of the value, or a disposition to abide by the reciprocal obligations involved in a government of the people. Their ideas of government, like those of the Arabs, and the nomadic hordes of Central Asia, are only consonant with the system called patriarchal: ideas which, at this day and in this country, are not only wholly inapplicable, but antagonistic to those upon which our system is founded. The only instance in which they have made a sensible progress in the right direction is that of the Cherokees, under the guidance of chiefs in whose veins flows a predominance of European blood. And while it may be admitted that the Indians of the old Floridian stock are in all respects superior to the islanders of the Pacific, yet neither in industry, docility, or traditional deference to authority are they equal to the Indian families of Mexico and Central America, where the attempt to put the latter on a political and social footing with the white man has entailed eternal anarchy, and threatens a complete dissolution of the political body.

In Guatemala, as in Yucatan, it has brought about a bloody and cruel war of castes, and in the former state has resulted in placing a treacherous and unscrupulous half-breed at the head of affairs, who rules over a desolated country with irresponsible sway. Not less disastrous has been the result in Mexico, while in Jamaica savage nature is fast resuming her dominion over deserted plantations, and the woods begin to swarm with half-naked negroes, living upon the indigenous fruits of the soil, and already scarcely one degree removed from their original barbarism in Africa.

To the understanding of intelligent and reflecting men, who are superior to the partisan and sectional issues of the hour, these considerations can not fail to appeal with controlling force; for if the United States, as compared with the Spanish American republics, has achieved an immeasurable advance in all the elements of greatness, that result is eminently due to the rigid and inexorable refusal of the dominant Teutonic stock to debase its blood, impair its intellect, lower its moral standard, or peril its institutions by intermixture with the inferior and subordinate races of man. In obedience to the ordinances of Heaven, it has rescued half a continent from savage beasts and still more savage men, whose period of existence has terminated, and who must give place to higher organizations and a superior life. Short-sighted philanthropy may lament, and sympathy drop a tear as it looks forward to the total disappearance of the lower forms of humanity, but the laws of Nature are irreversible. *Deus vult*—it is the will of God!

From this point of view, it appears that the only hope of Central America consists in averting the numerical decline of its white population, and increasing that element in the composition of its people. If not brought about by a judicious encouragement of emigration or an intelligent system of colonization, the geographical position and resources of the country indicate that the end will be attained by those more violent means, which among men, as in the material world, often anticipate the slower operations of natural laws. To avert the temporary yet often severe shocks which they occasion, by providing for the necessities of the future, is the true mission, and should be the highest aim of the patriot and statesman. Central America will be fortunate if she shall be found to number among her sons men adequate to the comprehension and control of the circumstances under which she is placed, and which are every day becoming more complicated and exigent.

HONDURAS.

CHAPTER IV.

DISCOVERY—BOUNDARIES—GENERAL ASPECT—TOPOGRAPHY, ETC.

IT was in Honduras that Columbus first planted his feet on the continent of America. In 1502, then sailing on his fourth voyage, he discovered the island of Guanaja (or Bonacca), which he named the Isle of Pines. From this island he descried to the southward the high mountains of the main land, and, pursuing his course in that direction, on the 14th of August landed at a point which he called *Punta de Casinas* (now Cabo de Honduras), and formally took possession of the country on behalf of the crown of Spain. He subsequently coasted to the eastward, touching at the mouth of Rio Tinto, or Black River, and finally, after great delays and dangers, reached a point where the coast, abruptly trending to the southward, formed a cape, to which, in gratitude for his safety, he gave the name of "*Cabo Gracias á Dios*," Cape Thanks to God. He lost a boat, with some sailors, in attempting to enter the Great Cape or Wanks River, which was, in consequence, called *Rio del Desastre*. From Cape Gracias he continued his voyage along what is now the Mosquito Shore, called by him *Cariay*, to the Isthmus of Darien.

Less than twenty years afterward, the conqueror of

Mexico, Hernando Cortez, inspired by the accounts of vast and populous kingdoms to the southward of the prostrate empire of Montezuma, undertook an expedition into Honduras, which at this time was called Hibueras or Higueras. This expedition, both for its length, and the difficulties which were encountered and overcome in its prosecution, stands, and will forever stand, unprecedented and unapproachable in the history of martial adventure.

Starting from the Isthmus of Tehuantepec, Cortez boldly entered the vast and unknown wilderness which intervened between the confines of Mexico and the country of which he was in search. For two years he struggled among deep morasses, broad and almost impassable rivers, and high and desert mountains, with almost superhuman courage and endurance. At the end of that time he reached the point where Columbus had made his first landing in Honduras, and there, after receiving the submission of the neighboring chiefs, he founded the ancient city, now the port, of Truxillo.

In addition to the names of Columbus and Cortez, those of Alvarado, Cristoval de Olid, and Cordova appear in the list of daring and zealous captains who distinguished themselves in the exploration of the country and its reduction to the Spanish crown. But it is not my purpose to write the history of Spanish power in Honduras. Suffice it to say that as early as 1540, sixty years before Jamestown was founded, and nearly a hundred years before Hudson entered the Bay of New York, Honduras had its large and flourishing cities, and the Audiencia of the Confines had been established within its borders.

Subsequently the seat of the Audiencia was transferred to Guatemala, and from that time forward, until the independence of the Spanish American states, Honduras constituted a part of the kingdom or captain-generalcy of Guatemala, which comprised the provinces or intendencias of Guatemala, Honduras, San Salvador, Nicaragua, and Costa Rica. These threw off their allegiance to Spain in 1821, and, assuming the rank of sovereign states, soon after united in a confederacy called the "Republic of Central America." This union, in consequence of internal dissensions and the struggles of factions, became practically dissolved in 1839, since which time, although various efforts have been made to revive its provisions, the several states have asserted and now exercise their original sovereign powers as distinct republics.

The Republic of Honduras, therefore, comprises the territory which pertained to it as a province. It is bounded upon the north and east by the Bay of Honduras and the Caribbean Sea, extending from the mouth of the Rio Tinto, lat. 15° 45′ N., and long. 88° 30′ W., to Cape Gracias á Dios, at the mouth of the Rio Wanks or Segovia, in lat. 14° 59′, and long. 83° 11′, being a coast-line of about 400 statute miles. Upon the south it is bounded by the Republic of Nicaragua. The line of division follows the Rio Wanks for about two thirds of its length, and thence deflects to the southwest to the sources of the Rio Negro, flowing into the Gulf of Fonseca. It has a coast-line of about sixty miles on this gulf, from the Rio Negro to the Rio Goascoran, and embraces the large islands of Tigre, Sacate Grande, and Gueguensi. Upon the west and southwest it is bounded by the republics of San Salvador and Guatemala. The line of separation is irregular. Commencing on the Gulf of Fonseca, at the mouth of the Rio Goascoran, it follows that river for about thirty miles in a direction due north, to the mouth of one of its affluents from the northwest, called Rio Pescado. From the head of this stream it strikes a branch of the Rio Torola (flowing southwest into the Rio Lempa), which it follows to its mouth. Thence it follows the Rio Lempa to the mouth of the Rio Sumpul, which it ascends nearly to its source, to a point where its waters approach those of the Rio Paza, separating San Salvador from Guatemala. From this point it runs nearly northeast, along the mountain chain of Merendon and Grita, leaving the town and ruins of Copan about fifteen miles to the southeast, until it strikes the headwaters of the small stream called Rio Tinto, which it follows to the Bay of Honduras.

The state is therefore embraced entirely within 83° 20′ and 89° 30′ west longitude, and 13° 10′ and 16° north latitude, and comprises not far from 39,600 square miles, or about the same area with the State of Ohio.

The large island of Roatan, with its dependencies, Guanaja or Bonacca, Utilla, Helena, Barbaretta, and Morat, also pertain to Honduras, but are now, under the denomination of the "Colony of the Bay Islands," forcibly occupied by Great Britain, in violation of the rights and sovereignty of Honduras, and of the explicit terms of the treaty with the United States of 1850. Great Britain has also set up claims to a considerable portion of the eastern coast of Honduras, from Cape Comorin, or Cape of Honduras, a few miles to the eastward of Truxillo, to Cape Gracias á Dios, on behalf of the suppositious "Mosquito King."

The general physical features of Honduras have been indicated in the preceding chapter, on the Geography and Topography of Central America. As, however, the greater part of what follows, in this brief memoir, pertains to this state, I am warranted in entering more into details concerning it. As I have said, its general aspect is mountainous; that is to say, it is traversed in various directions by ranges of mountains and hills, radiating from the common base of the Cordilleras. This great chain, which may be regarded as the foundation and support of the continent, does not, in Honduras, approach within fifty or sixty miles of the Pacific. Nor does it throughout maintain its general character of an unbroken range, but in its course sometimes turns back on itself, forming interior basins or valleys, within which are collected the head waters of the large streams that traverse the country in the direction of the Atlantic Ocean. Nevertheless, viewed from the Pacific, it presents the general appearance of a great natural wall, with a lower range of mountains, relieved by volcanic peaks of wonderful regularity of outline, intervening between it and the Western Sea. It would almost seem that, at one time, the waters of the Pacific broke at the very feet of this great mountain barrier, and that the subordinate coast-range had been subsequently thrust up by volcanic forces. In San Salvador this conjecture seems to be wholly verified; for the high ridge, averaging some two thousand feet in altitude, and which extends from the volcano of San Miguel to that of Apeneca, separated from the true Cordilleras by the parallel valley of the River Lempa, is throughout of volcanic origin. Not less than eleven volcanic peaks bristle along its summit; and the traveler rides from one end of the state to the other over an almost unbroken bed of scoriæ and ashes, largely mixed with pumice, occasionally relieved by beds of lava and volcanic stones. In Nicaragua this volcanic range subsides for intervals, and is only marked by high cones and broken craters, while the Cordilleras trend away to the southeast on the northern border of the transverse basin of the Nicaraguan lakes.

As I have said, Honduras has but a narrow frontage of about sixty miles on the Pacific, and within this limit the volcanic coast-range is wholly wanting. Its place is supplied by the high islands, of volcanic origin, pertaining to the state, in the Bay of Fonseca.

The northern and eastern coast of Honduras presents several bold groups of mountains, which are the ends of the dependent ranges radiating north and east from the Cordilleras. These subordinate ranges strike the northern coast diagonally, and lap by each other in such a manner as to appear from the sea like an unbroken chain. Hence it has occurred that in some of the charts of that coast, although the mouths of the large rivers flowing from the interior are indicated, the rivers themselves are rendered impossible by a continuous chain of mountains, represented as skirting the shore at a very short distance inland.

The Cordilleras proper, or the great dividing ridge which separates the waters flowing into the Pacific from those falling into the Atlantic, traverses the state in a general direction northwest and southeast. Its course, however, is serpentine, and at one point, at least, it is interrupted by a large transverse valley, of which, as offering probably the most favorable route for a railway between the two seas, I shall have occasion to speak farther. Starting from the high plateaus of Guatemala, this range pursues a course nearly east until it reaches the frontier of Honduras, where it is deflected to the southeast, while a higher spur, or range, not inferior in elevation to the "Sierra Madre," or

Mother Mountain, runs off east by north to the Bay of Honduras. At the point of separation, this range is called the Mountains of Merendon, afterward Grita, and nearer the coast, the Mountains of Espiritu Santo. On the coast itself, where it sustains the majestic height of between seven and eight thousand feet, it is called the Mountains of Omoa. Along its northern base flows the Rio Motagua, rising near the city of Guatemala, and falling into the Bay of Honduras; and at its feet, on the south, flows the Rio Chamelicon, which in turn is separated from the parallel river Santiago by only a range of hills, terminating in the broad plain of Sula, near the mouth of the River Ulua.

Following the course of the Sierra Madre, we find it, at the distance of a few leagues from the Mountains of Merendon, involving itself in a tangled mass or knot of mountains known as the Mountains of Selaque. Intermediately lies the large valley or plain of Sensenti, in which the Rio Santiago takes its rise. This great plain is not less than thirty miles long, by from ten to twenty wide, and is almost shut in by mountains. Its only outlet is the narrow valley, or rather gorge, through which it is drained by the Rio Higuito or Talgua.

The Mountains of Selaque constitute one of the principal centres of elevation in Honduras, their summits rising to the height of between eight and ten thousand feet. The uppermost branch of the River Santiago, called at various points Talgua, Higuito, Alas, and Rio de la Valle, bends around these mountains on the north and west. Another branch, the Rio Mejicote or Rio Grande de Gracias, separates them on the east from the Mountains of Puca, with their lofty peak, and from the terraced Mountains of Opalaca or Intibucat, with their truncated summits and elevated plains, on which flourish the cereal grains, and the fruits of the temperate zone.

Next in order comes the valley of the Rio Sta. Barbara, one of the principal affluents of the Santiago, which, below the point of junction, is often called the Venta. The Rio Sta. Barbara, like the Santiago, has its sources in high plains, the principal of which is the valley or plain of Otoro, only separated from that of Comayagua by the group of mountains known as the Montecillos. These are formed by the true range of the Cordilleras, which turns abruptly from its general east by south course to a direction due north, and finally loses itself in diverging ranges toward the coast. These divergences create another mountain-bound valley, in the centre of which lies the Lake of Yojoa or Taulebé.

We now come to the most remarkable topographical feature of the state, considered in reference to the facilities which it offers for the grand economic purposes of travel and commerce between the oceans. At the eastern base of the Montecillos range, where the interruption of the Cordilleras is complete, lies the plain of Comayagua, from which, extending due north to the Atlantic Ocean, is the valley of the Rio Humuya, and, extending due south to the Pacific, is the valley of the Rio Goascoran—altogether constituting a great transverse valley reaching from sea to sea. These two rivers may be said to rise in the same plain, for they both have their sources side by side in the slight dividing ridge or swell of land which defines its southern extremity.

The plain of Comayagua has an extreme length of perhaps forty miles, by a general width of from five to fifteen miles. Its longest axis is nearly due north and south, coinciding with the general direction of the two rivers already named. It slopes almost imperceptibly toward the north, and is watered by the Rio Humuya, which runs through its centre. It is separated from the considerable plain of Espino on the north by low hills, which alone prevent the two plains from being regarded as one. Together, these two plains, both of surpassing beauty of scenery, fertility of soil, and salubrity of climate, occupy nearly one third of the distance between the Bay of Honduras and that of Fonseca.

Passing the plain of Comayagua, the Cordilleras are resumed in a great mass or group of high mountains, known toward the north as the Mountains of Comayagua, and on the south as the Mountains of Lepaterique. They extend about eighty miles from north to south, and near the centre send off a high range known as the Mountains of Ule, around which, almost describing a circle, flows the Rio Choluteca.

The valley of the Rio Choluteca, after that river turns the flank of the Ule Mountains, is broad and fertile. As it approaches the Bay of Fonseca, it widens into extensive, densely-wooded alluvions, which nevertheless are so high as to be above overflows, and are without swamps or marshes. Dependent upon this valley is a subordinate one, of great beauty, called Valle de Yuguare.

Nearly to the eastward of the high mountains of Comayagua, after passing the river and valley of Sulaco, we come to a knot or group of high mountains, called the Mountains of Sulaco. Standing almost in the centre of the state, it sends the streams which have their rise in its gorges to every point of the compass. Here the great River Wanks or Segovia, reaching the Atlantic at Cape Gracias á Dios, takes its origin, as do also the large rivers Aguan or Roman, and Tinto or Black River, flowing north into the Bay of Honduras, and the tributaries of the Choluteca, flowing south into the Pacific. From this elevated centre also radiate several extensive ranges of mountains, scarcely inferior to their parent in elevation. That which extends to the northeast, separating the numerous rivers flowing into the Bay of Honduras from the valley of the Rio Wanks or Segovia, is called the Mountains of Misoco. The range which extends to the north, and which terminates its numerous spurs in the high peaks of Congrehoy, frowning over the Bay of Honduras, is called the Mountains of Pija, while the chain which pursues a tortuous course to the southwest, and finally skirts the northern border of the transverse valley of the Nicaraguan lakes, is called the Mountains of Chili. The latter may be regarded as the true Cordilleras. At the base of the Mountains of Sulaco, to the east and northeast, are the broad and elevated plains or terraces of Olancho and Yoro, celebrated, even in Central America, for the number and excellence of their cattle. The rivers on this slope of the continent abound in goldwashings, and may perhaps furnish, when the country becomes better known, a supply of gold scarcely less than that which has been obtained from California. Unfortunately, most of the wide region between the Mountains of Sulaco and the Atlantic, embracing nearly half of the whole territory of the state, is uninhabited except by detached Indian tribes. But little is known of the country, except that it is very diversified, and rich in the nature of its soil and the variety of its minerals.

The northern coast of Honduras presents a diversified surface. A portion is flat, and covered with vast growths of timber. Among the precious woods, the mahogany is most abundant. It would be a great mistake to suppose this coast to be of the same character with that known as the Mosquito Shore, where the land is low, and filled with hundreds of swamps and lagoons. The mountains, as I have already said, often come down to the sea, or rise not very far inland. The Mountains of Omoa shadow over the Bay of Amatique, and those of Congrehoy and Poyas are conspicuous landmarks from the ocean, which breaks almost at their feet.

PHYSICAL SECTIONS.

The topographical features which I have indicated will probably be best explained by the accompanying vertical sections, reduced from a series of barometrical observations:

I. A section of Honduras, commencing at Puerto Caballos, on the Bay of Honduras, and extending thence southward, following the valleys first of the Rio Ulua and afterward of the Rio Humuya, through the plains of Espino and Comayagua, and past the dividing ridge (which has its greatest elevation at the southern extremity of the plain last named), down the valley of the Rio Goascoran to the Bay of Fonseca on the Pacific Ocean, a distance of one hundred and fifty miles. This section runs through the lowest pass in the whole line of the Cordilleras, from the transverse valley of the Nicaraguan lakes to the Isthmus of Tehuantepec. It exhibits a longitudinal view of the plains of Espino and Comayagua, which may almost be regarded as one. These are remarkable, not only as having their longest axis due north and south, but as lying transversely to the general course of the Cordilleras, the altitude of which, where they are interrupted, is also indicated in the section.

This section shows the profile of the proposed interoceanic railway from Puerto Caballos to the Bay of Fonseca, and illustrates its eminent feasibility in respect of grades. Under this aspect, as affording an avenue between the seas, the great transverse valley of Comayagua may justly be regarded as the most important physical feature of Honduras.

II. A section commencing at the city of Leon, in Nicaragua, and following the mule-road thence nearly due north to the town of Ocotal, the capital of the Department of Nueva Segovia,* thence nearly due northwest, through the departments of Tegucigalpa and Comayagua, to the town of Santa Rosa, in the Department of Gracias, Honduras. This section, it will be observed, coincides very nearly with the course of the Cordilleras. From Leon to the summit of the mountains near the town of San Juan de la Maya, the mule-path runs on the western side of the Cordilleras, thence to the summit of the Mountains of Chili on their eastern declivity. From the point last named to the summit of the mountains overlooking the plain of Comayagua, the waters flow to the southward; from thence to the high mountains of Intibucat, to the northward. The next summit is crossed near the little town of San Juan (Department of Gracias), beyond which the waters flow toward the north. In other words, this section intersects the Cordilleras at six points:

1. Near San Juan de la Maya, in Nicaragua, at an elevation of . . . . 1900 feet.
2. At the crest of the Mountains of Chili, at an elevation of . . . . 3400 "

* The barometrical observations upon which is founded that portion of the section from Leon to Comayagua were made by Dr. S. W. Woodhouse, to whom I am indebted for the original notes.

3. At the crest of the Mountains of Comayagua, at an elevation of . . . . . . 4900 feet.
4. Height of Pass of Guajoca, plain of Comayagua, 2400 "
5. Crest of Mountains of Intibucat . . . 5900 "
6. Near village of San Juan de Gracias . . 4000 "

The road from Santa Rosa to San Salvador crosses the Cordilleras at the Pass of Canguacota, at an elevation of 4100 feet, but the mule-roads only cross the grand dividing ridge at its lowest passes. These have an average elevation of 3800 feet. Proceeding upon this basis and upon other observations, I think that the average elevation of the Cordilleras of Honduras, exclusive of isolated peaks, may be estimated at not less than 6000 feet. The plateau of Tegucigalpa has an average elevation of 3400 feet, that of Intibucat 5300 feet, and that of Sta. Rosa, or, rather, of the Department of Gracias in general, of 3200, and the plain of Comayagua of 1900 feet. The inhabited central portions of the state, or what may be called the grand plateau of Honduras, has an average elevation of 3200, or something less than one half that of the great plateau of Mexico. It is calculated that temperature diminishes in the proportion of one degree of Fahrenheit for every 334 feet of elevation. The average temperature at noon at the mouth of Black River, on the northern coast of Honduras, as shown in a preceding table, is a little less than 70° Fahr. These elements of calculation would therefore give 60° of Fahr. as the average noonday temperature of the plateau of Honduras, which is equal to about 55° of mean average temperature.

III. This section may be understood as coinciding with the meridian of 89° 10′ lon. W. from Greenwich, or 12° 10′ W. from Washington. It commences at the precise point where Section II. terminates, *i. e.*, at

Santa Rosa, Department of Gracias in Honduras, and extends thence, nearly due south, across the State of San Salvador to the Pacific Ocean. It exhibits a longitudinal profile of the valley or plain of Sensenti, as also a transverse section of the valley of the River Lempa, which may be understood as extending from the Pass of Monte Redondo to the crest of the volcanic range which intervenes between the true Cordilleras and the Pacific Ocean. The features illustrated by this section will be more fully explained when we come to speak specifically of the physical conformation of San Salvador.

It will of course be understood that these sections are only approximations in respect of horizontal distances, and that the general elevations, except at ruling points, are also laid down approximately. Any thing beyond these, in a general reconnaissance of a diversified country, is impossible.

Topographically, therefore, Honduras has the greatest diversity of surface and of elevation; broad alluvions, fertile valleys, wide and elevated plains, and mountains terraced to their summits, collectively affording almost every possible variety of climate, soil, and production. These are conditions favorable to nurturing and sustaining a large population, and point unerringly to the ultimate, if not the speedy development here of a rich and powerful state. A stable and liberal government, which shall make the material interests of the country its primary care, with the opening of new and improved means of communication, can not fail to attract to Honduras an emigration from effete and distracted Europe relatively not inferior to that which flows in a constant and increasing flood upon the shores of the United States.

CHAPTER V.

RIVERS, LAKES, AND LAGOONS.

THE rivers of Honduras are numerous; some of them of large size, and deserving of a particular notice. The Chamelicon, Ulua, Aguan or Roman, Tinto or Black River, Patuca, and Wanks or Segovia, flowing into the North Sea, and the Choluteca, Nacaome, and Goascoran, flowing into the Bay of Fonseca, are the most important. Of these, the Ulua, Aguan, Tinto, Patuca, Segovia, and Choluteca are naturally capable of navigation, to a greater or less extent, for vessels propelled by steam.

River Chamelicon.—The Chamelicon is a long stream, but drains a comparatively narrow section of country, and consequently does not pass a very large body of water. It is, moreover, rapid and full of shallows.

River Ulua.—The Ulua, on the other hand, which is the largest river in Honduras, drains a wide expanse of territory, comprehending nearly one third of the entire state, and probably discharges a greater amount of water into the sea than any other river of Central America, the Wanks or Segovia perhaps excepted. Its principal tributaries are the Santiago, Santa Barbara, Blanco, Humuya, and Sulaco, and below their point of junction it is a majestic stream. It appears, from the reconnaissance of Lieutenant Jeffers, that it has a bar at its mouth, on which there is but nine feet of water, but which, except during the prevalence of high winds, may be passed by vessels drawing seven feet. Light-draught steamers can ascend as far as the junction with the Humuya, and in the rainy season pass up this stream to its union with the Sulaco. It is also said that similar vessels may ascend the Santiago to a point some distance above its junction with the Sta. Barbara. Where the Santiago is crossed by the road leading from Yojoa to Omoa, it is a deep and wide stream, with from eight to twelve feet of water in its channel. The Rio Blanco is narrow, but deep, and could be used advantageously as a means of local communication. The capacity of the Lake of Yojoa or Taulebé, with which it communicates, is not well known. Accounts differ widely as to its length and breadth, but all concur in representing it to be of great depth. Don José de la Valle is said to have written a memoir on the practicability of opening a communication for river craft between this lake, *via* Rio Ulua, and the sea.

Altogether, the Ulua and its tributaries offer many facilities for water communication with the interior, which can not fail to be made useful as the resources of the country become developed. Nor is it impossible—on the contrary, from the volume of water which passes through them, it is more than probable—that both the Chamelicon and Santiago may be artificially improved so as to answer an adequate purpose in bringing down to the coast and to a market the valuable products of the naturally rich departments of Sta. Barbara and Gracias. But, should this anticipation not be verified, it is certain that the valleys of these rivers offer facilities for the construction of carriage or rail-roads whenever circumstances shall require their substitution for the present slow and expensive method of transportation on mules.

In regard to the Ulua, it may be added that there is a cove a little to the eastward of its mouth, which extends to within two hundred yards of the river. Here vessels may enter and land with comparative ease and safety. In case any traffic should be opened by means of the Ulua, this cove might answer the purposes of a harbor, and obviate the necessity of passing the bar. Blunt, in his "Coast Pilot," observes, "The River Ulua is large and deep, and in front of it is an anchorage on excellent holding-ground." The Ulua, from the junction of the Santiago or Venta, flows through a plain of great extent, which was called by the conquerors the plain of Sula. The soil on its banks is of extreme fertility. During the height of the rainy season, some portions of the country to the eastward of the river are overflowed, as also portions of the lands between it and the Chamelicon. Indeed, at this time the waters of the two streams frequently intermingle.

River Aguan.—Rio Aguan, or Roman River, is a large stream, rising in the Mountains of Sulaco, and falling into the sea a little to the eastward of Truxillo. Its total length is about one hundred and twenty miles. Its largest tributary is the River Mangualil, celebrated for its auriferous sands and extensive gold-washings. In its course, it flows past the town of San Jorge Olanchito, through the rich valley of the same name, and the equally rich valley of Sonaguera. The portion of Honduras lying around its sources and on its banks is unsurpassed by any portion of the world for its fertility, its valuable woods, mineral, and other products. It is reported to have a comparatively favorable bar (carrying from five to seven feet of water), and to be practicable for boats of light draught for eighty miles.

Its capacity for purposes of transportation is a question of much interest, for reasons which are obvious from what has been said of the resources of the country which adjoins it.

Rio Tinto, Negro or Black River, which, a short distance from the sea, takes the name of Poyer, Poyas, or Polyer River, is a considerable stream, and is said to have a course of about one hundred and twenty miles. In common with most of the rivers on the coast, it has a bad, variable bar at its mouth, on which the water ranges, at different seasons, at from five to nine feet. Small vessels may ascend from forty to sixty miles. It was on this river that the English had a fort and some settlements during the last century, which were, however, evacuated in 1786, in conformity with the treaty that year negotiated between England and Spain. Subsequent attempts were made to found permanent establishments there, one under the auspices of "the Cazique of Poyas," Sir Gregor M'Gregor, and another in 1839–41 by an English company, under the countenance of the British settlement at Belize, but all have proved signal failures.* The last adventurers named the district "Province Victoria," and made an unimportant establishment, to which they gave the name of

* The plans of M'Gregor, although shallow in their inception and poorly combined, nevertheless dazzled the imaginations of a considerable number of unreflecting persons, and his agents were able to dispose of many shares in the imaginary kingdom of Poyas. In furtherance of the scheme, a work was published in London, in the year 1822, entitled, "*Sketch of the Mosquito Shore, including the Territory of Poyas, etc., by Thomas Strangeways, K.G.C., etc.*," which contains some valuable information, chiefly drawn from miscellaneous sources, upon the character and products of the country. It appears that "M'Gregor, cazique of Poyas," set up pretensions not only to what is known as the Mosquito Shore, but to the fine islands in the Bay of Honduras. A pamphlet, without date, was published in London, entitled, "*Constitution de la Nation Poyaisienne dans l'Amerique Centrale*," which commences, "Gregor, par la grâce de Dieu, Cacique de Poyais;" and concludes, "in the year of grace 1825, and of our reign the sixth."

Fort Wellington. An account of this expedition was written by Thomas Young, a person connected with it in some official capacity, which conveys considerable information concerning this portion of the coast. He describes that portion of the stream called Rio Tinto as flowing through a low, but rich and densely-wooded country, which, a few miles higher up, becomes swampy, and covered with willow-trees. At the point where a branch of the main stream diverges to connect with the Criba, or Black River Lagoon, commences the savanna and pine-ridge country, where some Sambos have a settlement. The savanna supports a few cattle, but the land is poor, and unfit for cultivation; "but, notwithstanding its aridity, it is very beautiful. It extends several miles in every direction, and appears to have been laid out by some landscape gardener. It is relieved by clumps of papter-trees and low shrubbery, which are the haunts of many deer. There are also great quantities of lofty pine-trees. Some of the pine-ridges on this coast are very extensive, and are valuable for their timber, which is the red pitch-pine, rich in turpentine. This timber, from its length and straightness, is not only very useful for building, but also for masts and spars. In the pine-ridges, many mounds of earth rise above the level surface to the height of eight or ten feet, and have broad tops large enough for dwelling-houses. Some parts of the savanna, however, are swampy, and are the nurseries of an-

---

Article IV. divides the kingdom of Poyas into twelve provinces, viz.:

Island of Roatan.	Province of Neustria.
" " Guanaja.	" " Panamaker.
Province of Caribbania.	" " Towkas.
" " Romaine.	" " Cackeras.
" " Tinto.	" " Wolwas.
" " Carthage.	" " Ramas

noying insects."* Above this pine-ridge the river is bordered by a continuous "bush," relieved higher up by many gracefully-bending bamboos, and the tall cabbage-palm, the crown of which affords food, and the straight trunk, when split, boards for native buildings. At a point sixteen miles above the mouth of the river, the English anciently had an establishment, and here the sarsaparilla and cacao begin to make their appearance. Near this point had been anciently a coffee plantation, at a place called "Lowry Hill," and near by had been a sugar estate, the boilers for which still remained at the time of Young's visit. "Thousands of banana-trees, loaded with fruit, were growing spontaneously." The ground here becomes elevated, and the Poyer, or Sugar-loaf Peak, two thousand feet high, shuts off the view seaward. Up to the "Embarcadero" the river is much obstructed by snags, which, even in small boats, it is difficult to avoid. Young adds, that "the passage from Fort Wellington to the Embarcadero, during a flood in the river, takes a pitpan, with six men, three days and a half. The descent, under similar circumstances, can be made in a day and a half." The Embarcadero is estimated by Roberts (Strangeways following his authority) as ninety miles from the sea, but this is probably an over-estimate.

In the Poyas River proper the snags are not numerous, but the current is strong. The mahogany, which has been cut off below, begins to appear. The scenery also changes, the banks becoming high and rocky, and the beds of the stream studded with sunken rocks. The river now begins to wind among what are called the Poyer Hills or Mountains, and little is known of its character beyond that it is rapid and tortuous. At

* Young's Narrative, p. 91.

some point above the Embarcadero it divides into two principal branches, respectively called Agalta and Paon. This point is represented by Señor Herrera, Gefe Politico of the Department of Olancho, who went down the Paon and Poyas in 1840, as "thirty-five leagues from the valley of Olancho, the path lying through steep and broken mountains, and crossing the Paon not less than seventy-three times—a river," he adds, "of much water, and very stony." He reported emphatically against any attempt to open communication between the settled districts of Olancho and the sea by way of the Poyas River and its branches.

The Poyas Indians have a number of settlements among the hills of the same name, on the upper tributaries of this river. Young reports the land about the Poyer Hills as exceedingly fertile, and the country healthy.

Black River Lagoon, called Criba by the Spaniards, according to Roberts, who visited it, is about fifteen miles long by seven wide. It contains several small islands, which were cultivated during the English occupation of Black River. At this period they erected considerable works of defense, which were enlarged by the Spaniards after the English evacuation, the ruins of which are still conspicuous. On the borders of the lagoon are some extensive savannas and pine-ridges, from which the former settlers obtained considerable quantities of pitch, tar, and turpentine.

The Patook River (written *Patuca* by the Spaniards) enters the sea by a principal mouth about midway between Cartine (also called by the Spaniards Brus, and by the English Brewer's) and Cartago, or Carataska Lagoons. It appears to be the largest river on the entire northern coast of Honduras, between the Ulua and Herbias, or Cape Gracias á Dios Rivers. It takes its rise in the very heart of the Department of Olancho, in the vicinity of the large Spanish town of Juticalpa (capital of the department), and the great Indian town of Catacamas. The principal streams which unite to form the Patuca are the rivers Jalan, Tinto de Olancho, and the Guyape (or Guallape) and Guallambre. The two last named are celebrated for their extensive gold washings, to which reference is elsewhere made. The geographical basin in which this river collects its waters is one of the richest and most beautiful in all Central America. It is separated from the transverse valley of the Rio Herbias or Segovia by a high, narrow chain of mountains, steep on the south, but subsiding by terraces toward the north. Señor Herrera, in his report already alluded to, states that the Patuca is navigable for canoes as high as the junction of the Jalan with the Guyape. The river, however, above the coast alluvions has a powerful current, and is interrupted by rapids called "chiflones." At the mouth of the Guallambre is what is called Puerto de Delon; below this point are numerous "chiflones," the principal of which are those of Campanera and Caoba. At one point the river is compressed between high, precipitous walls of rock for a long distance. The place is called "*Portal del Infierno*," or Hell's Mouth, and probably gave rise to the story recorded by Roberts, "that at one part of its course the river has forced its way through a range of hills, one of which is completely excavated by the stream, which thus passes through a natural arch, as through a cavern, for a distance of nearly five hundred yards."* The principal affluents below the Guallambre are the following, in

* Roberts's Narrative, p. 159.

the Poyas dialect, viz., Rio Guineo, Rio Cuyamel, Rio Amac-was (River of Bee-hives), Rio Was-pres-senia (Roaring Water), Rio Uampu, and Rio Upurra (River of Retreat).

The principal mouth of the Patuca opens directly into the sea, and is obstructed by a bad, shifting bar, on which there is generally from eight to ten feet of water. Sometimes, after heavy gales, it is deeper. The tide, which is slight, nevertheless ebbs and flows in the river for some miles. The land about the mouth of the river is mostly savanna, which, however, according to an account given in 1844 by Messrs. Haly, Upton, and Deacon, unlike most of the savannas on the coast, is not swampy, and furthermore has a black and fertile soil. An extensive pine-ridge is found about thirty miles up the river, above which, as also down to near the sea, the banks are thickly wooded, having a great variety of soil—red clay, loam, and black mould—all admirably adapted to the cultivation of sugar, coffee, cotton, cacao, indigo, etc. Large quantities of mahogany, cedar, rose, and Santa Maria wood are found throughout the whole length of the river valley, while the pine-ridges are capable of furnishing inexhaustible quantities of pine wood and oak. Exclusive of valuable woods, the forests produce abundance of sarsaparilla, India rubber, gum copal, and vanilla. Mr. Haly pronounces the Patuca "navigable for small steamers" to the vicinity of the Spanish settlements in Olancho, "or at least to the foot of the falls" (*Portal del Infierno*), and that "it is the best river on the entire coast, excepting that of San Juan de Nicaragua, for commercial intercourse with the interior." He thinks, also, that an establishment at its mouth, supported by improvements in the river and by roads in the interior, would soon become the most important point on the coast east of Omoa. According to Haly, it takes *seventeen days* to ascend the river to the Spanish settlements in Olancho, which implies that the current must be very strong and navigation far from easy. He estimates a day's voyage up the stream at thirty miles, and adds that "the Spanish towns are therefore five hundred and ten miles above the mouth of the river." This estimate is simply absurd, as that distance in the direction of the course of the river would carry the traveler not only across the continent, but far out of sight of land in the Pacific Ocean! As I have already observed, distances in Central America are always overestimated, or, to use a saying of the country, "depend upon the quality of your horse." In other words, what is five leagues with a good animal is ten with a bad one. Roberts, more moderate, estimates the length of the Patuca at one hundred and fifty miles, and Strangeways at one hundred miles. Various establishments of Caribs and Sambos exist on the lower part of the river, and the Toacas and Poyas (called Payas by the Spaniards) on its upper waters and its various tributaries.

An arm of the Patuca, called Toomtoom Creek, diverging from the main stream a short distance above its mouth, connects it with Brus, or Brewer's Lagoon. This lagoon has a wide mouth, but will not admit vessels drawing more than six or seven feet. Three or four miles from its entrance is an island of moderate height, about two miles in circumference, fertile, formerly fortified by the English, and seems to have been extensively cultivated. This lagoon abounds with fine fish, has plenty of water-fowl, and large beds of oysters. "The country to the northward," says Roberts, "is beautifully diversified by gently-rising hills, valleys, and savannas, and the soil, generally speaking, is excellent."

Carataska or *Cartago Lagoon* "is of very considerable extent, varying in breadth, and having, in some places, the appearance of several lagoons running into each other, in various directions, for the most part parallel to the coast, but nowhere exceeding twelve miles in breadth." It has two entrances, one a small creek called "Tibacunta." The principal mouth is wide, with thirteen to fourteen feet of water on the bar. The lagoon is estimated at about thirty-six miles in length. It is for the most part shallow, varying in depth from six to twelve and eighteen feet. Captain Henderson, who visited it in 1804, describes the country near the Sambo village of Crata (Croatch or Cartago) as "a spacious savanna, of very considerable extent, forming an entire level of unbroken verdure and finest pasturage, skirted on one side by the waters of the lagoon, and on the other bounded by gently-rising hills. The clumps of pine and other lofty trees, interspersed at pleasing distances over the whole, gave the view all the appearance of cultivated art, and afforded a most agreeable relief to the eye." Several small streams discharge into the lagoon from the south, viz., Ibentara, Cartago, Locca, Warunta, and Kaukari. It has also three considerable islands. There are a number of villages of Sambos around this lagoon, who raise a few cattle, but do not cultivate the soil to any extent, being grossly indolent and improvident. "The land in the vicinity of the lagoon," according to Roberts, "consists almost entirely of extensive and beautiful savannas, covered with the finest pasturage, and abounding in deer and other game. There are few pine-trees at Crata, but on the opposite or south side there are ridges growing timber as large as any on the coast. Behind these ridges the savannas are bounded by hills, whose summits are covered by the most luxuriant vegetation. On the banks of the streams in the interior there is excellent mahogany, and cedar of the finest quality and largest size. Pimento and various other valuable plants are also indigenous."

Rio Wanks or *Segovia* (also called Herbias, Yare, Cape, Coco, and Oro), which enters the sea at Cape Gracias á Dias, is certainly the longest, if not in other respects the largest, river in Central America. It rises in the Department of Nueva Segovia, in the extreme northwest corner of Nicaragua, within fifty miles of the Bay of Fonseca, and flows northeast into the Caribbean Sea. For the greater part of its course it is the boundary between Honduras and Nicaragua. Its total length can not be less than three hundred and fifty miles. For two hundred and fifty miles above its mouth it flows through an almost unbroken wilderness, among high mountains, and for a great part of its way in a rapid current over a very broken and rocky bed. It is nevertheless occasionally navigated by canoes to within a few leagues of the town of Ocotal (or Nueva Segovia). Señor Don Francisco Irias, of the town of Ocotal, descended it in 1842 in a canoe, and returned by the same means. He started from a place called Coco, which, from his account, appears to be not far from Ocotal. From that point to another called Pailla, he represents the river as not much obstructed. "Just above Pailla there falls into the principal river a large and beautiful stream, called Bocay, the mouth of which is near that of the large river Pantasma, which enters from the right. There are other medium-sized tributaries, among which is the Poteca, rising on the left base of the mountains bounding the great valley of Jalapa, at a point called Macarali. The Poteca is too rough for navigation. There is also another stream, called Coa, which flows from the south, among high and steep mountains. It abounds in fish, and the forest which borders it is rich in honey, and also in valuable woods."

Below Pailla commence a series of rapids or falls, which follow each other in quick succession, some of which can only be passed by unloading the canoes and carrying them over land. "These are the sole obstructions," continues Señor Irias, "to the navigation of the river from the point of embarkation to the sea at Cape Gracias á Dios. At present, the descent occupies about ten days. Two days are taken up in descending the rapids, and four in ascending them. It will be observed that only about one fifth of the river is in any way obstructed. The delay in the voyage is chiefly occasioned by unloading and loading at some of the rapids. From Tilras and Quipispe, the final rapids, to the Cape, there is scarcely any current, and it is necessary to use the oars. This part of the country through which the river passes is very beautiful, consisting of open plains covered with grass and scattered trees. It is well adapted for grazing, and cattle and horses might be raised here for exportation to Cuba and Jamaica. * * In ascending the river from the Cape, I was occupied twenty days. * * Cape Gracias á Dios unfortunately has no commerce, but it has a favorable and picturesque situation. It has in front a salt lagoon of great capacity, separated from the sea by a sandy strip of land covered with mangrove-trees. The entrance is to the south. * * It is lamentable that so beautiful a section as that around the Cape should have no other population except a few worthless Moscos (Mosquitos or Sambos), unable from want of instruction, as unfitted by disposition, to attain to any improvement in the future."

In 1688, a body of French and English pirates, about three hundred in number, abandoned their vessels in the Gulf of Fonseca, forced their way across the continent, through Nueva Segovia, and down this river to Cape Gracias. They descended the stream on small rafts, which they called "*pipiries*, pitiful machines," each supporting two or three men. Many were drowned in the descent, of which De Lussan, one of the leaders, has left us an animated, though perhaps somewhat exaggerated description. He says: "This river springs in the Mountains of Segovia, and discharges itself into the North Sea at Cape *Gracias á Dios*, after having run a very long way in a most rapid manner ovee a vast number of Rocks of prodigious bigness, and by the most frightful Precipices that can be thought of, besides a great many Falls of Water to the Number of at least an Hundred of all sorts, which it's impossible for a Man to look on without trembling, and making the Head of the most fearless to turn round, when he sees and hears the Water fall from such an height into these tremendous Whirlpools. In short, the whole is so formidable that there are none but those who have some Experience can have right conceptions of it. But for me, who have passed these Places, and who, as long as I live, shall have my mind filled with these Risques I have run, it's impossible I should give such an Idea hereof but what will come far short of what I have really known of them."*

* *A Journal of a Voyage made into the South Sea by the Bucaniers or Freebooters of America*, by the Sieur Raveneau de Lussan, London, 1704, p. 171.

De Lussan speaks of the large quantities of bananas which they found on the banks of the river, "which kept them from starving," for, although there was "very good game," their "powder was wet, so that they could not go a Hunting." He describes the lower part of the river as "very good, and the stream very gentle."

Roberts, who spent some months at Cape Gracias, describes "the soil in that neighborhood as very poor, and, with the exception of a few spots, on which there are small patches of cassava, incapable of producing any thing better than a coarse, rank grass, fit, however, for pasturage." The few people who live there depend upon those who dwell a considerable way up the river for their supply of plantains, maize, and other provisions. Game is scarce, and there is a deficiency of good water, so that the Cape presents no advantages for an agricultural settlement, although holding out inducements for grazing establishments and commerce.

The river enters the ocean some distance to the northward of the bay or harbor, with which, however, it is connected by a creek or shallow canal, passable for canoes, and which might be deepened so as to enable small vessels to avoid the dangerous bar of the river itself, on which there is seldom more than four or five feet of water. "For forty or fifty miles above its mouth," continues Roberts, "the land is low, sandy, and poor, with occasional ridges of pitch pine, and some patches of good mould." There is little doubt that the Rio Segovia might be made to answer a useful purpose in the development of the country.

Three rivers of note flow from the interior of Honduras southward into the Pacific. These are the Goascoran, Nacaome, and Choluteca. The last named is much the largest. It rises in the Lepaterique Mountains, at the head of the plain of Comayagua, flows eastward until it reaches the meridian of Tegucigalpa, then turns abruptly north, flowing past that city, and after describing a circuitous course, runs nearly south into the Gulf of Fonseca, having a total length of about one hundred and fifty miles. Its course illustrates what I have already said of the peculiarities of the mountain groups of Honduras. The Lepaterique Mountains become *knotted* and much broken up in the great bend of this river, which embraces one of the richest mineral districts of Central America. The mines of Yuscuran, San Antonio Mineral, Sta. Lucia, San Juan Cantaranas, etc., all lie within this bend. The valley of the Choluteca is narrow until it reaches the point where it takes a southern direction, whence it gradually expands into broad alluvions on the gulf. In the midst of these alluvions is situated the town of Choluteca (anciently Xeres de la Frontera), a place of considerable size. The Yuguare is a tributary of the Choluteca. It flows through a broad valley, distinguished, even in Honduras, for its beauty and fertility. "Bongos," and other native boats of light draught, ascend the Choluteca to considerable distances. Indeed, the river, for ten or twelve miles from the gulf, can only be regarded as an estuary. Its banks, throughout the lower part of its course, are well wooded with cedar, mahogany, and other trees, the value of which is much enhanced by the facility with which they may be reached from the sea. The river will be of great utility in working the numerous rich silver mines which are found in the vicinity of Corpus, and in the hills which skirt its valley.

The Rio Nacaome collects its waters on the south side of the Lepaterique Mountains, while the Choluteca drains their northern slope. It is not a long stream, but passes a considerable body of water. It is very rapid, and is not available for purposes of navigation except during the rainy season, when it may be ascended by canoes as high as the town of Nacaome. Below that place it flows through alluvions; and above, to the town of Pespiri, it has a broad valley. Beyond that point it finds its way in deep gorges among the hills and mountains. Its principal tributary is the Moramulca.

The River Goascoran rises among the low hills which lie at the head of the great plain of Comayagua, and its valley may almost be regarded as a prolongation of this plain. It has its sources in the same savannas with those of the Humuya, which flows northward into the Bay of Honduras. Its course is nearly due south, and, in conjunction with the River Humuya, it opens a great transverse valley, completely cutting through the Cordilleras, and extending from sea to sea. From this circumstance it derives its principal importance. Its valley consists of a succession of terraces, of greater or less width, with no alluvions proper until within ten miles of the Gulf of Fonseca, where the ground spreads out in a broad, low, and fertile plain. At Caridad, where the river breaks through the Lepaterique Mountains, the valley is much compressed, but this is only for a few hundred yards. The first town on the river is Goascoran, above which occur Aramacina, Saco, Caridad, San Antonio del Norte, Aguanqueterique, and San Juan. The entire length of the Goascoran is between seventy and eighty miles. During the rainy season it passes a large body of water, but during the dry season it can every where be forded without difficulty. It could doubtless be made navigable as far as the town of Goascoran by artificial aids, but naturally it can not be regarded as a navigable river. From the Gulf upward to the Rio Pescado, which enters it from the west, a few miles below Caridad, it constitutes the boundary between the states of San Salvador and Honduras. The principal importance of this stream, as already intimated, consists in its dependence on the plain of Comayagua, whereby a favorable railway route is opened between the two seas.

Lake of Yojoa.—The Lake of Yojoa or Taulebé is the only lake of note in Honduras. Its extent is unknown, nor can any definite information respecting it be obtained from the people of the country. It is probably about twenty-five miles in length by from three to eight broad, and closely shut in by mountains. The River Blanco, a narrow but deep stream, flows from its northern extremity, and unites with the Ulua at the same point with the Humuya. This outlet, I am informed by Mr. Follin, United States consul in Omoa, loses itself in a subterranean passage a few miles from its point of debouchure, through which it flows for a number of miles. Another singular circumstance is affirmed of this lake, and accepted by Mr. Baily in his Map of Central America, viz., that, besides the Rio Blanco, it has three other distinct outlets, one flowing northwest into the Rio Sta. Barbara, and two southeast into the Humuya. However common such peculiarities may have been in the earlier eras of map-making, modern investigation fails to discover them, and we may safely believe that the Lake of Yojoa has but a single outlet until the existence of the others is better authenticated. An investigation of this interesting lake is certainly a geographical desideratum, and could not fail to be interesting. It seems to occupy one of those numerous interior basins, of which I have had several occasions to speak as peculiar features in the physical conformation of Honduras, in which the mountain ridges appear to have turned back on themselves in knotted groups, instead of pursuing the rectilinear course observable in most mountain ranges. Around the head of the lake the country seems to be comparatively plain. Here are found several towns, while its lateral shores are uninhabited. I infer from this that its sides are lined by steep and rugged mountains, affording little arable ground, and no favorable positions for villages. It would seem as if these questions might be answered by the people of the country, but the lake is entirely out of the line of ordinary travel, and the greatest ignorance prevails in respect to it.

CHAPTER VI.

BAYS, PORTS, AND HARBORS.

THE Bay of Fonseca, sometimes called *Golfo de Amapala*, or *Conchagua*, is beyond dispute one of the finest ports, or, rather, "constellation of ports," on the entire Pacific coast of this continent. It is upward of fifty miles in greatest length, by about thirty miles in average width. A reference to the accompanying chart, reduced from a survey made by Captain Sir Edward Belcher, R. N., in 1838, will explain its peculiarities better than any description. It will be seen from the general map that this bay lies within the great longitudinal valley which intervenes between the volcanic coast-ridge and the true Cordilleras, and which extends from Guatemala to Costa Rica. In San Salvador this valley is drained by the River Lempa, which breaks abruptly through the coast-ridge and flows into the Pacific. In Nicaragua the same valley is represented by the basin of the Nicaragua lakes, drained by the River San Juan, which breaks as abruptly through the Cordilleras and flows into the Atlantic. Intermediately between San Salvador and Nicaragua, it is farther represented by the Bay of Fonseca, where the sea has broken through the volcanic coast-range, and spread itself out behind it. The bay, no doubt, owes its origin to volcanic causes, and its study, under this aspect, must hereafter prove of the highest interest to science.

The entrance to the bay, from the sea, is about eighteen miles wide, between the great volcanoes of Conchagua (3800 feet in height) and Coseguina (3000 feet in height), which stand like giant warders upon either hand, and constitute unmistakable landmarks for the mariner. On a line across this entrance, and about equidistant from each other, lie the two considerable islands of Conchaguita and Mianguera, and a collection of high rocks called "los Farellones," which, while they serve to protect the bay from the swell of the sea, divide the entrance into four distinct channels, each of sufficient depth of water to admit the passage of the largest vessels. These islands are high; Conchaguita being not less than 1500, and Mianguera about 1200 feet in height. They were formerly inhabited by Indians, who withdrew to the main land to avoid the oppressions of the freebooters during the period of their ascendency in the South Sea. Both of these islands belong to San Salvador.

The three states of San Salvador, Honduras, and Nicaragua touch upon this bay. Honduras has, however, much the largest frontage. The port of La Union, on the subordinate bay of the same name, is the principal Pacific port of San Salvador. Nicaragua has also a nominal port on the "Estero Real," an estuary of the bay, which penetrates that state in the direction of the Lake of Managua. Honduras has the free port of Amapala on the island of Tigre, which occupies a commanding position nearly in the centre of the bay.

The subordinate bay of La Union, from the island of Punta Sacate to its head, is about eight miles in length by four in breadth. Its northern half, however, is shallow, and almost dry at low water, and it is said that the anchorage is yearly becoming narrower from the sand washed down by the rivers Goascoran and Sirama, both of which flow into it. There are also two other subordinate bays, viz., that of Chismuyo, to the northward of the large island of Sacate Grande, and which receives the Rio Nacaome, and that of San Lorenzo, a fine body of water to the eastward of the same island. At the head of this bay is situated the nominal port of San Lorenzo, which is only a dependency of that of Amapala. The principal estuary of the bay is that called "El Estero Real," which extends into Nicaragua behind the volcano of El Viejo. It starts from the extreme southern point of the bay, and penetrates inland for a distance, including its windings, of not far from fifty miles. It has an average width of two hundred yards, and, for at least thirty miles from its mouth, a depth of not less than three fathoms. Sir Edward Belcher went up this estero in 1838, in the "Starling," a vessel drawing ten feet of water, for thirty miles. In his own language, he "might easily have gone farther, had the wind permitted." This estero extends to within twenty or twenty-five miles of Lake Managua, from which it is separated by the plain of *Conejo.**

The principal islands in the Bay of Fonseca are Sacate Grande, Tigre, Gueguensi, and Esposescion, belonging to Honduras, and Punta Sacate, Martin Perez, Conchaguita, and Mianguera (already described), belonging to San Salvador.

Sacate Grande is considerably the largest, and, in common with the others, is of volcanic origin. It is seven miles long by about four in breadth. The southern half is elevated, rising in a number of peaks to the

* I have elsewhere indicated this line as the most feasible route for a ship canal, *via* the River San Juan and Lakes Nicaragua and Managua. See Part III. of "*Nicaragua, its People, Scenery, Monuments, and proposed Inter-oceanic Canal.*"

height of two thousand feet. These elevations slope off gently to the northward, and subside finally in level alluvial grounds of exceeding fertility. These, as well as the slopes descending toward them, are densely wooded with cedar, mahogany, willowisti, and other valuable trees. The peaks themselves, as well as their more abrupt southern slopes, are covered with grass, called by the Indians *sacate*, whence the island derives its name. These grassy slopes afford pasturage for great numbers of cattle, and it is said that as many as four thousand have been pastured upon the island at a single time. For most of the year, and except in very dry seasons, there are running streams of water on the northern slopes of the island. Abundance of water, however, may be obtained by digging through the upper lava crusts, beneath which, as is frequently the case in volcanic countries, flow constant streams. The grassy peaks of Sacate Grande, as well as of the other islands, afford a source of ever-varying and eternal beauty. With the commencement of the rainy season, they are clothed with the delicate translucent green of the springing grass, which deepens as the season advances both in color and thickness, until all the asperities of the ground are matted over with an emerald robe of luxuriance. Then, when the rains cease and the droughts commence, the grass becomes sere, and finally of a brilliant yellow, and the islands appear as if swathed in a mantle of golden grain, which Ceres herself might envy. Then comes the torch of the *vaquéro*, and the sky is lurid with the blaze of the rapid flame, which clears the ground for the future fresh and tender blade, but leaves it browned and purpled, in sober contrast with its previous gayer garniture of gold and green.

The island of Gueguensi may be regarded as a dependency of Sacate Grande, from which it is separated only by a narrow and shallow strait. It has a single eminence of great beauty and regularity. The rest of the island is level, chiefly savanna, fertile, and well adapted to the cultivation of rice, cotton, and sugar. It is fringed by a narrow belt of mangroves, which would lead the careless observer to suppose the ground within to be low and swampy.

The island of Tigre, from its position, is the most important island of the bay. It is perhaps twenty miles in circumference, rising in the form of a perfect cone to the height of two thousand five hundred feet. The slope from the water, for some distance inward, is very gentle, and admits of cultivation. Upon the southern and eastern shores, the lava forms black, rocky barriers to the waves, varying in height from ten to eighty feet; but upon the northward and eastward there are a number of "playas" or coves, with smooth, sandy beaches. It is facing one of the most considerable of these that the port of Amapala is situated. The water in front is deep, with clear anchorage, where vessels of ordinary size may lie within a cable's length of the shore.

This island was a favorite resort of the pirates, and it was here that Drake had his depôt during his operations in the South Sea. At that time, in common with Sacate Grande, and the other principal islands in the bay, it had several considerable towns of Indians, who, however, soon afterward retired to the main land to avoid their piratical persecutors. From that time it remained almost entirely uninhabited until about 1838, when some enterprising merchants, under the suggestions of Don Carlos Dardano, a Sardinian trader, conceived the idea of making it a free port. They ac-

From Nature and on Stone by D.C. Hitchcock

Printed by Sarony & Co. N.Y.

ISLAND OF TIGRE

cordingly obtained the requisite action from the government of Honduras, and the free port of Amapala was accordingly established. Since then it has rapidly increased in population, and is now by far the most important point in the Gulf, and undoubtedly destined to become the most important port in the Pacific between San Francisco and Valparaiso. It has a salubrious climate, resulting from its admirable ventilation, the proximity of high grounds, and absence of swamps. The markets of three states are accessible from it, and it may be reached from the sea much more easily than any other point in the bay, while the largest vessels of the line may lie in perfect security in its waters. The actual population may be estimated at about one thousand. It contains several large wholesale mercantile establishments, with the requisite warehouses, and a number of substantial and commodious dwellings. A direct trade is carried on between Amapala and Bremen, Liverpool, Marseilles, Genoa, New York, and Valparaiso. No data exist for determining its extent or value. The exports are indigo, hides, tobacco, bullion, silver and copper ores, and Brazil-wood, together with maize to ports on the coast. The cultivation of sugar has been introduced on the main land, with a view of supplying the Californian market.

Lying in front of the port of Amapala, to the northwest of the island of Tigre, is the island of Esposescion. It is high, with a large "playa" on its southern side, but is deficient in water. This, however, might be supplied to every necessary extent by wells of the requisite capacity. The same remarks hold good in respect to the considerable island of Punta Sacate. The little island of Martin Perez is comparatively low and level, and has a rich, productive soil. It retains its verdure during most of the year, and is green when the other islands are sere and yellow from the drought. The remaining islands, of which there are many, may be described as volcanic domes, supporting only enough soil to nourish the grasses which disguise the rough and blistered rocks of which they are composed.

The bay abounds in fish, and its shores swarm with every variety of water-fowl—cranes, herons, pelicans, ibises, spoonbills, ducks, curlews, darters, etc., etc. Large beds of oysters are found in the shallow waters in the dependent bays of La Union and Chismuyo. Their quantity seems to be inexhaustible. Huge piles of their shells are scattered along the shores of the islands and main land, showing how extensively they were used by the aborigines. They are about the size of the ordinary oysters found around New York, and of excellent flavor. Crabs and cray-fish are also abundant.

The whole region around this bay is eminently productive, and capable of furnishing supplies of every kind to every desirable extent. The lands on the banks of the Choluteca, Nacaome, and Goascoran are of the highest fertility, and adapted to the production of every tropical commodity. The savannas back of these comparatively low grounds are peculiarly fitted for grazing, while wheat, potatoes, and other products of the temperate zone may be cultivated on the slopes of the mountains and the plateaus of the interior. Wood of value for purposes of export or for the construction of dwellings and ships, including pine, exists in exhaustless quantities on the very shores of the bay, or may be rafted down the rivers from the interior. These rivers also afford facilities for navigation by small boats for considerable distances inland, to points near the metal-bearing spurs or outliers of the Cordilleras. The silver and gold mining district of Tabanco, in the Department of San Miguel (San Salvador), the silver mines of Aramacina and San Martyn, and the famous mine of Corpus, all lie within from ten to twenty miles of this bay. Limestone is found in large beds on the navigable waters of the estero of Cubulero, and a fine rose-colored sandstone abounds in the vicinity of the town of Nacaome, on the banks of the river of the same name. This bay must also ultimately become the dépôt of the coal from the great beds which exist in the valley of the River Lempa, when these shall come to be worked for supplying the Pacific steamers. It is alleged that coal is to be found both on the Rio Sirama and Choluteca, but the reports remain to be verified.

As affording admirable ports, abundant means for ship-building and repairs, with supplies of every kind, not less than for its value in respect to existing and local commerce with San Salvador, Honduras, and Nicaragua, the Bay of Fonseca has a singular value and commercial importance. But our estimate of that importance becomes greatly enhanced when we consider its commanding position, both in a political and geographical point of view, and especially when we regard it, as it is inevitably destined to become, as the terminus on the Pacific of the most available route of permanent railway communication between the two great oceans. I have no hesitation in repeating now, what I had occasion to say to the government of the United States when acting as its representative in Central America, that "the Bay of Fonseca is, under every point of view, by far the most important position on the Pacific coast of America, and so favored by Nature as ultimately to become the great emporium of trade, and centre of enterprise upon that side of the continent." This was written before the fact of a feasible interoceanic railway route through Honduras, terminating on this bay, had been demonstrated or even conceived.

The principal ports of Honduras, on the Atlantic, are Omoa, Puerto Caballos, and Truxillo; and on the Pacific, Amapala, or the island of Tigre.

Puerto Caballos.—The first port established by the Spaniards on the northern coast was Puerto Caballos, lat. 15° 49′ N., and lon. 87° 57′ W. It was selected by Cortez in his expedition into Honduras, and he founded a settlement there, with the purpose of making it the grand *entrepôt* of New Spain, which he called Natividad. For more than two centuries it was the principal establishment on the coast, but it was removed to Omoa, a few miles to the westward, during the time of the buccaneers, because of the large size of the bay, which could only be adequately defended by the construction of several forts, while a single work was sufficient for the protection of the comparatively small port of Omoa.

The port, or rather bay, is of large capacity, being not less than nine miles in circumference. Its depth is ample, ranging, for more than two thirds of its area, from four to twelve fathoms, with secure holding-ground. Toward its northern shore the depth of water is greatest; and by the construction of docks sixty feet in length, the largest ocean steamers may enter, and receive and land passengers and cargo, more easily than in the docks of New York, inasmuch as, in this portion of the Bay of Honduras, the rise and fall of the tide is almost imperceptible.

Connected with the port or bay is a large salt-water

lagoon, upward of two miles in length, by about a mile and a quarter broad, of equal depth of water with the port itself.

The winds which prevail on the north coast of Honduras are from the northeast, north, and north by west, from all of which the port is perfectly protected. West and southwest winds are scarcely known, and are furthermore entirely cut off from the port by the high hills and mountains skirting the coast in that direction.

Omoa.—The port of Omoa is in lat. 15° 47′ N., long. 88° 3′ W. It is small but secure, and defended by a strong work, called "El Castillo de San Fernando." The anchorage is good, in from two to six fathoms. The town is situated about a fourth of a mile back from the shore, and numbers fifteen hundred or two thousand inhabitants. The site of the town is level, but the country back rises rapidly into a chain of high mountains, which, commencing abruptly at Puerto Caballos, trend off to the westward, and connect with the Sierra Madre in the Department of Gracias. Very little agriculture, therefore, is carried on in the vicinity of Omoa, which draws its supplies chiefly from the Indians settled around Puerto Caballos, and from the vicinity of Cheloma and San Pedro, in the plain of Sula. It is through Omoa that the merchants of Gracias, Sta. Barbara, Comayagua, and Tegucigalpa obtain their principal supplies of merchandise, and most of them have agencies at the port. Goods landed here, nevertheless, sometimes find their way across the continent into San Salvador and Guatemala. It is from this port, also, that most of the exports of the departments which I have indicated are made. They consist of bullion, mahogany, hides, tobacco, indigo, sarsaparilla, etc. ; but the amounts of these articles which pass here, in the absence of published data, are unknown. A large number of cattle are shipped annually to supply the markets and the mahogany establishments around Belize with provisions and with oxen for trucking the mahogany.*

Omoa, from its position, receives the full ventilation afforded by the trade winds, and its climate in general is cool and salubrious. It has seldom been visited by those epidemics which so often desolate the islands of the Caribbean and the Mexican ports on the Gulf of Mexico. This exemption is no doubt due, in a great degree, to the proximity of the mountains, and the absence of marshes in its vicinity.

Omoa receives an abundant supply of fish, turtle, and wild fowl from the cays off the coast and the waters in its neighborhood.

Truxillo.—This ancient port is situated in lat. 15° 55′ N., long. 86° W., upon the western shore of a noble bay, formed by the projecting land of Punta Castilla. Young estimated the population in 1842 at two thousand five hundred, of which one thousand were whites and Ladinos, and fifteen hundred Caribs. The latter are described as tall, athletic, hardy, and industrious. The trade of the place is chiefly carried on

* "The harbor of Omoa is formed by a little bay, with a low sandy point stretching out about half a mile to the north, covered with mangrove-trees and bushes, which make a good shelter from the northern gales. The fort, or castle, stands at the head of the bay, near which is the best anchorage, in from four to sixteen fathoms of water. As you approach the shore it shallows, and you may choose your own depth, say from sixteen to four fathoms, soft, muddy bottom, and good holding-ground. In fine, it is a snug, safe harbor. The castle is large, and, like most other of the fortifications built by the Spaniards, very strong. When this province was under Spain, its convicts were imprisoned in this castle. The town is located about a mile to the eastward of the landing-place at the castle. It is now a small place, containing about two hundred indifferent houses. The people of Omoa generally are a simple-hearted, honest people, and wish to do justice and deal fairly with all foreigners who visit their place."—*Coggeshall's Voyages, 2d Series*, p. 142 (1852).

with Olancho, of which department it may be considered as the port. Its exports, in common with those of Omoa, are hides, sarsaparilla, cochineal, indigo, copper, and silver. The subjoined description of Truxillo is extracted from the Narrative of G. W. Montgomery, Esq., United States Commissioner to Central America, who visited it in the year 1838:*

"The town of Truxillo stands close by the sea, at the foot of a lofty mountain crowned with trees, and clothed with rich vegetation, reaching to the very edge of the water. It is an isolated, solitary place, of antique appearance, with a few houses, and these in ruinous condition. * * In former times, Truxillo was a place of some importance, both in a military and commercial point of view. It contained a considerable garrison, and the ruins of extensive barracks may yet be seen there. It carried on a flourishing trade with the metropolis, the manufactures of which were exchanged for the products of the country. Of these products the principal are mahogany, cedar, and other woods, sarsaparilla, hides, and tallow. There are also some mines of gold in the neighborhood, which, under proper management, might be worked with a profit. This place, however, has long been on the decline, and its prosperity is not likely to return in many years. Its population, which now does not much exceed a thousand souls, was formerly twice or three times that number.

"The principal street—and, strictly speaking, the only one, for the others scarcely deserve the name—extends from one end of the town to the other, and is paved. The houses, for the most part, are but one story high, and their sombre, dilapidated appearance, together with the grass-grown pavement, impart to the place a melancholy air of abandonment. It has, at the same time, something romantic in its situation, being inclosed by mountains, and imbosomed in an exuberant vegetation, which the efforts of man seem to have been unable to check.

* *Narrative of a Journey to Guatemala, etc., in* 1838, by G. W. Montgomery. New York, 1839, p. 31.

"There is scarcely any open ground in the vicinity, except here and there a cultivated spot, where the plantain, the yucca, and a little corn are raised for individual consumption. As the woods afford a rich pasture, the cattle are good, and milk is abundant; and as the soil, by its fertility, liberally repays the little labor bestowed on it, the very moderate wants of the inhabitants are easily supplied.

"During my stay in Truxillo, I took a ramble in the woods, accompanied by the captain of the vessel. There is a brook in the neighborhood of the town which pursues a winding course through the woods and among the rocks until it falls into the sea. We resolved to explore its banks as far as circumstances might permit. We set out accordingly, each of us armed with a stout stick, in the apprehension of encountering snakes. Indeed, so exaggerated were the accounts I had received of the number of these reptiles infesting the woods, that I had conceived it impossible to move a step without danger of being attacked by them. As we proceeded in our excursion, I was agreeably surprised by the beauty of the scenery. The size and loftiness of the trees, some of them in blossom, and the deep verdure of their foliage, surpassed any thing I had ever seen of the kind. There was the tamarind-tree, the wild lemon, loaded with fruit, and the sassafras. There, too, was the mahogany-tree, which, like the sassafras, furnishes a staple commodity of the country, and a variety of other trees, with whose properties and names we were wholly unacquainted. There was a vast number of plants, also, that seemed to me curious, and well worth the attention of a botanist. Parrots, pelicans, and other birds of brilliant plumage, were flying all around us; there were singing-birds among the trees, while in the limpid waters of the brook might be seen, now and then, the silvery sides of a fish glistening in the sun as it darted across the stream. The brook sometimes rushed and foamed noisily among groups of rocks or through narrow passes, and at other times glided peacefully on, with an almost imperceptible current. At one place a little bay was formed, deep and cool, where the smooth and placid surface of the water, which was beautifully transparent, reflected, as in a mirror, the overhanging trees. It was impossible not to be affected by the solitude and beauty of the scene; the charm was felt and acknowledged by my companion as well as myself. A pleasant breeze, blowing at the time, effectually prevented our being annoyed by mosquitoes; and, singular as it seemed to me, we met with no snake, nor any dangerous animal in our path."

Puerto Sal is a small harbor a few miles to the eastward of Puerto Caballos. The depth of water is not sufficient for large vessels. Some high rocks lie to the northward of the point which shuts in the harbor, called the "Bishops," under the lee of which there is a very good anchorage.

Triunfo de la Cruz is a large bay, which commences at Puerto Sal, and bends thence inward, forming a coast-line of upward of twenty miles, terminating in a cape called Cabo Triunfo. It is very well sheltered from the winds, and has good anchorage for ships of every denomination.

Besides these harbors, there are many points on the north coast of Honduras where vessels may anchor under favorable circumstances. At the mouths of the Chamelicon, the Ulua, Lean, Black River, Patook River, and off Carataska Lagoon, there are roadsteads, with good holding-ground, which are secure, except during the prevalence of north winds.

The islands of Roatan and Guanaja both afford excellent harbors, and there is also a good port on the south side of Utilla. The references had elsewhere to these islands preclude the necessity of any special reference to their ports. It is only necessary to say that these islands are surrounded by coral reefs and cays, which render approach to them difficult except under the direction of experienced pilots.

Amapala is a free port, situated on the island of

Tigre, in the Gulf of Fonseca, and is the principal, and, in fact, the only port of Honduras on the Pacific. The nominal port of La Paz, on the main land, is a simple office for the collection of duties on goods which may be introduced for sale. A sufficient account of this port is given in the paragraphs on the Bay of Fuseca, and in the description of the island of Tigre, in a subsequent chapter.

CHAPTER VII.

ISLANDS OF HONDURAS.

TO the northward of the main land of Honduras, in the bay of the same name, there is a cluster of islands lying nearly parallel to the coast, at a distance from it of from thirty to fifty miles. Their names, in the order of their size, are Roatan (sometimes written Ruatan and Rattan), Guanaja (or Bonacca), Utilla, Barbaretta, Helena, and Morat. Dependent upon them are numerous coral islets or "cays" of small size. These islands have good soil, fine climate, advantageous position, and some of them excellent harbors, rendering them both valuable and important to that portion of the continent upon which they are geographically dependent.

Roatan, the largest of these islands, is about thirty miles long by nine broad at its widest part. "It may be considered," says Alcedo, "as the key of the Bay of Honduras, and the focus of the trade of the neighboring countries." "This beautiful island," echoes Macgregor, "has an excellent harbor, easily defended, and is well adapted to the culture of cotton, coffee, and other tropical products." And Captain Mitchell, of the British Navy, whose account was written in 1850, adds, that "the local position of the island seems one of importance in a commercial, and perhaps in a political, point of view. It is the only place where good harbors are found on an extensive and dangerous coast." And also "that its proximity to Central

America and Spanish Honduras seems to point it out as a good dépôt for English goods and manufactures, where they would find a ready market, *even in opposition to any duties placed on them.*" "Roatan and Bonacca," writes another English author, "in consequence of their fine harbors, good soil, pure air, and great quantities of animals, fish, and fruits, and commanding ground, are proverbially known in that part of the world as the 'Garden of the West Indies,' 'the Key to Spanish America,' and a 'New Gibraltar.' From their natural strength they might be made impregnable, being tenable with a very small force."*

Strangeways affirms that here are found "great quantities of cocoanuts, wild figs, and excellent grapes. The forests produce white oaks and pine-trees fit for masts of merchant ships. It abounds with deer, wild hogs, Indian rabbits, and birds of many species. A constant breeze from the east cools and tempers the air, and there is abundance of excellent water." Young describes the island "as one beautiful mass of evergreens, from the shore to the tops of the high hills, interspersed with many cocoanut gardens; and there are many patches of coffee, which, although abandoned, continue to thrive well."

The account of this island by Captain Mitchell, R. N., is the latest and fullest. He says that it has little waste land on it, and that the whole might be advantageously cultivated.

"Limestone is the principal formation: there are also sandstone and quartz, and a great deal of coral on the lower parts. The island seems originally to have been elevated by a volcanic eruption, and the lower portions washed up by the subsequent action of the sea. On the coral formations sand has been thrown

* *Memoir on the Mosquito Territory*, by Captain John Wright, p. 16.

up; then decayed vegetable matter and seeds, drifted or brought by birds from the continent and surrounding lands. These, springing up and decaying, have assisted in forming a fruitful soil, on which man has at length landed, erected his dwelling, and has found the land subservient to his wants. These remarks are applicable to the lower portions of the island. I have not heard of any minerals having been collected on the island.

"The island has a singularly beautiful appearance at a distance, as you approach it in a ship. The mountains rise in a gradual height to the summit of nine hundred feet, and they seem successively to follow each other, intersected by valleys, the whole thickly and most luxuriantly wooded. As you draw near to it, you discover that palm and cocoanut-trees encircle the shores, and forest trees of various descriptions grow on the higher hills. The natural beauty of its appearance is greatly enhanced when you cast anchor in one of its many harbors on the southern side.

"In the valleys, alluvial deposits and decayed vegetable matter form the soil, which is exceedingly rich and deep. On the mountains and their declivities, a red clay or marl predominates.

"A great deal of good and useful timber is found spontaneously growing on the island, such as Santa Maria wood, extensively used for ship-building, three varieties of oak, cedar, Spanish elm, and lancewood, and the shores of the island are lined and surrounded with groves of cocoanut-trees; a tree which, in administering to the wants of man, is hardly surpassed in tropical regions. The seeds of this tree in remote times have been probably drifted here, and they have sprung up in abundance on a sandy and low shore, which is found so congenial to their growth.

"At present, the island produces in abundance cocoanuts, plantains, yams, bananas, pine-apples, etc., etc.; but I feel convinced that bread-fruit, European vegetables, and, indeed, many fruits, vegetables, and productions of more temperate regions, would grow here.

"The country is capable of raising all tropical productions, such as sugar, coffee, tobacco, etc., which might become staple commodities of export.

"There was found on the island previous to its being inhabited a great quantity of deer, wild hogs, Indian rabbits, parrots, pigeons, birds of various descriptions, etc. Some years ago, previous to its settlement, men from small vessels and fishing-boats, employed on the surrounding coasts, originally resorted to this island for the purpose of supplying themselves with game and stock.

"A great quantity of domestic animals, such as poultry, pigs, etc., are raised; cattle might be raised, but the inhabitants have not yet the means of keeping them from destroying their plantations.

"It seems probable the island at some remote period was thickly inhabited by the Indian race. In clearing away the land for plantations, many domestic and culinary utensils have been found. There is a tradition that the Spaniards (in accordance with their system of cruelty), on their first discovery of America, depopulated the island; they seized upon the aborigines, and took them to the continent to work in the mines, whence they never returned.

"A great deal of rain falls in the winter months from September to February. This has the effect of cooling the air beyond what is felt in the other parts of the West Indies, and the breeze tempers the influence of the sun. If the people could keep themselves dry and free from damp, the climate must not only be exceedingly agreeable, but singularly pure and healthy. The dry months are much warmer; the natives, however, do not complain of the heat; they aver that it is the healthier portion of the year. The thermometer since we have been here (January) has averaged 80° of Fahrenheit.

"Rheumatism is very common, and a species of low fever or ague; the latter probably arises from the land not being sufficiently cleared away, and a luxuriant and decaying vegetation; the former from constant damp and exposure. Yet I should think, from my limited observation, that the climate is not only healthy to those born in warm latitudes, but that Europeans, with proper precautions, might enjoy not only health, but live to a good old age.

"The population of the island is now estimated at 1600 or

1700. In 1843 it was only eighty. It has gone on steadily and rapidly increasing, and there are at present three births to one death. With the means of existence at hand, and almost prepared for them, the young people have a disposition to marry at an early age; their families are large, many consisting of nine to ten, and even more children. They seem to be a proof of what has been often asserted in civilized countries, that a diet of vegetables and fish, or what is usually termed scanty food, is favorable to population.

"The population is scattered in different parts along the whole sea-shore of the island; from obvious reasons, they find these localities more convenient than the interior. They here erect their dwellings, in the midst of their palm and plantain groves, having their little vessels and fishing-boats in quiet and sheltered nooks, and convey their produce and seek for their wants by water-carriage.

"At Coxen Hole, or Port M'Donald, the greatest numbers seem located: there are here perhaps five hundred. It is a safe and sheltered harbor; yet chance seems to have directed them, in the first instance, to this spot, as I am inclined to believe, from my limited observation, there are other places more eligible for a township.

"The mass of the population is composed of liberated slaves from the Grand Cayman, and a small portion of the inhabitants are colored people, also natives of that island, and formerly slave-owners. These latter people seem to be the most wretched on the island; unaccustomed to labor, and having lost their property and their slaves, or squandered away what they obtained for them, they have no longer any means of existence. From a false feeling of pride, so universal in man, and found alike in all countries, they were unwilling to labor in a small island where they were once regarded with comparative consequence, and they emigrated and sought their fortunes on the unpeopled shores of Ruatan. The slaves who had obtained their freedom, but could not procure labor in a small island like the Grand Cayman, hearing of the success of their former masters, followed in their footsteps.

"The dark population, or those who were formerly slaves,

from their physical powers and their habits of labor from childhood, soon surpassed the white population in the accumulation of the means of existence, and are now the most thriving and successful.

"If riches be estimated from man's wants being easily supplied, and the accumulation of more than he requires, these people are not only wealthy, but in far better circumstances than many of those who are relieved from manual labor in Europe.

"Added to these two classes, a third, and much smaller one, must be named, which consists purely of Europeans. They are men who have tried various pursuits and professions of life, which they have given up for various reasons, have taken to others, and have become familiar with the hard usages of adversity; and they sought this remote island, some in their old and some in their middle age, either to commence again, or to retrieve their broken fortunes, or to speculate in an imaginary construction of wealth. This class, though small in numbers, exercise a great influence over the minds of the community.

"The mass of the population is a fine race. They are strong, active, and athletic, temperate, quiet, and regular in their habits, not given to excess. The sexes are equally divided, and the old, who have lived with women in the days of slavery, evince a disposition to be married. I should say they have fewer vices than one usually meets among their class. As a proof that their character is good, they have lived and are living without any form of government or restraint, and the crimes that have been committed are comparatively few.

"Their occupation consists in cultivating their grounds and plantations, fishing, turtling, etc. Necessity, in all countries and in the first rude ages of civilization, has been fertile in invention, consequently it is by no means extraordinary to find the mass of these people familiar with those rude mechanical arts of which they stand so much in need. Every man erects his own dwelling, plants and lays out his ground—most are carpenters, some good rope-makers. They have a knowledge of boat and ship building, the making of lime, etc., and other useful attainments. Their dwellings are well and comfortably made.

"Their trade or commerce is in their plantains, cocoanuts, pine-apples, etc., and this trade is steadily increasing. With these articles they trade to New Orleans, bringing back lumber, dry and salt provisions, etc.

"Their relations with other countries consist principally with New Orleans, Belize, and Spanish Honduras.

"I should conceive the island might maintain a population of 15,000 or 20,000 when cultivated.

"The harbors on the south side of this island are many and good. I have visited Coxen Hole, or Port M'Donald, and Dixon's Cove. In both of these you are sheltered from all winds. They have great facilities for heaving down and repairing ships, and fresh water is found in abundance.

"Dixon's Cove is a good harbor. It is about six miles to the eastward of Port M'Donald, in some points preferable to the latter. A ship having lost her anchors might run into this harbor and ground upon the soft mud without injury. Many ships might find anchorage here.

"There is, again, Port Royal, a much larger harbor, and where twenty or thirty sail of the line might be moored. Its entrance is exceedingly narrow, which is its drawback, and the land is said not to be so fertile. Generally speaking, these harbors are surrounded by reefs of coral; their channels are narrow, and ought never to be attempted by strangers; but a local knowledge is easily obtained. The channels between the reefs are deep, and show themselves by the blueness of the water."*

Twenty-two vessels left Roatan in the year 1854, with fruits and vegetables for New Orleans.

Guanaja or Bonacca was discovered by Columbus, then sailing on his fourth voyage, in 1502. It was surveyed in 1840 by Lieutenant Thomas N. Smith, R. N., and, according to the chart published under order of the British Admiralty, is nine miles in length by five in breadth. It is distant about fifty miles

* *Statistical Account and Description of the Island of Roatan*, by Com. R. C. Mitchell, R. N., *United Service Magazine, August*, 1850.

from the nearest point on the main land, and about fifteen miles to the northeast of Roatan, with which it is connected by a series of reefs, through which there are only a few narrow passages. The land is high, and can be seen from a great distance at sea. Henderson touched its shores during his voyage, anchoring in "a little bay of great depth of water, which, however, was so transparent that the shell-fish and coral rocks at the bottom could be clearly discerned. This part of the island," he continues, "is highly romantic and picturesque, and, like Roatan, profusely covered with trees. Its natural productions appear to be the same."* Roberts also visited it, "landing opposite a watering-place, in an excellent harbor on the south side. The beach, above high-water mark, was thickly covered with cocoanut trees, and innumerable tracks of the wild hog were visible on the ground. The island contains hills of considerable elevation, thickly covered with trees, and is said also to have beds of limestone and ores of zinc."†

The account of Young, who was forced to take shelter there through stress of weather, is fuller, and gives a picture of the island as it was in 1841.

"It is covered with high hills, producing much valuable timber, and in the rich valleys and fertile savannas are numerous fruit-trees of various kinds. Along the water's edge, in many parts of the island, are numbers of cocoanut-trees. One spot, in particular, in the middle of the island, is called the cocoanut garden, where there are many other fruit-trees, indicating the hand of industry. Viewed from any part, the island has a pleasing appearance, and, though small, might be made of importance if the English were to establish themselves upon it. The woods abound in wild hogs of large size, and thousands of Indian rab-

* Henderson's Honduras, p. 194. † Roberts's Narrative, p. 276.

bits; the trees are full of pigeons and parrots; and the lagoons and harbors are celebrated for an immense variety of fish, which may easily be caught by going toward the edges of the coral reefs in a *dory* (canoe), where the bottom is plainly visible. Here the splendid sea-fans expand themselves, and almost invite the beholder to grasp them, so seducing are they in appearance, and so deceptive is the depth of the water. In some places large clusters of sponge can be seen; in others, handsome sea-eggs, inviting but to betray; and, altogether, with the numerous cays, studded with graceful cocoanut-trees around, there can not be imagined a scene more novel and beautiful. Under the rocks, on the reefs round the cays, are plenty of craw-fish; conchs and wilks are found in all parts, and a species of iguana, called *il-lishle*, abounds in every cay. The climate is exceedingly good, and during the ravages of the cholera at Truxillo a few years ago, the commandant of that place sent many to this island for the recovery of their health. Of the whole number, but three died. When Black River was occupied by the British, before the evacuation took place in 1778 by order of the British government, in consequence of its agreement with Spain, those of the colonists who were seized with the intermittent fever were sent to Guanaja, whence they generally returned improved in health and strength. It is surprising, considering the salubrity of this island, the richness of its soil, its woods, and fisheries, and its adaptation to many purposes, that it has never been settled by the English. By many traces, it is clear that it was formerly populated by the Indians.

"In one part of the island, near Savanna Bight Cay, there is a very rich and fine savanna, with several fruit-trees in it; and, what is more singular, near the place a stone wall has been discovered, evidently, by its shape and appearance, the work of uncivilized man. This wall runs along for some distance a few feet high, and here and there are fissures, or rude niches, made for the admission of peculiarly-cut three-legged stone chairs, which, I suppose, must have been seats for their idols. Several places have been discovered cut out of the solid rock representing chairs, and numerous articles of roughly-burned clay, in various fantastical devices, for holding liquids, have been found, as also broken English crockery and iron; and I have seen several curious things in the possession of various people, which have been dug up, and are doubtless of Indian manufacture. I understand the adjacent island, Roatan, exhibits yet more proofs of having been inhabited by an uncivilized race.

"In the months of April and May, thousands of birds, called boobies and noddies, generally lay their eggs on the southwest part of Half-moon Cay, thus affording a most delicious provision for nearly two months.

"The number of cocoanut-trees is really incredible, so much so that great advantage might be derived from making oil, which might be effected at a small expense, especially as living, after the first twelve months, would cost little or nothing but labor, allowing that time for the establishment of plantations on the main land for any sort of bread kind, as the soil is so well adapted for such a purpose. Plantains, which may be considered as the standard, thrive wonderfully; this, with keeping some hogs and fowls on a cay, and feeding them on the refuse of the cocoanut, etc., would, in a short period, show the advantage to be reaped. A few good Spanish dogs for hunting the wild hog, two or three turtle-nets, harpoons, hooks and lines, and fish-pots, are indispensable. On the island may also be grown coffee, cotton, tobacco, cacao, etc. During the greater part of the year plenty of fish and wild hogs can be caught, but when bad weather sets in, which is sometimes the case, little good can be done.

"With respect to making oil, it takes about fourteen common sized nuts to make a quart, by the method in vogue at Roatan, etc.; but by the introduction of the hydraulic press, I should say, a quart might be expressed from nine or ten, and with a great saving of labor.

"The many uses to which the cocoanut-tree and its fruit can be applied are pretty well known; suffice it to say, it may be considered as one of the most valuable productions which a bountiful Providence has lavished on tropical climates. At the present time the island abounds with wild hogs, they not having been hunted much lately. Caribs occasionally resort to Guanaja for the purpose of hunting these animals, but they have not been so frequently as in former years, thus the hogs have much increased. The only things that can be said to militate against the island and its cays are, firstly, the myriads of bottle and horse-flies on the former, and mosquitoes and sand-flies on the latter, which appear to deter people from settling; although it is evident that, when a place is covered with vegetation, these annoying insects must exist, and that, as the land becomes cleared, the flies will gradually diminish.

"From March to June the cays are subject to the pest of whole armies of soldier-snails, creeping and crawling over every thing the moment the sun sets, and with such an indescribable noise as to surpass belief; the dead branches on the ground creak and break under the legion as they advance, consuming all in their progress. They were a great nuisance to us, as we were obliged to hang up our hammocks pretty high.

"On the whole, Guanaja may be considered a fine island, and one on which any man could soon obtain the necessaries of life, and with energy, activity, and a strict determination to sobriety, even the luxuries, without fear of a bastile in his old age.

Helena, *Morat*, and *Barbaretta*, are comparatively small islands, and may be regarded as detached parts of Roatan. They are, in fact, connected with it by reefs, through which there are only a few narrow and intricate passages. Captain Henderson, who visited Barbaretta in 1804, has left us a very animated and quite an enthusiastic account of its beauty. He describes it as high, and covered with a dense forest.

"After a walk of a mile and a half along the beach, in a course contrary to that which I had pursued the day before, we came to the rocks, and here, although our progress seemed less difficult to the eye, it scarcely presented fewer obstacles to the feet. Difficulties, however, sink before determination. After some trouble, I gained a firm station on a tolerable eminence, and without resorting to the extravagant and affected language sometimes used on similar occasions, I might truly say the whole was enchantingly beautiful and picturesque. The spot on which I stood might be connected with a space of somewhat more than half an acre, entirely clear of trees, and covered with luxuriant grass. Beyond this the whole became a thick, continued grove,

'Where scarce a speck of day
Falls on the lengthened gloom.'

At the base of the rock the sea rolled with loud and haughty sway, and the confused masses of stone which lay scattered about at once confessed its uncontrollable dominion."*

It was subsequently visited in 1841 by Young, who found some Spaniards from the main land established there. One of these, Señor Ruiz, showed him over his "large and extensive plantations, full of all manner of bread kind, besides greens, peas, and beans of various descriptions. He had a large expanse of ground covered with cotton-plants, and hundreds of papaya-trees, the fruit of which he gave to his fowls and hogs. He had also a cane-patch, and a small mill for crushing it, as he made his own sugar. There was a large turtle-crawl opposite his dwelling containing eight turtles. In rainy weather, he employed his people in the manufacture of cocoanut oil." Finding him surrounded with all these means of comfortable and even luxurious existence, Young was astonished to learn that he had arrived there only three years previously, "with his wife, his son, about eleven years of age, some provisions, a gun, two or three machetes (large knives), and a few hooks, and other trifles." "I thought," continues this author, "of the thousands of my poor countrymen struggling in vain for a decent subsistence, and who would live in independence if similarly situated, instead of being brought to an early grave by disappointed hopes, or the weight of a large family."† Roberts, who also visited Barbaretta, speaks of finding "three or four sorts of wild grapes."

* Henderson's Honduras, p. 194. † Young's Narrative, p. 151.

Helena is smaller than Barbaretta, distant from it between four and five miles, near the extreme north-eastern extremity of Roatan. Young found there a Frenchman, in the Honduras service, who had "plantations and large nets for turtling." His principal business, however, was that of making lime, which he sold at Omoa and other places at from two to three dollars a barrel: "rather a high price, but which he obtained in consequence of its strength, the kind of stone from which it is made being found chiefly in this island."

Honduras has two large islands in the Gulf of Fonseca, on the Pacific, viz., Tigre and Sacate Grande, which are described in the account elsewhere given of that gulf.

CHAPTER VIII.

POLITICAL DIVISIONS—DEPARTMENTS OF COMAYAGUA, GRACIAS, CHOLUTECA, TEGUCIGALPA, OLANCHO, YORO, AND STA. BARBARA.

THE political divisions of Honduras are seven, viz.: the Departments of Gracias, Comayagua, Choluteca, Tegucigalpa, Olancho, Yoro, and Sta. Barbara. The subjoined table expresses the capital, area, and population of each, as also the aggregate area and population of the state:

HONDURAS—CAPITAL, COMAYAGUA.

Departments.	Capitals.	Area in Square Miles.	Population.	Inhabitants to Square Mile.
Comayagua .	Comayagua .	4,800	70,000	$14\frac{1}{2}$
Tegucigalpa .	Tegucigalpa .	1,500	60,000	43
Choluteca . .	Nacaome . . .	2,000	50,000	25
Sta. Barbara.	Sta. Barbara .	3,250	50,000	$13\frac{1}{2}$
Gracias. . . .	Gracias	4,050	55,000	$13\frac{1}{2}$
Yoro	Yoro	15,100	20,000*	$1\frac{1}{3}$
Olancho . . .	Olancho	11,300	45,000*	4
Total		39,600	350,000	9

Each department has a distinct representation in the general Congress of the state, and is governed by an officer appointed by the central government, who bears the title of *Jefe Politico*, or political chief. Each department is also subdivided into districts, for the convenience of the inhabitants and the better administration of justice.

* The population in Yoro and Olancho is calculated exclusive of the Indian tribes; and the area of the unsettled country, comprising nearly the whole of the eastern and politically unorganized half of the state, is divided between these two departments.

DEPARTMENT OF COMAYAGUA.

Districts.—Comayagua, Lajamini, Yucusapa, Siguatepeque, Miambar, Aguanqueterique, Goascoran.

Principal Towns.—Las Piedras, or Villa de la Paz, Villa de San Antonio, Opoteca, Espino, San Antonio del Norte, Goascoran, and Caridad.

The Department of Comayagua, lying in the very centre of Honduras, and comprehending its capital, the ancient city of Comayagua, is entitled to the first place in a notice of the various departmental divisions of the state. Its distinguishing geographical feature is the plain of the same name, to which I have elsewhere adverted, and in which a great part of the population of the department is concentrated. The capital itself, the considerable towns of Las Piedras and San Antonio, and the smaller towns of Ajuterique, Lajamini, Yarumela, Cane, Tambla, Lamani, and Lo de Flores, are all found in this plain, embracing a population of not far from 25,000 souls.

The city of Comayagua (anciently called Valladolid) is situated on the southern border of the plain. It was founded in 1540 by Alonzo Caceres, in obedience to instructions "*to find out an eligible situation for a town midway between the oceans.*"

It now contains between 7000 and 8000 inhabitants. Previous to 1827 it had about 18,000, and was embellished with fountains and monuments. In that year it was taken and burned by the monarchical faction of Guatemala, and has never been able wholly to recover from the shock.

In the maps its position has been put too far to the eastward and southward. It is in lat. 14° 28′ N., and long. 87° 39′ W., and in a right line, or within a few miles of a right line, drawn between the mouth of the

Ulua and that of the Goascoran. Its distance from the Bay of Fonseca is seventy miles, and it is, within a few miles more or less, midway between the two seas.

Comayagua is the seat of a bishopric, and has a large, and, according to Spanish taste, an elegant Cathedral. It has also a University, founded many years ago, but which declined in consequence of the adverse political circumstances of the country, until it was revived in 1849, under the auspices of Dr. Don Juan Lindo, a man of enlightened spirit, then president of the state. The trade of the city is small. Hitherto the difficulty of communication with the coast has prevented it from gaining any commercial eminence. But when the incentives and means for developing the resources of the adjacent country shall be afforded, it must become a place of much importance.

The plain, upon its eastern and western borders, is skirted by mountains five or six thousand feet high, and it consequently enjoys a climate cool, equal, and salubrious, comparing in respect of temperature with the Middle States of our Union in the month of June. The hills and mountains adjacent to the plain are covered with pines, and on their summit and slopes, wheat, potatoes, and other products of the temperate zones are cultivated, and may be produced in abundance. The productions of the plain, however, are essentially tropical. Its soil is extremely fertile. In short, the plain of Comayagua offers all the conditions for attracting and sustaining, as there is abundant evidence that it formerly sustained, a large and flourishing population.

Indeed, hardly a step can be taken in any direction without encountering evidences of aboriginal occupation, and the names of the principal towns in the valley

From Nature and on Stone by D. C. Hitchcock

Printed by Sarony & Co. New York.

PLAIN OF COMAYAGUA.

are only perpetuations of those which they possessed before the conquest. In some of them the predominating portion of the population is still unmixed Indian. Lamani, Tambla, Yarumela, Ajuterique, Lajamini, and Cururu, are all Indian names. There are also many Indian towns which have been entirely abandoned as the population of the country has decreased, and of which the traces are now scarcely visible.

The principal ruins, strictly aboriginal and of ancient architecture, are in the vicinity of Yarumela, Lajamini, and near the ruined town of Cururu. They consist of large pyramidal, terraced structures, often faced with stones, conical mounds of earth, and walls of stone. In these, and in their vicinity, are found carvings in stone, and painted vases of great beauty.

The principal monuments, however, retaining distinctly their primitive forms, can hardly be said to be in the plain of Comayagua. They are found in the lateral valleys, or on the adjacent tables ("mesas") of the mountains. Of this description are the ruins of Calamulla, on the road to the Indian mountain town of Guajiquero; of Jamalteca, in the little valley of the same name; of Maniani, in the valley of Espino; of Guasistagua, near the little village of the same name; of Chapuluca, in the neighborhood of Opoteca; and of Chapulistagua, in a large valley back of the mountains of Comayagua. I have visited all of these, but in many respects the most interesting, and by far the most extensive, are those of Tenampua.

The ruins of Tenampua are popularly called Pueblo Viejo, Old Town. They are situated on the level summit of a high hill, almost deserving the name of mountain, about twenty miles to the southeast of Comayagua, near the insignificant village of Lo de Flores, by the side of the road leading to the city of Tegucigalpa. The summit of the hill is a plain or savanna, covered with scattered pines, and elevated about sixteen hundred feet above the plain of Comayagua, of which, in every part, a magnificent view is commanded. The hill is composed of the prevailing soft, white, stratified sandstone of this region, and its sides, except at three points, are either absolutely precipitous, or so steep as to be nearly if not quite inaccessible. At the accessible point, where narrow ridges connect the hill with the other hills of the group, are heavy artificial walls of rough stones, varying in height from six to fifteen feet, and in width, at the base, from ten to twenty-five feet. These walls are terraced on the inner side, for convenience of defense. At various points there are traces of towers, or buildings designed perhaps for the use of guards or sentinels. The dimensions of the wall correspond to the greater or less abruptness of the slope along which it is carried, and are greatest where the ascent or approach is easiest. Where narrow gullies or natural passes existed, the hollows have been filled with stones, so as to present a vertical outer face, corresponding with the rocky escarpment of the hill. Naturally, I think this place is the strongest position I have ever seen. That it was selected, in part at least, for defense is obvious. Under any system of warfare practiced by the aborigines, it must have been impregnable. The defensive design is made still more apparent by the existence, in the centre of the area of the summit, at a place naturally low and marshy, of two large square excavations, now partially filled up, which were clearly designed for reservoirs.

But the most interesting features of Tenampua are not its ruined walls and defenses. The level summit of the hill is about one and a half miles long, by half a mile in average width. The eastern half of this large area is crowded with ruins. They consist chiefly of terraced mounds of stone, or of earth faced with stone, of regular rectangular forms, their sides conforming to the cardinal points. Although the stones are uncut, they are laid with great precision. Most of the small mounds, which occur in groups, and are arranged with obvious design in respect to each other, are from twenty to thirty feet square, and from four to eight feet in height. There are none of less than two, but most have three or four stages. Besides these, there are a considerable number of large pyramidal structures, varying from sixty to one hundred and twenty feet in length, of proportional width, and of different heights. These are also terraced, and generally have ruins of steps on their western sides. There are also several rectangular inclosures of stone, and a number of platforms and terraced slopes.

The principal inclosure is situated in the very midst of the ruins, at a point conspicuous from every portion of the hill. It is three hundred feet long by one hundred and eighty feet broad. The wall is fourteen feet broad, but now elevated only a few feet above the ground. It seems to have consisted of an outer and inner wall, each about two feet thick, between which earth had been filled to the depth of two feet. Transverse walls then appear to have been built at regular intervals, dividing it into rectangular areas, resembling the foundations of houses. It is not improbable they were surmounted by structures of wood, devoted to the use of the priests or guardians of the great temple, in the same manner that, according to the chroniclers, "the cloisters of the priests and attendants" surrounded the court of the great temple of Mexico. The line of the wall is only interrupted by the gateway or entrance, which is on the western side, between two oblong terraced mounds, in which the ends of the wall terminate. To preserve the symmetry of the inclosure, the opposite or eastern wall has in its centre a large mound, also terraced and regular in form, equaling in size both those at the entrance.

Within the inclosures are two large mounds, the relative positions and sizes of which can only be explained by a plan. The largest has three stages and a flight of steps on its western side. From its southwest angle a line of large stones, sunk in the ground, is carried to the southern wall. The north line of this mound coincides with one drawn from east to west through the centre of the inclosure. Between it and the gateway is a square of stones, sunk in the ground, which may mark the site of some edifice. The second pyramid is situated in the northeast corner of the inclosure; it has the same number of stages with the larger one just described, and, like that, has a flight of steps on its western side.

At the extreme southeast corner of the hill is another inclosure similar to this, except that it is square, and has openings in the centre of each side. It also contains two terraced mounds, ascended by steps. Between the great inclosure, or central structure, and the precipice which faces the hill on the south, is a depression or small valley. This is terraced upon both sides, the terraces being faced with stone, ascended by various flights of stone steps. The principal mound beyond this depression is situated upon the edge of the precipice, due south of the great mound in the principal inclosure. It commands a view of the entire southern half of the plain of Comayagua, and fires lighted upon it would be visible to all the inhabitants below. I could not resist the conviction that its position had been determined by this circumstance.

There are many other striking features in these ruins, of which no adequate idea can be conveyed except from plans, and which, therefore, I shall not attempt to describe. The most singular, perhaps, consists of two long parallel mounds, each one hundred and forty feet in length, thirty-six feet broad at the base, and ten feet high in the centre. The inner sides of each, facing each other, appear to have consisted of three terraces, rising like the seats of an amphitheatre. The lower terraces are forty feet apart, and faced with huge flat stones, set upright in the ground, so as to present an even front. The outer sides of these mounds have an appearance corresponding with that of the walls of the great inclosure, and each seems to have been the site of three large buildings. The whole rests on a terrace three hundred and sixty feet long. Exactly in a line with the centre of the space between these parallels, and distant twenty-four paces, are two large stones placed side by side, with an opening of about one foot between them. Fronting these to the northward, and distant one hundred and twenty paces, is a large mound occupying a corresponding relative position in respect to the parallels, and having a flight of steps on its southern side. Upon these mounds, as indeed upon many of the others, are standing large pine-trees, upward of two feet in diameter. Without attempting to define the special purposes of these parallels, it seems to me probable that they had a corresponding design with the parallel walls found by Mr. Stephens at Chichen-Itza and Uxmal in Yucatan. Doubtless games, processions, or other civic or religious rites or ceremonies, took place between them, in the presence of priests or dignitaries who were seated upon the terraces on either hand.

The form of the various mounds at Tenampua precludes the idea that they were used as the foundations of dwellings. It seems quite clear that they were either altars or sites of temples—counterparts of those of Guatemala, Yucatan, and Mexico, and of a large portion of those found in the Mississippi Valley, with all of which they accurately coincide in the principles of their construction. I was able to excavate but one, situated in the vicinity of the great temple. The mass of the mound, after penetrating the stone facing, was found to be simple earth; but the interior of the upper terrace was composed almost entirely of burned matter, ashes, and fragments of pottery. Great quantities of these fragments were discovered, and I was able to recover enough of some vessels to make out their shape, and the paintings and ornaments upon them. Some were flat, like pans; others had been vases of various forms. All were elaborately painted with simple ornaments or mythological figures. One small, gourd-shaped vase, of rude workmanship, I recovered nearly entire. It was filled with a dark-colored, indurated matter, which it was impossible to remove. Fragments of obsidian knives were also found.

Near the western extremity of the summit of the hill are two deep holes with perpendicular sides, sunk into the rock. They are about twenty feet square and twelve feet deep. Although now partially filled with earth, a passage is to be discovered at the bottom of each, leading off to the north. These passages seem to have been about three feet high by nearly the same width.

How far they may go, or whither they lead, is unknown. The water which flows into them during rains finds a ready outlet. I am unprepared to decide whether these openings are natural or artificial, but incline to the opinion that they are natural, with perhaps artificial improvements or adaptations. A ruined pyramid stands near the principal mouth. The tradition concerning them is that they were dug by the "antiguos," and lead to the ruins of Chapulistagua, beyond the mountains, and were designed to afford an easy means of flight in case of danger.

Altogether there are here the remains of between three and four hundred terraced, truncated pyramids of various sizes, besides the other singular inclosures which I have mentioned.

The whole place probably served both for religious and defensive purposes. This union of purposes was far from uncommon among the semi-civilized families of this continent. I have presented, in my work on the Monuments of the Mississippi Valley, many instances in which structures strictly religious are found within works clearly defensive. It was within the area, and on the steps and terraces of the great temple of Mexico, that the Aztecs made their final and most determined stand against the arms of Cortez. It is not to be supposed, however, that this was a fortified town, or a place permanently occupied by any considerable population. The summit of the hill is rocky, and the soil thin and poor, affording few of the usual accessories of a large Indian population, viz., abundant water and rich lands. The builders doubtless had their permanent residences in the plain below, and only came here to perform religious or sepulchral rites, or to find safety in times of danger.

Falling within the Department of Comayagua is the plain of Espino. It lies to the northward of the plain of Comayagua, from which it is separated by only a narrow range of hills, and of which it may be regarded as an extension or dependency. It is watered by the same river, the Humuya, which traverses its entire length. The plain of Espino is sometimes called Maniani. It is much smaller than that of Comayagua, being but about twelve miles long by eight broad, but in other respects, such as climate, productions, etc., what is true of one is equally true of the other.

Dependent also upon the plain of Espino is the small lateral valley of Jamalteca, a spot of surpassing beauty, abounding in springs of water, which sustain its vegetation fresh and vigorous, and enable the inhabitants to keep an uninterrupted succession of crops during the dryest seasons, when the country elsewhere is parched, and agriculture is suspended. In this valley are some very interesting monuments of the aborigines, indicating a large ancient population.

Nearly the whole length of the valley of the Rio Goascoran, which flows southward from the plain of Comayagua into the Gulf of Fonseca, falls within this department. This valley is narrow, and, except at its mouth, where it expands into the Pacific plains, does not embrace much valuable land. It is chiefly interesting as offering an easy route for the projected line of railway.

The mountains of San Juan or Guajiquero, in the southeast portion of this department, are occupied exclusively by Indians descended from the aboriginal Lencas. These mountains of stratified white sandstone are naturally terraced, presenting to the eye bold escarpments of rock, but supporting beautiful level areas, covered with rich soil, on which the Indians cultivate wheat and other grains, and the fruits of higher latitudes. They also rear a fine and very hardy race of mules, and altogether evince a degree of perseverance and industry, very wide nevertheless of enterprise, which we look for in vain among the semi-European inhabitants.

Every department in Honduras possesses more or less mineral wealth. In this respect, although not ranking so high as some of the others, the Department of Comayagua is abundantly favored. The considerable town of Opoteca is literally built upon a silver mine, which was most extensively worked under the crown, and with signal success. At present the attention of the inhabitants, for obvious reasons, is directed to agriculture. Near Aramacina, Las Piedras, and in the mountains near Lauterique, are numerous mines of silver, now wholly abandoned or imperfectly worked. They only need the touch of intelligence, enterprise, and capital to become of value. Copper ores exist in abundance, but no attempt has ever been made to reduce them. Throughout the entire department there are vast beds of blue and veined marble, proper for every class of constructions and for conversion into lime. The predominating rock is sandstone, generally milky white, but sometimes of cream color verging on orange. Near Guajiquero are also found inexhaustible beds of variously-colored ochres, of fine quality. These were and still are used for painting by the aborigines. The colors are remarkably vivid.

Pine and oak are abundant on the hills throughout this department, and mahogany, cedar, and lignum-vitæ, as well as other useful woods, are found in all desirable quantities in the valleys bordering the streams. Many varieties of cactus are found in the plain of Comayagua. The most common is the variety called the *nopal* in Mexico, and which is cultivated in the southern states of that country, and in Guatemala, for the production of cochineal. The numerous wild plants of this variety found in Honduras produce what is called *grana silvestre*, or wild cochineal. The plains of Comayagua and Espino are admirably adapted, therefore, for the cultivation of cochineal, as well as coffee, and all the other great staples of semi-tropical regions.

DEPARTMENT OF GRACIAS.

Districts.—Ocotepeque, Guarita, Erandique or Corquin, Gualalcha, Sensenti, Camarca, Intibucat, Gracias, Sta. Rosa, and Trinidad.

Principal Towns.—Gracias, Sta. Rosa, Intibucat, Sensenti, Corquin, San José, Ocotepeque, Cololaca.

The Department of Gracias lies in the northeastern angle of the state, touching upon Guatemala and San Salvador. Its territory is, in many respects, the most interesting in all Central America, of which it may be regarded as, in some degree, an epitome. In respect to it we have more information than in regard to any of the others. This is due to Señor Don José M. Cacho, present Secretary of State of Honduras, who, as Commissioner of the Census of 1834 for this department, discharged his duties, considering all the difficulties of the case, in a very creditable manner.

Its surface is much diversified, and it is distinguished by several groups of majestic mountains. The Mountains of Selaque occupy very nearly the centre of the department; and on the north it has the range of Merendon, which, as I have elsewhere said, extends from the borders of San Salvador to the Bay of Honduras, a distance of not far from one hundred and fifty

From Nature and on Stone by D. C. Hitchcock. Printed by Sarony & Co. New York.

PLAIN OF INTIBUCAT.

miles. It is called by different names at different points, as Merendon, Gallinero, Grita, Espiritu Santo, and Omoa. No towns occur in these mountains, except the small village of Dolores Merendon. At its feet, upon the north, are several beautiful valleys, among which is that of Copan, distinguished for its ancient monuments. Upon the south, nearly coinciding with the boundaries between this department and that of Comayagua, are the Mountains of Opalaca and Puca, both of commanding height. They extend to the north-eastward, nearly parallel to those of Omoa, until intercepted by the valley of the Rio Sta. Barbara.

All of these mountains are heavily timbered with pines and oaks. Their lower slopes, and the valleys at their feet, produce the cedar, mahogany, and other valuable woods in great abundance. In the Mountains of Merendon is found the *Quetzal*, the royal and sacred bird of the aboriginal kingdom of Quiché, and one of the most beautiful found in the world.

Like all other parts of Honduras, this department is profusely watered. In it rise some of the largest streams of Central America. To the west of the Mountains of Merendon, and rising in its gorges, are the small rivers Gila and Gualan, which flow into the Motagua. Flowing along the eastern base of the same range is the Rio Chamelicon, which has its rise a few leagues to the northward of the town of Sta. Rosa. It forms a valley of great beauty and fertility, which, like that of Copan, abounds in monuments of a large aboriginal population. The river Santiago or Venta, which, after its junction with the Humuya, is called the Ulua, has its sources in the great plain of Sensenti, where it bears different names—Rio de la Valle, Alas, Higuito, and Talgua. Its first great tributary in this department is the Rio Mejicote, or Gracias, flowing along the eastern base of the Mountains of Selaque. Below the point of junction, the Santiago is a large, unfordable stream. Along the southern border of the department, and constituting the boundary separating it from San Salvador, is the River Sumpul, one of the largest affluents of the great river Lempa, flowing into the Pacific. It receives several considerable tributaries from the territories of this department. Among them may be mentioned the Guarajambala, Pirigual, Moscal, and Cololaca.

Perhaps the most interesting topographical feature of this department is the plain or valley of Sensenti, lying between and almost encircled by the Mountains of Selaque, Pacaya, and Merendon. It is about thirty-five miles long by from five to fifteen in width. It is nearly divided by a range of hills, which extend partially across it in the neighborhood of Corquin. The upper valley might, with propriety, be called that of Sensenti, the lower one the plain of Cucuyagua. The latter has an average altitude of 2300 feet, and the former of 2800 feet above the sea. The soil throughout is good, and the climate delightful. It constituted part of the dominions of the aboriginal cazique Lempira, who resisted the Spaniards longer than any chief in Central America. The army with which he encountered the Spanish general Chaves was more numerous than the present entire population of the department.

The climate of the department is unexcelled for salubrity. The general temperature, as might be inferred from the elevated character of the country, is cool, although no two places can, in this respect, be said to be alike. Their climate varies with their elevation. Intibucat, an Indian town, situated in the midst of a considerable plain or terrace of the Opalaca Mountains, is 5200 feet above the sea. Occasional slight falls of snow take place here during the months of December and January. I passed through the town in the early part of the month of July, when the thermometer at sunrise stood at 56° of Fahrenheit. Peaches, apples, and plums flourish in this plain, and the blackberry is indigenous among the hills. The towns of Caiquin and Colocte have a temperature still lower than that of Intibucat. During three weeks which I spent at Sta. Rosa, from July 9 to August 1, the average temperature at sunrise was 68°, at noon 72°, and at 3 P.M. 73° of Fahrenheit. From September to February the thermometer has a still lower range.

The vegetable products of this department, actual and possible, exhaust the list of productions of the temperate zones and the tropics. Wheat, rye, barley, the potato, etc., grow on the mountains, while sugar-cane, indigo, tobacco, cotton, coffee, cacao, plantains, oranges, etc., flourish in the plains and valleys. Of valuable timber there is also great abundance. Pine, equal to the best North Carolina, covers the hills. There is also much mahogany, cedar, granadillo, Brazil wood, mora, etc., for purposes of dyeing, manufacture, and construction. Copal, balsam, and liquid amber are among the most common gums. The tobacco of Gracias, as will be seen farther on, has a wide and deserved celebrity.

Apart from its agricultural wealth, Gracias is distinguished for its minerals and precious metals. Gold and silver mines are numerous and rich, although but little worked, for want of scientific knowledge, intelligence, machinery, and capital. The silver and copper mines of Coloal, in the Mountains of Merendon, are very valuable, the copper ores yielding 58 per cent. of copper, besides 98 ounces of silver to the ton. The silver ores of Sacramento yield 8674 ounces of silver to the ton. Coal is also found in the plain or valley of Sensenti, near the half-deserted town of Chucuyuco. I visited the beds at a place where they were cut through by ravines, and found the principal deposit from eight to ten feet thick, separated by bituminous shale from a superior bed about two feet in thickness. The coal is bituminous, and, at the outcrops, of fair quality. Asbestos, cinnabar, and platina are also found in this department. Opals are obtained at various localities, and have been exported to a considerable extent. The most and best have been found near the mountain town of Erandique.

It appears from the official paper of Honduras that, from the 1st of April, 1851, to the 31st of January, 1853, there were "denounced," or entered, in accordance with the mining laws, not less than *sixteen* opal mines in the single district of Erandique. In the department at large, for the same period, were entered thirteen silver mines, one gold mine, and one coal mine. Amethysts are reported as having been found near Campuca.

Near the little town of Virtud, in the extreme southern part of the department, is a curious natural phenomenon, known as *Mina ó Fuente de Sangre*, Mine or Fountain of Blood.* From the roof of a small cavern

* "A little to the south of the town of Virtud is a small cavern (*gruta*), which during the day is visited by the buzzards and *gabilanes*, and at night by a multitude of large bats (*vampiros*), for the purpose of feeding on the natural blood which is found here dropping from the roof of the cavern. This grot is on the borders of a rivulet, which it keeps reddened with a small flow of a liquid that has the color, smell, and taste of blood. In approaching the grot a disagreeable odor is observed, and when it is reached there may be seen some pools of the apparent blood in a state of coagulation. Dogs eat it eagerly. The late Don Rafael Osejo undertook

there is constantly oozing and dropping a red liquid, which, upon falling, coagulates, so as precisely to resemble blood. Like blood, it corrupts; insects deposit their larvæ in it, and dogs and buzzards resort to the cavern to eat it. In a country where there is so little scientific knowledge as in Central America, a phenomenon of this kind could not fail to be an object of great, if not superstitious wonder, and many marvelous stories are current concerning the Fountain of Blood. Attempts have several times been made to obtain some of this liquid for the purpose of analysis, but in all cases without success, in consequence of its rapid decomposition, whereby the bottles containing it were broken. By largely diluting it with water, I succeeded in bringing with me to the United States two bottles of the liquid, which I submitted to Professor B. Silliman, Junior, for examination. It had, however, undergone decomposition, and was very offensive. It had deposited a thick sediment, containing abundant traces of original organic matter. The peculiarities of the liquid are doubtless due to the rapid generation in this grotto of some very prolific species of colored infusoria.

DEPARTMENT OF CHOLUTECA.

Districts. — Nacaome, Amapala, Choluteca, Savana Grande, Texiguat, Cururen, Santa Anna.

Principal Towns.—Choluteca, Nacaome, Texiguat, Amapala, Langue, Pespiri, Savana Grande.

Choluteca is the extreme southern department of Honduras, fronting on the Bay of Fonseca. It lies on the western slope of the Mountains of Lepaterique or Ule, among which the streams that water it take their

to send some bottles of this liquid to London for analysis, but it corrupted within twenty-four hours, bursting the bottles."—*Gaceta de Honduras*, February 20, 1853.

rise. It is, consequently, extremely diversified in surface. The valleys of the rivers Choluteca and Nacaome are broad and fertile, and the district fronting on the bay is distinguished for its extensive savannas and densely-wooded alluvions. For an average distance of fifteen miles inland, the soil is admirably adapted for plantations, and undoubtedly capable of producing in profusion all the staples of the tropics. As the country rises, which it does by a series of terraces, the savannas become broader and more numerous, affording vast pastures for herds of cattle, which at present probably constitute the chief wealth of the department.

The Mountains of Ule, or Lepaterique, which bound the department on the north, are not less than 5280 feet in height at the point where they are crossed by the high road from Nacaome to Tegucigalpa. Their summits are broad, undulating plains, cool, salubrious, and fertile, and literally constitute the granaries of the adjacent mineral districts. Wheat, potatoes, and especially maize, have there a vigorous and most productive growth. Hail, and occasionally snow, falls there, and in a few instances it has been known to fall in sufficient quantities to whiten the ground for several days. From the summits of the Ule Mountains the eye takes in a landscape more than a hundred miles broad, from the great blue masses of the Mountains of Sulaco on the north, to the volcanoes of Nicaragua and the Gulf of Fonseca on the south and southeast.

From these mountains the traveler also obtains a fine view of the valley of Choluteca, which sweeps in luxuriant beauty around its base, the course of its river being clearly defined by the belts of evergreen forests which grow upon its banks. This view is obtained through the broad, dependent valley of Yuguare, celebrated, even in Honduras, for its surpassing beauty and exhaustless resources. In this valley are several considerable Indian towns, whose inhabitants are distinguished alike for their industry, bravery, and republican spirit. Those of Texiguat and of Cururen obtained great distinction in the wars which preceded the dissolution of the republic of Central America, and are now among the most loyal and faithful citizens of the state, and its bravest defenders.

Apart from its agricultural wealth, the Department of Choluteca is rich in minerals, but chiefly in mines of silver. Among the latter is the famous mine of Corpus, near Choluteca, which, under the crown, was regarded of so much importance as to induce the Audiencia to establish a branch of the treasury there, in order to receive the royal fifths. It is now worked in a very small way, the shafts having been filled with water, and the adits obstructed with fallen rock. The mines of Cuyal and San Martyn, also found in this department, are now worked profitably on a small scale. Their value is much enhanced by their proximity to the Gulf of Fonseca, through which the requisite machinery can be brought within reach. Mills have recently been established on the island of Tigre for sawing the cedar, mahogany, and other valuable woods which are found in great abundance on the coast, for exportation to Chili, Peru, and California.

The islands of Tigre and Sacate Grande, which have already been noticed (see p. 96), as also the free port of Amapala, fall within the jurisdiction of this department. Choluteca, which has a population of about four thousand souls, is nominally the capital, but the seat of administration has for a number of years been at Nacaome. This town is situated on the river of the same name, about eight miles above its mouth, and has a population of about two thousand inhabitants. A few leagues above, on the same stream, is the considerable town of Pespiri. In the vicinity of Nacaome, at a place called "Aguas Calientes," there are several hot springs, much esteemed for their medicinal properties.

DEPARTMENT OF TEGUCIGALPA.

Principal Towns.—Tegucigalpa, Yuscuran, Cedros, San Antonio Mineral, Yuguare, Agalteca.

The Department of Tegucigalpa is the smallest, but relatively the most populous of the political divisions of Honduras. It may be described as occupying a great interior basin or plateau, bounded on the north and west by the Mountains of Sulaco and Comayagua, and the south and east by those of Ule and Chili. The average elevation of this mountain-bound plateau is not less than three thousand feet above the sea. It is drained by the River Choluteca, which nearly describes a circle in tracing its course among the mountains, through which it breaks by a deep and narrow gorge or valley into the broad and rich plains of the Pacific coast.

The temperature of the department is cool, and its climate can not be surpassed for salubrity. Its soil is not generally so productive as that of the remaining departments, but it excels them all in the number and value of its mines. It is, in fact, essentially a mining district; and, until the political disturbances of the country rendered the prosecution of that branch of industry almost impossible, mining was the chief employment of its people, and their principal source of wealth. The mines of Yuscuran are still worked, as are also those of San Antonio and Santa Lucia. The gold and

City of Tegucigalpa, Honduras.

Plaza of Tegucigalpa.

silver mines of San Juan Cantaranas are second to none in the state in value, but they are not largely worked, for precisely the reason which is most likely hereafter to commend them to American and European enterprise. The natives can not be induced to establish themselves in their vicinity, *on account of the coldness of the climate.* The Mountain of Agalteca, in the northwest portion of this department, is a vast mass of very pure and highly magnetic iron ore. Some of the ore has so large a per centage of metal, that it is forged directly from the mine, without undergoing the previous process of smelting.

Since the decline of the mining interest, the proprietors of this department have engaged largely in the raising of cattle, many of which are driven to San Salvador and Nicaragua for sale.

Tegucigalpa, the capital of the department, is the largest and finest city in the state, numbering not less than twelve thousand inhabitants. It stands on the right bank of the Rio Choluteca, in an amphitheatre among the hills, and is substantially and regularly built. It has not less than six large churches. The Parroquia is hardly second to the Cathedral of Comayagua in size. A fine stone bridge, of ten arches, spans the river, and connects the city with the suburb called Comayaguita. It had formerly several convents and a University, the last of which has still a nominal existence. It has also a mint, but it is now only used for the coining of the copper or provisional currency, which circulates in the central departments at a greatly depreciated value. The trade of Tegucigalpa was formerly carried on through the ports of Omoa and Truxillo, but, since the establishment of the free port of Amapala, it has chiefly taken that direction

DEPARTMENT OF OLANCHO.

Principal Towns.—Juticalpa, Catacamas, Campamiento, Silca, Monte Rosa, Yocon, Laguata, Danli, Teupac.

The Department of Olancho joins that of Tegucigalpa on the east. It has an area of not less than 11,300 miles, or something more than that of the State of Maryland. But a small portion of this wide district is inhabited by a civilized population, the greater part, comprising the entire eastern half, being in the possession of Indian tribes, known as Xicaques, Payas, Pantasmas, and Toacas. The Spanish settlements are almost entirely confined to the large interior plateau, generally called Valley of Olancho, in which the great river Patuca, and the hardly less important streams known as Rio Tinto and Roman or Aguan, take their rise. This valley is represented as undulating, fertile, and chiefly covered with luxuriant savannas, supporting vast herds of cattle, which constitute the chief wealth of the people. In this respect, indeed, Olancho is distinguished above any other equal extent of Central, or perhaps of Spanish America.

From its elevation and the proximity of the mountains, Olancho has a cool and healthful climate. Its people are industrious, and live in the possession of all of the necessaries and many of the luxuries of life. From their geographical position, away from the centres of political commotion, they have enjoyed comparative quiet during all the disturbances to which the country at large has been subjected. This circumstance has been favorable to the accumulation of property, and the department is therefore relatively the richest in the state.

Its exports are cattle, hides, deer-skins, sarsaparilla, tobacco, and bullion, which are chiefly taken to Omoa and Truxillo; a portion, nevertheless, goes, by the way of Tegucigalpa, to the Gulf of Fonseca. Next to its herds of cattle, its principal sources of wealth are its gold-washings. Nearly all the streams in the department carry gold of a fine quality in their sands. These washings were distinguished for their richness at the time of the conquest, and have ever since maintained a local celebrity. But the jealous policy of Spain was effectively directed to the suppression of all knowledge of the wealth and resources of these countries, and their condition since the independence has been unfavorable to their development. There can, however, be but little doubt that the gold-washings of the rivers Guayape and Mangualil, and their tributaries, are equal in value to those of California, and must soon come to attract a large share of attention both in the United States and in Europe. At present the washings are only carried on by the Indian women, who devote a few hours on Sunday mornings to the work, living for the remainder of the week upon the results. A farther notice of the mineral wealth of this department will be found in the chapter on mines and minerals.

Juticalpa, capital of the department, ranks third in the state in respect of size. It is delightfully situated on a small tributary of the Guayape, not far from the principal stream, and is reputed to contain 10,000 inhabitants. Near it is the large Indian town of Catacamas, and there are other considerable towns of Indians scattered throughout the valley. These Indians are proverbial for their peaceful disposition and industrious habits.

The communication between the valley of Olancho

and the coast is chiefly carried on by mules, through the valley of the River Aguan, to Truxillo. A road was formerly opened through the valley of the Rio Tinto, but it was rough and difficult, and soon abandoned. There exists a much easier means of communication by way of the Rio Patuca, which is navigable as far as the Puerto de Delon, within a few leagues of Juticalpa. But the absence of a good port, as well as of commercial establishments at the mouth of the river, has rendered this natural highway of but little value. It is now chiefly used in floating down mahogany, which grows in large quantities on its banks. But even this trade is embarrassed by the difficulty of loading the wood in the open roadstead off the bar of the river. How far the Wanks River may ultimately be made useful to the trade of this department and that of Segovia, in Nicaragua, can only be ascertained by a survey of that stream, the capacities of which are now but little known.

DEPARTMENT OF YORO.

Principal Towns.—Yoro, Olanchito, Truxillo, Negrito, Jocon, and Sonaguera.

The Department of Yoro comprehends all the northern part of Honduras lying eastward of the River Ulua. Its area is upward of 15,000 square miles—equal to the three states of Massachusetts, Connecticut, and Rhode Island; but, while the largest department in size, it is the smallest in respect of population. Its surface is exceedingly diversified. It is made up of a series of valleys, formed by the numerous streams which flow down from the interior into the Bay of Honduras. These have a direction from south to north, and, except on the very shores of the bay, where the country is plain and alluvial, are separated from each other by a corresponding number of ridges, or mountain spurs or ranges, of various elevations. Communication transversely to these valleys and mountain ridges is exceedingly difficult, and the population of the department, therefore, has been chiefly concentrated in the valleys of those larger streams which have ports near their mouths, and through which pass the roads leading from the interior to the coast.

The Mountains of Pija and Sulaco rise in the western part of this department, and form the eastern boundaries of the valleys of the Sulaco and Ulua Rivers. They are terraced and truncated, constituting elevated savannas, sparsely covered with pines; but their soil is comparatively poor, and they have consequently failed to attract population from the more favored portions of the state. Tradition points to them as containing great mineral wealth, but they have never been adequately explored, and nothing can be affirmed in this respect with any degree of certainty.

The valleys of all the streams abound in precious woods, and the department may be described as comprising the great mahogany district of Central America. There are "*cortes*," or cuttings, on nearly all the streams which from their size admit of the wood being floated down to the coast. The inhabitants are chiefly mahogany-cutters by occupation, having their temporary residences at the various "*cortes*" during the season of cutting, and retiring to their homes and plantations when it is ended.

On the upper waters of the streams, and among the mountains and hills which intervene between the coast and the valley of Olancho, are found the remnants of the once famous and indomitable nation of Xicaque Indians. Their numbers are not known, but are estimated at not far from seven thousand. They are peaceful and inoffensive, and traffic freely with the Spaniards, collecting sarsaparilla, India-rubber, and skins, for the purpose of exchange for such few articles of civilized manufacture as they may require.*

The greater portion of the great plain of Sula, described below, falls within this department. To the eastward of this plain, and, in fact, constituting an extension of it, is a vast tract of rich and valuable territory, known as *Costa de Lean.* It has equal capacities with the plain of Sula for agricultural purposes, and in this respect holds out inducements inferior to no other part of Central America or the West Indies. The proximity of the mountains, absence of marshes, abundance of good water, and exposure to the sea-breezes, are circumstances favorable to its salubrity, and must have an influence in directing to it the attention of emigrants and planters. The valleys of Sonaguera and Olanchito may also be mentioned as equally remarkable for their beauty, fertility, and general resources.

Yoro, a town of about three thousand inhabitants, is the capital of this department. Truxillo, already described (p. 102), is its principal seaport.

DEPARTMENT OF SANTA BARBARA.

Districts.—Omoa, Sta. Barbara, Yojoa, San Pedro.

Principal Towns.—Sta. Barbara, Yojoa, Omoa, San Pedro Sula, Quimistan.

This department lies to the northward of Gracias and Comayagua, and intervenes between these departments

* A large number of Carib Indians, emigrants from the island of San Vincent, are also established in this department; but, as a full account of them has been given elsewhere, it is unnecessary to speak of them in this connection.

and the Bay of Honduras. It is traversed by several large streams. The Ulua runs through it from south to north, and the Blanco, Santiago, Sta. Barbara, and Chamelicon also flow through it in other directions. The valleys of these rivers afford large tracts of level and fertile lands, well wooded, and capable of vast production.

The great plain of Sula, which may be said to commence at Yojoa, is a distinguishing feature of this department. It is not only of great extent, but of unbounded capacity. The early accounts of the country represent it to have been densely populated by the aborigines. It is now mostly covered by a heavy forest, relieved only by a few narrow patches of cultivated grounds in the vicinity of the towns which are scattered along the *camino real.* This forest abounds in valuable woods, and from it a greater part of the mahogany exported from Honduras has been derived. The Chamelicon and Ulua are the natural channels through which the mahogany has been, and still is, carried to the sea-side. That portion of the plain of Sula lying to the eastward of the River Ulua is included in the Department of Yoro. Taking it as a whole, it may be estimated as having a base of sixty or seventy miles on the Bay of Honduras, reaching inland, in the form of a triangle, to Yojoa, a distance of upward of fifty miles, and comprising an area of not less than fifteen hundred square miles. In the future development of the country, this plain will attract the first attention, not less on account of its valuable natural products, than its easy access through good ports, its navigable rivers, and rich and easily-cultivated soil, adapted to the production of cotton, rice, sugar, cacao, and the other great staples of the tropics. A variety of the cacao, called *cacao mico*, and said to be equal, if not superior, to the celebrated cacao of Nicaragua and Soconusco, is indigenous here, and the inhabitants draw their supply from the wild trees in the forest. The vanilla and sarsaparilla are also abundant. Copal-trees, India-rubber, rosewood, dragon's-blood, and other useful trees and precious woods, are found in profusion, and will ultimately contribute to swell the exports and augment the wealth of the state. Vast numbers of palms, of every variety, relieve the monotony of the forest with their graceful forms. At one point on the banks of the Ulua, a few leagues above its mouth, is a natural park of the cocoanut-palm, which extends along the river for several miles.

In the neighborhood of Yojoa the country rises by a series of magnificent terraces, which open out in broad, undulating savannas. Their soil is good, and, apart from their natural adaptation for grazing purposes, they admit of profitable cultivation. These terraces are represented as constituting the distinguishing features of the country around the city of Santa Barbara, where the principal part of the population of the department is concentrated.

The great dependent mountain chain of Merendon, elsewhere alluded to as dividing the valleys of the Chamelicon and Motagua, and terminating abruptly on the sea at Omoa, affords, on its slopes, favorable conditions, both of soil and climate, for the cultivation of the grains and fruits of higher latitudes. It moreover seems to be rich in gold, which is found, more or less abundantly, in all the streams which flow down its southern declivity. In the neighborhood of Quimistan there are washings which have long been celebrated for their productiveness. In that portion of this chain back of Omoa, and overlooking the plain of Sula, are vast beds of white marble of spotless purity, fine, compact, and susceptible of exquisite finish. It more closely resembles the marbles of Carrara in Italy than any of those found in the United States. It is easy of access, and may be obtained in any desirable quantity.

The fine, capacious harbor of Puerto Caballos, and the small but secure port of Omoa, both fall in this department. They are fully described under the subdivision of "Ports of Honduras."

The inhabitants of this department are chiefly devoted to the raising of cattle, of which large numbers are exported to Belize and Yucatan, and driven into Guatemala, where they command prices ranging from five to ten dollars per head. A large part of the people in the towns in the plain of Sula, or bordering upon it, are employed in the mahogany cuttings, while a few, chiefly Indians, collect sarsaparilla, or occupy themselves, at intervals, in washing gold. Altogether, the department is healthy, and possessed of vast resources, the value of which is enhanced by the natural facilities which it possesses, both in respect of geographical position and the means of interior communication.

CHAPTER IX.

ASPECTS OF NATURE IN HONDURAS.

THE aspects of nature in Honduras are varied and striking. The conditions of conformation of coast, of elevation and consequent temperature, the amount of rain falling upon the respective declivities of the Cordilleras, all contribute to diversify the forms under which vegetable life presents itself to the eye of the traveler. The three great features, nevertheless, are the coast alluvions, generally densely wooded, the elevated valleys of the interior, spreading out in broad savannas, and the high plateaus of the mountains, sustaining an unending forest of scattered pines, relieved by occasional clumps of oak.

Upon the northern coast, in the broad plain through which the Ulua and Chamelicon find their way to the sea, the country is so low as occasionally to be overflowed for considerable distances. Here grow immense forests of cedar, mahogany, ceiba, India-rubber, and other large and valuable trees, thickly interspersed with palms, whose plumes rise through every opening, and fringe the bases of all the hills. The smaller streams are arched over with verdure, and completely shut out from the sun, while the large rivers gleam like silver bands in fields of unbroken emerald. But even here, where the land is lowest, spread out broad, grassy meadows, the retreats of innumerable wild-fowl, and during the dry season, when the grass on the hills becomes sere and withered, offering abundant support for herds of cattle. In the depths of these primeval forests the mahogany-cutters prosecute their laborious calling, rousing the echoes with the ringing strokes of the axe and the shouts of the truckmen, who, with twenty oxen attached to a single log, drag the heavy trunks to the edges of the rivers. The broad meadows supply them with food for their cattle, while every company has its hunter and fisher to help out the fixed rations with which it is provided by the proprietors of the establishments.

Farther to the eastward, on the same coast, the heavy forests are confined chiefly to the valleys proper of the rivers, and give place, at little distances inland, to sandy savannas, covered with coarse grass, and clumps of pines and acacias. But the plain country of the coast is every where narrow. The spurs or dependent ridges of the mountain groups of the interior often come down to the very shore. Immediately back of Omoa, within cannon-shot of its fortress, the mountains begin to rise abruptly, and speedily attain the height of nine thousand feet, looking down majestically upon their shadows in the clear waters of the beautiful Bay of Amatique. Such also is the case at the port of Truxillo. The peaks of Congrehoy, and the Mountains of the Holy Cross or Poyas, form gigantic landmarks for the mariner in his approach to the coast of Honduras.

The alluvions of the Pacific coast are also densely wooded, but not extensive. At short distances inland they give place to numerous savannas and *jicarales*, in which the low calabash-tree, with its fruit resembling the apple, conveys to the traveler the idea of a New England orchard. These savannas are studded with clumps of acacias (gum-arabic bushes), and covered with grass; but the pine does not appear on this side of the continent, except upon the slopes of the hills at an altitude of about twelve hundred feet.

The valleys of all the rivers, on both coasts, are heavily wooded, and covered with *lianes* or vines; but as they are ascended toward the interior, vegetation diminishes, and is reduced to a narrow fringe of trees and bushes upon their immediate banks. These valleys, in the high interior country, often expand into broad and beautiful plains, half savanna, half woodland, the common grounds where the products of the tropics and of the temperate zone, the palm and the pine, flourish side by side. Such are the plains of Espino and Comayagua on the Humuya, of Otoro on the Sta. Barbara, Sensenti on the Ulua, La Florida on the Chamelicon, Olancho on the Aguan, and Yuguare on the Choluteca. In some of these, as in that of Comayagua, the variant forms of cactus become distinguishing features, frequently attaining to gigantic size, and almost taking the character of forests. Here they stud the ground, spherical and spinated, warning man and beast against incautious tread, yet radiating from their grooved sides flowers and fruits of delicate ruby, in shape and color like glasses of tenderest crystal, flowing over with ruddy wine of golden Burgundy. There they rise in tall, fluted columns, appearing in the exaggerating twilight like the ruins of ancient temples. And still beyond we see them, articulated and jointed, spreading their broad succulent palms, silvered with the silky habiliments of the scarlet cochineal, as if in imploration to the sun. And yet again, lavish of contrasting forms, they trail like serpents over the ground, and twine themselves in knotty coils around fallen trunks and among the crevices of the barren rocks. Here, too, the agave appears, with its dense green cluster of spiny-edged leaves, shooting up its tall stem, to flower but once, scatter forth its thousand bulbs, and then to die.

The mountains which rise around these valleys are ascended by terraces, crowned with forests of pines and oaks, and carpeted with grass. The summits of the mountains sometimes run up in peaks, but generally constitute broad table-lands, more or less undulating, and often spreading out in rolling savannas, traversed with low ridges of verdure, and green belts of trees, which droop over streams as bright and cool as those of New England. Here the familiar blackberry is indigenous, and the bushes which impede the traveler are covered with fruit. Wheat-fields, billowing beneath the cool mountain winds, and orchards of peach and apple trees, struggling against man's neglect, give to these districts all the aspects of the temperate zone; and when, at night, bright fires of the pine illuminate every hut, and the picturesque inhabitants cluster around them to receive the warmth which the temperature here renders necessary to comfort, the stranger can scarcely appreciate that he is under the tropics, and within fourteen degrees of the line. The contrast which his experiences of to-day afford with those of yesterday, when he rode among groves of palms, plantains, and oranges, become still more decided when the cold, sleety rain descends from leaden skies, or the sharp hail falls from tumultuous clouds, swept over his head by blasts as chill and pinching as those of a northern November.

But whether in plain, in valley, or on mountain, every where the trees are covered with parasitic plants. Some varieties of cactus, particularly that of which the long, tangled arms are prismatic in form, do not disdain to fix themselves in the forks of the calabash-tree, and overwhelm it with their own more rapid growth. So abundant are these air-plants, that it is sometimes difficult to discover the verdure of the tree to which they are attached. Some are delicate as threads of silk, and others coarse and rank, but all of wax-like beauty, and many producing flowers of brilliant colors. Science would exhaust its nomenclature in distinguishing them, and the traveler is happy to think of them as yet unburdened with the portentous designations of studious Dryasdusts, to whom nature was not given as "a joy forever," but a thing to be classified, and named, and mummified in Greek and Latin cerements.

Upon the higher mountain crests, where the short and hardy grass betokens a temperature too low for luxuriant vegetation of any kind, the air-plants themselves disappear, and the pines and gnarled oaks are draped in a sober mantle of long gray moss, which waves mournfully in the wind, like frayed and dusty banners from the walls of old cathedrals. The rocks themselves are browned with mosses, and, except the bright springs gushing from beneath them and trickling away with a silvery murmur, there is no sound to break the eternal silence. The traveler sees, perhaps, a dark shadow sweep over his path; it is that of the eagle or of the voiceless raven, poising in the sky. Upon some distant rock his eye catches a slight and graceful figure; there is a sudden but noiseless bound, and the antelope of the mountain has disappeared.

The geological features of Honduras are equally marked and impressive. Starting from the Gulf of Fonseca and advancing northward, we leave behind us the volcanic coast-range, with its high, grassy peaks of scoriæ, and reach at once vast masses of white and rose-colored rock, the outliers of the great sandstone nucleus of the central plateaus. Viewed from a distance, they appear like cliffs of trap or basalt, and take a thousand castellated forms with the changing positions of the traveler. Among these we find occasional beds of blue limestone, and ribs of quartz and greenstone are here and there boldly protruded through the superincumbent rocks, richly veined with ores of silver and of gold.

As we proceed farther inland, the mountains rise by a succession of terraces, deeply furrowed by streams descending to the sea. These terraces prove to be a succession of vast stratified sandstone deposits or beds, presenting abrupt edges, up which the sure-footed mule toils painfully and with difficulty. But when the ascent is accomplished, the traveler finds spread out before him extensive savannas, interspersed with groves of pines, and clumps of oaks and bushes. Often the layer of soil is thin, and a scant vegetation strives in vain to divest nature of its savage aspect. The rocks, exposed and bare, reflect the light of the sun, which shines down through the clear and rarefied atmosphere of these elevated regions with a blinding glare. The weary traveler looks forward with aching eyes, tracing the white line of the solitary path across the arid plain, and urges on his faithful mule, in the hope of finding some narrow valley, worn in the rock by mountain streams, where he may form his lonely camp for the night, in the pleasant company of living trees and running waters.

Suddenly the plateau along which he is journeying breaks away in a few rapid terraces, and reveals, almost beneath his feet, a wide and level plain, mottled with savanna and forest, threaded with bright streams, and dotted with villages, whose white churches catch the light like points of silver in the landscape. It seems but a little distance there: a stone thrown from the hand might fall in the square plaza, so distinctly defined, of the first village; but hour after hour the traveler toils downward, and night falls, and he sees the gleaming of lights in the valley before the familiar barking of dogs and the instinctive accelerated pace of his mule apprise him that at last he has reached the level ground.

In the western part of Honduras, among the mountains of Corquin, the outline of the country is exceedingly bold and diversified. The rivers, collecting their waters in interior basins, break through the porphyritic mountains and hills which surround them in deep valleys or gorges, with steep and precipitous sides. Yet in these fissures, whose bottoms are only reached by dangerous zigzag paths, are found strips of alluvial soil, where the Indian builds his hut, and the necessary plantain has a luxuriant growth, beneath high and frowning cliffs, bristling with peaks, like gigantic sentinels, along their rocky ramparts.

A greater variety of trees and abundance of verdure cover the hills and mountains of the northern coast, which have, in consequence, a less rugged aspect than those on the Pacific declivity, where the rains are not so constant. The hills are more swelling, and the mountains, though equally elevated, have a softer and more harmonious outline. They present few cliffs or rocky crests, and in their denser forests afford more congenial retreats to the multitudinous forms of animal life which are nurtured in the genial tropics.

Birds of brilliant plumage sparkle in the foliage of

the trees, and crowds of monkeys troop among their branches. The tapir, the peccary, and the ant-eater live in their shade, and the puma and the cougar lurk in their recesses. Here, too, are found the boa, the bright corral, and the deadly tamagas. The vanilla hangs in festoons from the limbs, and the sarsaparilla veins the earth with its healing root. And while silver, imprisoned in flinty quartz or crumbling greenstone, tempts men to labor with the promise of rich reward on the other slope of the continent, here gold glitters in the sands of almost every stream.

It is thus that Nature, lavish of her gifts, has comprised within the comparatively narrow limits of Honduras a variety of scenery, as well as of climate and production, unsurpassed by any equal portion of the earth. Upon the coasts she robes herself in luxuriance, draped in vines, crowned with flowers, and her breath is fragrant with aromatic gums, while the sea kisses her feet with its frothy lips. But among the mountains, in sober, monastic robes, she is no longer the productive mother. The wind lifts the gray hair on her serene brow; but even here her lips, though motionless, still utter a language of lofty and holy import to the sensitive ears of her true votaries.

CHAPTER X.

MINES AND MINERALS.

IN respect of mineral resources, Honduras ranks first among all the states of Central America. Indeed, the mineral wealth of the country at large seems chiefly confined to that system or cluster of mountains which constitutes what may be called the plateau of Honduras. Nueva Segovia and Chontales, the mineral districts of Nicaragua, naturally belong to this mountain system; and the same is true of the mineral district of the Department of San Miguel in San Salvador, which embraces the only mines found in that state. There are a few mines of gold and silver in Guatemala and Costa Rica, but, as compared with those of Honduras, they are insignificant in number and value.*

Mining has indeed been always, and until recently, the predominant interest in Honduras; but no branch of industry suffers so directly from wars and civil dissensions, such as have agitated Central America for the last thirty years. As a consequence, mine after mine has been abandoned, and the works once fallen into decay, there has been neither the enterprise, capital, or intelligence necessary to restore them. The mining districts are studded with decayed mining villages,

* "El estado de Honduras es el mas rico en puntos minerales; alli esta el famoso del *Corpus*, que en otros tiempos produjo tanto oro, que se estableció en él una tesoreria para solo el cobro del derecho de quintos; el departamiento de Olancho en el mismo estado posee el rio *Guayape*, de cuyas arenas se saca, sin beneficio, el oro mas apreciable."—*Montéfur*, *Centro-America*, xxiii.

whose proprietors have become *hacienderos*, owners of immense grazing estates, on which their former laborers are now employed as herdsmen. A few establishments are still kept up, but the operations are conducted on a very small scale and in a very rude manner, and afford a very imperfect indication of the capabilities of the mines.

Few of the mines were ever opened in conformity with any well-established or intelligent system, nor with any reference to continuous or extended operations. Without adits or machinery for draining, the only means of removing the water which invaded many of the richest were leathern buckets carried on the backs of men, in which manner also the ore was brought up from shafts so narrow as rarely to allow more than one man to work in breaking out the ore. When obtained, it was frequently crushed by heavy stones, beveled on their lower edge, and vibrated backward and forward by men, or else slowly reduced by the rudest and most cumbersome machinery, driven generally by oxen or mules, but occasionally by water. In the latter case the apparatus consisted of a vertical shaft (driven by a wheel moving horizontally), through which passed an arm, having at each end heavy stones attached by chains, which were thus dragged over the ore, in a basin of masonry, until it was reduced sufficiently for amalgamation. This last operation was performed by placing the amalgam in heaps in a "*patio*," or yard, upon a floor of boards, where it remained for several weeks, until the amalgamation became complete, when the mass was washed in troughs, and the result reduced by fire.

But, even under all these difficulties, and rude and expensive processes, mining in Honduras, as I have said, was formerly carried on extensively and profitably. The mines were seldom worked to any great depth, and their proprietors were often obliged to abandon most of them before they had been carried to the depths where the richest ores are generally found. Others were given up from lack of knowledge of treating the ores; and still others from the lack of roads whereon the ores could be transported to the mills.

There are hundreds of mines scattered over the country, abandoned and filled with water, most, if not all of which could be profitably worked by the application of proper machinery. But as there are now no roads over which machinery can be transported, many of them must await the general development of the country to become of value. The rough and narrow mule-paths in the neighborhood of the ports on both oceans are lined with fragments of heavy and expensive machinery, which men more enterprising than prudent have vainly essayed to introduce into the country. They are enduring monuments of that blind energy which neglects necessary means in its eagerness to attain desirable ends.

Silver ores are most abundant and valuable of any which exist in the state. They are chiefly found upon the Pacific ranges or groups of mountains, while the gold-washings, if not the gold mines proper, are most numerous on the Atlantic slope. The silver is found in various combinations, with iron, lead, copper, and, in a few instances, with antimony. Chlorides of silver are not uncommon, and rank among the richest ores in the country.

The group of silver mines in the neighborhood of Ocotal in Segovia (Nicaragua) enjoy a high celebrity, and are undoubtedly of great value. They yield their silver in the forms of sulphurets, bromides, and chlorides. Some of the mines give an argentiferous sulphuret of antimony. The mine of Limon, in the vicinity of Ocotal, formerly yielded large quantities of chloride of silver, but is now unworked for want of requisite machinery to keep it free from water. The ores of this district yield variously from 28 to 727 ounces of silver per every ton of 2000 lbs. or 32,000 ounces.

The mineral district of Yuscuran, in the Department of Tegucigalpa, has a high and deserved reputation for the number of its mines and the value of its ores. These are, for the most part, an argentiferous galena, and, when worked, yield from 63 to 1410 ounces per ton. The mines throughout this department and that of Choluteca yield a similar ore, generally occurring in a matrix of quartz, with varying proportions of brown blende, and sulphurets of zinc and iron, and oxydes of iron.

The mines of the Department of Gracias are equally celebrated with those of Tegucigalpa. Some remarkable combinations of silver are found in their ores. The upper, or old mine of Coloal has sulphuret of copper (copper glass), galena with sulphuret of silver, and in parts copper pitch ore and black copper, the whole yielding fifty-eight per cent. of copper, besides from seventy-eight to eighty-four ounces of silver to the ton. The ores of the new mine of Coloal are a combination of chloride of silver, a little sulphuret of silver, oxyde of iron and antimony, mixed with earthy matter, and yield the somewhat startling proportion of 23.63 per cent., or 8476 ounces per ton of 2000 lbs.!

Dependent upon the silver deposits of Honduras are those of the Department of San Miguel, in San Salvador. The silver occurs generally in the form of sulphurets, in combination with galena, iron, black blende (sulphuret of zinc), in quartz and greenstone matrices, interspersed with threads and crystals of native silver. The particular mines known as those of "El Tabanco" are richest, and yield from 100 to 2537 ounces per ton. These have been extensively and profitably worked, and derive a large part of their value from their proximity to the Bay of Fonseca.

Gold mines are not uncommon in Honduras, but, excepting those of San Andres in the Department of Gracias, and in the vicinity of San Juan Cantaranas in Tegucigalpa, they are no longer worked. The principal supplies of this metal in the state are drawn from the gold-washings of Olancho, which are exceedingly productive. The River Guyape has always enjoyed great celebrity for the amount of gold contained in its sands; but, since the early periods of Spanish occupancy, washing has not been carried on except on a very small scale by the Indians, and even with them the process is generally left to the women and children, who only work for a few hours on Sunday mornings. Yet the amount thus obtained and carried into Juticalpa in the year 1853 was valued at $129,600.

The following paragraphs in reference to the gold district of Olancho are extracted from a private letter from Dr. Charles Doratt, who visited that region in 1853:

"Among the rivers of Olancho, which we visited and 'prospected,' the Guyape and Jalan are decidedly the richest in auriferous sands. These two rivers unite a little below Juticalpa, the capital of Olancho, and form the Rio Patuca or Patook (see *ante*, p. 79). The gold deposits on the Guyape commence properly at a point called Aleman, continuing thence up the river, the banks upon both sides containing much fine gold. We found gold in the alluvions half a mile distant from the present bed of the river. Leaving Juticalpa in a northeast direction, and crossing the department near Yocon, over an area of twenty leagues long and ten broad, there is not a streamlet, however insignificant, which does not contain gold both in its sands and in the banks which border it. For the most part, these streams follow the courses of the mountains, and fall into the Guyape and Jalan. The remaining ones, including the Sisaca and Mangualil (the latter carrying gold of larger size than the others), run into the 'Rio Mirajoco,' which, taking the name of Taguale, after fertilizing the beautiful valley of Olancho, reaches the sea near Truxillo. In these larger rivers the gold is found in deposits near the bends and rapids. The finest gold is from the Guyape, Jalan, and Mangualil, in the Department of Olancho, and the Sulaco, Caymito, and Pacaya in that of Yoro. * * * At Aleman the women only wash the sand on Sunday mornings, and, with the aid of their miserable *batteas*, in a few hours procure a sufficient quantity of the metal to supply their wants for the ensuing week. It is sold on the spot at from $11 50 to $12 per ounce. At Guijana the gold is found in a soft slate, and at San Felipe in a red, ferruginous earth. About five leagues from Danli, the Jalan produces well, and at the time of my visit there were more than a hundred men and women engaged in washing. They also used the *batteas*, and never went more than two or three feet below the surface."

The southern districts of Honduras, bordering on Nicaragua, bear also rich *placers* of gold, whence the Indians annually take considerable quantities. The same is true of the northern districts of the Department of Sta. Barbara. The streams which flow from the Mountains of Omoa into the Rio Chamelicon, and especially those in the vicinity of the town of Quimistan, all carry gold in their sands. Miners properly provided with implements for washing could not fail to secure here a rich reward for their labor and enterprise.

Honduras has also mines of copper of unsurpassed richness and value. The ores in all cases contain considerable proportions of silver. Those of Coloal, in Gracias, already alluded to, contain 58 per cent. of copper, besides about 80 ounces of silver to the ton. The ores from the mine of Guanacaste, Department of Olancho, give upward of 80 per cent. of pure copper, besides 2.9 per cent. of silver, equal to 1039 ounces of silver per ton. But, notwithstanding their great richness, these mines have been always neglected by the mining interest, or worked primarily for the silver which they contain in combination with the copper. Under the peculiar circumstances of the country, and principally from the difficulty of communication, the production of this metal has hitherto been regarded as unprofitable, and the pure copper as hardly worth its transportation to the coast; but, with improved means of communication, and the introduction of modern improvements in reducing the ores, the copper mines of Honduras must become one of the principal sources of wealth to the state. There are some mines of this metal in the neighborhood of the Gulf of Fonseca from which it has been customary for the merchants to ballast vessels, or fill out the freight of those bound for England or Germany, where the ores have always commanded a good price, and yielded a fair return to the shippers, notwithstanding the difficulty and cost of transportation to the coast.

Byam, who visited Nicaragua and Honduras for mining purposes, describes the copper ores as, for the most part, "uncombined with sulphur," and not requiring calcination. He adds, that "they may all be smelted in a common blast furnace, with the aid of equal quantities of iron stone, of which there is abundance in the hilly country. The ores are what the Spanish miners call *metal de color*, red and blue oxydes, and green carbonates, with now and then the brown or pigeon-breasted. They cut easily and smoothly with the knife, and yield from 25 to 60 per cent. The veins are generally vertical, and the larger ones run east and west."

Iron ores are common, but none of the mines of this metal are worked, except those of Agalteca in Tegucigalpa. The ore is highly magnetic, and so nearly pure that it is forged without smelting. It occurs in vast and exhaustless beds, and the metal might be produced in any desirable quantity; yet, within ten leagues of the mine, in the same department, it sells at the rate of from $10 to $12 per *quintal*, equal to $200 per ton!

Platina is said to exist both in the departments of Choluteca and Gracias, but the mines have never been worked. Cinnabar has also been found at several points, but probably not in sufficient quantities to admit of being reduced with profit. Zinc occurs in various combinations, and superior ores of the metal are found in great abundance on the islands of Guanaja (Bonacca) and Roatan. Antimony and tin also exist, but whether in such combinations as will admit of their economic production remains to be proved by experiment.

The opal mines of Gracias are worked to a large extent, and have been very productive. Some of the stones are large and beautiful, but most have suffered at the hands of the Indians, who estimate their value rather from their numbers than their size, and consequently break them in small pieces.

No means exist for determining the annual product of the opal mines, but it may be partially inferred from the fact that the mines or workings in the department are not less than one hundred in number. Amethysts are also reported as having been found in this department, but none have fallen under my notice. Asbestos is known to exist, and, there is reason to believe, might be produced in quantities sufficient to meet all demands.

Coal has been discovered in several localities. The beds in the valley or plain of Sensenti are very extensive. I visited those in the neighborhood of the village of Chucuyuco, at a point where they are cut through by the streams flowing down from the Mountains of Merendon into the Rio Higuito. The lower bed is about eight feet in thickness, separated from an upper stratum, which is two feet in thickness, by a layer of bituminous shale. The coal is what is called "brown coal," which is of a later formation than that familiarly known as "*pit coal*," which occurs beneath the new red sandstone. It is a tertiary formation of the era of the chalk of the Mississippi Valley. This coal occurs in vast layers in various parts of Germany, where it is extensively used for smelting metals in reverberating furnaces. Specimens of the Sensenti coal gave the following results:

Specific gravity	1.504
Ashes	25 per cent.

But these specimens were taken from the exposed faces

of the beds, where they were washed by the streams, and were consequently much infiltrated with foreign substances. The area of the beds is not known, but they probably extend below the greater part of the plain or valley. Situated so far inland, it is not presumed that these beds can ever have more than a local value in the reduction of the rich silver and copper ores found in the neighboring mountains.

Other beds of coal are said to exist in the valley of the Sulaco River, Department of Comayagua, and in the neighborhood of Nacaome, Department of Choluteca, but I am in possession of no positive information in respect to them. There are some beds in the valley of the River Torola, which will be more fully noticed when I come to speak of the coal deposits of the valley of the River Lempa, State of San Salvador.

In addition to these brief notices of the mines and minerals of Honduras, I may mention that an abundance of fine white, blue, and veined limestone is scattered throughout every department of the state. Large beds are found within a few miles of the Gulf of Fonseca, and extend thence through the valley of the Rio Goascoran, plain of Comayagua, and valley of the Humuya, to the Bay of Honduras. The hills and mountains back of Omoa have exhaustless quarries of a fine, compact white marble, remarkably free from faults and stains, and well adapted for statuary and ornamental use.

It is impossible, from the same want of data which I have deplored in respect to every other branch of industry, to form an accurate or satisfactorily approximate estimate of the past or present production of the mines of Honduras. It is alleged by persons whose antecedents entitle their statements to weight, that upward of $3,000,000 in gold and silver were annually exported from the northern parts of the state during the later years of its provincial existence. Since the independence, a small export duty has existed on bullion, but the facilities for evading the law have been such that it is not likely that one tenth part of the amount sent out of the country has come upon the records of the customs. Any statement upon the subject must therefore be purely conjectural.

In 1825, a statement was made by the Master of the Mint of the Federal Republic of the amount of gold and silver coined for the period of fifteen years previous and subsequent to 1810. He reported as follows:

"For fifteen years, ending 1810, were coined 285 marks of gold, 253,560 marks of silver, collectively valued at $2,193,832.

"For fifteen years, ending 1825, 1524 marks of gold, 423,881 marks of silver, equal in value to $3,810,383."

But the amount coined in the mint of Guatemala was insignificant in comparison with the aggregate product of the country during the same period. Where there was one dollar of coin from the mint in circulation, there were twenty dollars which were without the government stamp, mere rough pieces of pure gold and silver, which were received and paid out by weight.* Furthermore, during that period, with the exception of indigo and cochineal, the precious metals constituted the principal export of the country. Upon this point the report above quoted observes: "It must not be deduced from these statements that the amount of gold

* Thomas Gage, an English friar, who resided for twelve years in Guatemala, about the middle of the seventeenth century, has left us some facts which go to show the large and unrecorded production of the precious metals at that period. He speaks of one hundred mules entering the city of Granada "laden with gold and silver, which was the king's tribute."—*New Survey of the West Indies*, p. 421.

and silver coined indicates the amount produced in the country. Apart from the amount manufactured into ornaments and used for other purposes, there has been a great quantity exported, particularly since 1821. It is positively known that the merchants of Honduras and other parts have exported great quantities of gold and silver bullion, so that, according to the calculations of intelligent persons, not one tenth part of the production of these metals has passed into the mint. On this account, it is impossible to state exactly the actual produce of each year, and much less the amount exported, because the greater part has been effected clandestinely. In all the territories of the republic there are mines in abundance, but particularly in the State of Honduras, where the greatest number are to be found, and where Nature presents her greatest mineral wealth.* * * M. Gourmez, a mining engineer, who has visited most of the mines of Honduras, assures me that it is easier to find mines than men to work them; and that, if labor and means of communication existed, our mineral productions might in a short time rival those of Mexico and Peru."*

It should be observed that Honduras has adopted, without modification, the famous "*Ordenanzas de la Mineria*," or mineral ordinances of Spain, for the government of the mining interest.

* It is affirmed, in the report here quoted, that upward of two thousand metallic veins had been registered in Honduras up to the year 1825.

CHAPTER XI.

PRECIOUS WOODS — VEGETABLE PRODUCTIONS — ANIMALS — FISHES — REPTILES — INSECTS.

THE precious woods of Honduras rank next only to its minerals in point of value. At present they probably constitute the principal item in the exports of the state. Those best known are the mahogany and rosewood; but the proportion of the former which enters into commerce is much the greatest, and, both in this respect, and as giving employment to a considerable body of the inhabitants of the state, it is entitled to a first consideration.

And here it may be observed that the mahogany-tree of Honduras (*Swietinia Mahogoni*), in respect of its vast size and magnificent foliage, is entitled to be called "King of the Forest." In comparison with it, all other trees dwindle into insignificance. The enormous size and height of the trunk, the vast spread of its branches, and the space of ground occupied by its roots, are equally remarkable. It is of exceedingly slow growth, hardly undergoing a perceptible increase of size in the narrow span of man's life. It has been calculated that it requires three hundred years wherein to attain a growth proper for cutting. Some idea may be formed of the great size which it sometimes attains from the fact that the lower section of a tree, seventeen feet long, has been known to measure "in the square" five feet six inches, equal to five hundred and fifty cubic feet, and a weight of seventeen tons!

From Nature and on Stone by D. C. Hitchcock.

Printed by Sarony & Co. New York.

MAHOGANY CUTTINGS RIVER ULUA.

The mahogany grows in nearly all parts of Honduras, in the valleys of the various streams. It is, however, most abundant upon the low grounds which border the rivers flowing into the Bay of Honduras, where it also attains its greatest size and beauty, and where the mahogany-works, called "cortes" (cuttings) by the Spaniards, are chiefly confined. As these lands are for the most part the property of the state, the wood is cut under licenses obtained from the government, which exacts a fixed sum for each tree. Except those made at the mouths of the various rivers for receiving, marking, and shipping the wood as it is floated down, the mahogany establishments are necessarily temporary, and changed from time to time as trees become scarce in their neighborhood.

Of all occupations known to man, that of the mahogany-cutter is perhaps the wildest in its nature, and yet among the most systematic in its arrangements. When the cutter has fixed upon the valley of some river as the field of his operations, he makes a dépôt for storing provisions, and for securing and embarking the wood. Here he maintains a little fleet of *pitpans* for carrying supplies and keeping up relations with the "works" proper, the sites of which are determined chiefly by the abundance of trees, their accessibility, and the means that exist for feeding the cattle which it is necessary to use in "trucking" the wood. To these points it is often necessary to drive the oxen through thick and untracked forests, and to carry the chains and trucks, by means of small boats, against strong currents, or over shallows and rapids, which are only surmounted with infinite labor.

The site once definitively fixed upon, the next step is to erect temporary dwellings for the men: a task of no great difficulty, as the only requisite is protection from the sun and rains, which is effected by a roof thatched with long grass from the swamps, or with "cahoon" leaves, or the branches of the thatch-palm. A hammock swung between two posts, two stones to support his kettle, and the hut of the cutter is both finished and furnished!

The mahogany season, which lasts some months, commences in August of each year, it being the opinion of cutters that the wood is not then so apt to split in falling, nor so likely to "check" in seasoning, as when cut from April to August, in what is called "the spring." Furthermore, by commencing at this period, the cutter is enabled to get down his wood, and prepare it for trucking by the setting in of the dry season.

The laborers are divided into gangs or companies of from twenty to fifty each, under the direction of a leader styled "a captain," who directs the men in his company, assigns them their daily tasks, and adds to or deducts from their wages in proportion as they accomplish more or less than what is supposed to be a just day's work. Each gang has also one person connected with it, who is called a hunter, whose duty it is to search the "bush" for trees proper to be cut. His work, therefore, commences somewhat earlier than that of the others, and, as it involves activity and intelligence, he is paid much higher wages than the mere cutters. His first movement is to cut his way through the thickest of the woods to some elevated situation, where he climbs the tallest trees he finds, from which he minutely surveys the surrounding country.

"At this season of the year (August), the leaves of the mahogany-tree are invariably of a yellow-reddish hue, and an eye accustomed to this kind of exercise can, at a great distance, discern the places where the wood is most abundant. He now descends, and to such places his steps are at once directed, and, without compass or other guide than what observation has imprinted on his recollection, he never fails to reach the exact spot at which he aims. On some occasions, no ordinary stratagem is necessary to be resorted to by the huntsman to prevent others from availing themselves of the advantage of his discoveries; for, if his steps be traced by those who may be engaged in the same pursuit, which is a very common thing, all his ingenuity must be exerted to beguile them from the true track. In this, however, he is not always successful, being followed by those who are entirely aware of all the arts he may use, and whose eyes are so quick that the slightest turn of a leaf or the faintest impression of the foot is unerringly perceived; even the dried leaves which may be strewed upon the ground often help to conduct to the secret spot; and it consequently happens that persons so engaged must frequently undergo the disappointment of finding an advantage they had promised to themselves seized on by others. The hidden treasure being, however, discovered, the next operation is the felling of a sufficient number of trees to employ the gang during the season.

"The tree is commonly cut about ten or twelve feet from the ground, a stage being erected for the axe-man employed in leveling it; this, to an observer, would appear a labor of much danger, but an accident rarely happens to the people engaged in it. The trunk of the tree, from the dimensions of the wood it furnishes, is deemed most valuable; but, for purposes of an ormental kind, the limbs or branches are generally preferred, their grain being much closer, and the veins richer and more variegated."

A sufficient number of trees being cut, the preparations for "trucking" commence by the opening of roads from the places where they lie to the nearest river. The distance of road to be cut depends on the situation of the trees. When they are much dispersed, miles of roads and many bridges are required. A firm and well-graded main road is first built, from whence radiate numerous wing-roads. These are all built by task-work, and the principal amount of the labor of the cutters is expended upon them. The clearing away of the bushes and undergrowth is the work of one set of men, who are expected to clear one hundred yards per day. They are followed by another set, who cut down the larger trees as even with the ground as possible, the task being also one hundred yards per day to each laborer, although this is more difficult and laborious, from the number of hard woods growing here, which, on failure of the axe, are removed by the application of fire. The trunks of these trees, although many of them are valuable for different purposes, such as bullet-tree, iron-wood, redwood, sapodilla, etc., are thrown away as useless, unless they happen to be adjacent to some creek or small river which may intersect the road; in that case they are applied to the constructing of bridges across the same, which are frequently of considerable size, and require great labor to make them of sufficient strength to bear such immense loads as are taken over them.

The roads being finished generally by the month of December, the trees are sawn into logs of various lengths, in order to equalize the loads which the oxen have to draw. This being completed, the logs are separated one from the other, and placed in whatever position will admit of the largest square being formed according to the shape which the end of each log presents, and is then reduced, by means of the axe, from the round or natural form into "the square;" although some of the smaller logs are brought out in "the round," yet, with the larger description, the making them square is essential, not only to lessen their weight, but also to prevent their rolling on the truck or carriage.

"In the months of April and May, all the various preparations having been completed, and the dry season having become sufficiently advanced, the "trucking" commences in earnest. This may be said to be the mahogany-cutters' harvest, as the result of his season's work depends upon a continuance of the dry weather, for a single shower of rain would materially injure his roads. The number of trucks worked is proportioned to the strength of the gang, and the distance generally from six to ten miles. We will, for example, take a gang of forty men, capable of working six trucks, each of which requires seven pair of oxen and two drivers, sixteen to cut food for the cattle, and twelve to load or put the logs on the carriages, which latter usually take up a temporary residence somewhere near the main body of the wood, it being too far to go and return each day to the river side, or chief establishment. From the intense heat of the sun, the cattle would be unable to work during its influence; consequently, they are obliged to use the night-time in lieu of the day, the sultry effects of which it becomes requisite to avoid. The loaders, as before mentioned, being now at their stations in the forest, the trucks set off from the *embarcadero* about six o'clock in the evening, and arrive at their different places of loading about eleven or twelve o'clock at night. The loaders, being at this time asleep, are warned of the approach of the trucks by the cracking of the whips carried by the cattle-drivers, which are heard at a considerable distance; they arise, and commence placing the logs on the trucks, which is done by means of a temporary platform laid from the edge of the truck to a sufficient distance upon the ground, so as to make an inclined plane, upon which the log is gradually pushed up from each end alternately. Having completed their work of loading all the trucks, which may be done in three hours, they again retire to rest till about nine o'clock next morning. The drivers now set out on their return, but their progress is considerably retarded by the lading, and, although well provided with torch-light, they are frequently impeded by small stumps that remain in the road, and which would be easily avoided in daylight; they, however, are in general all out at the river by eleven o'clock next morning, when, after throwing the logs into the river, having previously marked them on each end with the owner's initials, the cattle are fed, the drivers retire to rest until about sunset, when they feed the cattle a second time, and yoke in again.

"Nothing can present a more extraordinary appearance than this process of trucking, or drawing down the mahogany to the river. The six trucks will occupy an extent of road of a quarter of a mile. The great number of oxen, the drivers half naked (clothes being inconvenient from the heat of the weather and clouds of dust), and each bearing a torch-light, the wildness of the forest scenery, the rattling of chains, the sound of the whip echoing through the woods—then all is activity and exertion so ill corresponding with the silent hour of midnight, makes it wear more the appearance of some theatrical exhibition than what it really is, the pursuit of industry which has fallen to the lot of the Honduras wood-cutter.

"About the end of May the periodical rains again commence. The torrents of water discharged from the clouds are so great as to render the roads impassable in the course of a few hours, when all trucking ceases; the cattle are turned into the pasture, and the trucks, gear, and tools, etc., are housed.

"The rain now pours down incessantly till about the middle of June, when the rivers swell to an immense height. The logs then float down a distance of 200 miles, being followed by the gangs in pitpans (a kind of flat-bottomed canoe) to disengage them from the branches of the overhanging trees, until they are stopped by a boom placed in some situation convenient to the mouth of the river.

"Each gang then separates its own cutting by the mark on the ends of the logs, and forms them into large rafts, in which state they are brought down to the wharves of the proprietors, where they are taken out of the water, and undergo a second process of the axe to make the surface smooth. The ends, which frequently get split and rent by the force of the current, are also sawed off, when they are ready for shipping."

The wages paid in Belize by the English cutters on the eastern coast of Yucatan do not vary much from the prices common in Honduras. A "gang" there is understood to comprehend a "captain" and fifty men, divided into thirty first class, ten second class, and ten third class. The captain receives from $30 to $45 per month, and the men $15, $12, and $10, according to their rank. The hunter for the gang has $15 per month, or most frequently is paid at from half a dollar to a dollar for each tree he finds, according to its size and value. The men here, as in Honduras, are supplied with tools and rations, and receive their pay in the same relative proportion of goods and money.

Around Belize the mahogany-cutters are chiefly negroes, descendants of the slaves who were formerly employed there. But in Honduras they are principally Caribs, who in activity and strength are said to excel the negroes; they are also more intelligent, and require less care and superintendence. Many of them go annually to Belize, and hire themselves for the season, returning to their homes at its close.

In reference to the mahogany trade of Honduras, as, indeed, in respect to every other branch of industry and commerce, we are absolutely without information both as to its amount and value. It may nevertheless be regarded as steadily increasing, and as promising to become every year more important as the supplies of wood from the islands and from the peninsula of Yucatan diminish, and as the demand for it in the markets of the world is augmented. The principal establishments are now on the River Ulua and its branches, and on the Aguan, Black, and Patuca rivers. The other streams have been neglected, in consequence of the difficulty of floating down the wood, as well as of embarking it on an unprotected shore.

Besides the mahogany, Honduras supplies nearly every other variety of wood common to the tropics, all of which are too well known to need more than an enumeration. Rosewood (*Amyris Balsamifera*, L.) is common on the northern coast, where it is beginning to become an article of commerce. Lignumvitæ (*Rhamnus Sarcomphalus*, L.) abounds in the valley of the Ulua, and on the banks of the rivers in the plain of Comayagua, and, no doubt, is common in all other parts of the state.

Among the numerous dyewoods, or trees producing dyes, for which Honduras is famed, may be enumerated the Fustic (*Morus Tinctoria*, L.); Yellow Sanders (*Santalum*); Brazil-wood (*Cæsalpina Echinata*, L.); Dragon's-blood-tree (*Pterocarpus Draco*, L.); Nicaragua-wood (a variety of Brazil-wood); and the Anotta (*Bixa Orellana*).

Trees producing gums and medicines are not less numerous. The Gum Arabic bush (*Acacia Arabica*) abounds on all the open savannas on the Pacific slope. And in the forests may be found the Copaiba-tree (*Copaifera Officinalis*, L.); the Copal-tree (*Hedwigia Balsamifera*); Liquid Amber (*Styrax Officinalis*); Palma Christi (*Ricinus Communis*); Ipecacuanha, and, finally, the *Ule*, Caoutchouc or India-rubber (*Siphonia Elastica*). The latter is abundant in the low lands of both coasts. Small quantities are collected for sale by the Caribs on the Bay of Honduras, but it has as yet received very little attention.

Among the common and most useful woods, the long-leaved or pitch pine deserves the first mention, not less on account of its excellent quality than its great abundance. It may almost be said to cover all the more elevated portions of Honduras, from one sea to the other. Upon the Pacific slope of the continent it makes its appearance on the hills and mountains at the height of about 1200 feet above the sea. Toward the interior it is found at lower elevations, and on the Atlantic declivity it is abundant nearly down to the sea level. I found it on the low hills bordering the great plain of Sula, on the west, at the height of 250 feet; and it is well known that on the savannas bordering the rivers and lagoons to the eastward of Truxillo, as well as on the Mosquito Shore, it is a characteristic feature. The trees do not grow closely together, but stand well apart, permitting the mountain grasses to grow beneath and around them, so that a pine forest in the interior more resembles a well-kept park than the thickets to which we are accustomed to give the name of forest. The trees grow frequently to great size, but average about twenty inches in diameter. They are rich in pitch, and the wood is firm, heavy, and durable, and the heart is never attacked by insects. It furnishes, therefore, a cheap and convenient timber for all kinds of constructions in the country, as well for bridges as for buildings and for boats. Captain Henderson observes of the Honduras pine: "The timber which it furnishes can scarcely be exceeded in size, and is generally considered, for every necessary purpose, greatly superior to what can be imported from the United States;" and Strangeways expresses the conviction that the endless tracts of pine forest on the northern coast will ultimately come to furnish a large supply both of pitch, tar, and timber for the wants of commerce.

The *Cedro*, or cedar (*Cedrela Odorata*, L.), ranks next to the pine in the list of common and useful woods. It is found in all the valleys, but more particularly in those of the principal rivers near the coasts. It attains the height of seventy or eighty feet, and a diameter of from four to seven feet. It is not attacked by insects, is light and easily worked, as well as ornamental in color and agreeable in smell. For these reasons, it is more extensively used than any other wood in Honduras. It is now exported in small, but increasing quantities. Most of the canoes and *pitpans* of the natives are hollowed from the trunks of the *cedro*, and are both light and durable, but liable to be split in beaching.

The *Ceiba*, or silk-cotton-tree (*Bombax Ceiba*, L.), is abundant, and distinguished for its vast size, which leads to its common use for "*bongos*" and "*pitpans*." I have seen boats, hollowed from a single trunk, which would measure seven feet "in the clear" between the sides. This tree blossoms two or three times a year, when its carnation flowers give a bloom to an entire forest. It produces a pod containing a kind of downy fibre or cotton, which is sometimes used to stuff cushions and pillows, and may possibly be made useful for other purposes.

In addition to these woods, all of those enumerated below are more or less abundant, and fitted for use, viz.: Live-oak (*Bignonia*); Santa Maria; Sumwood; Sapodillo (*Achras Sapota*); Mangrove (*Rizophora Mangle*); Mangrove Grape-tree (*Coccoloba Uvifera*); Iron-wood (*Syderoxylum*); Calabash (*Crescentia*); Button-wood or Mangle Saragoza; Mohoe (*Althœa rucemosa*); Locust (*Hymenœa Courbaril*); Pole-wood; Almond or *Almendrillo;* various kinds of Oak; Granadillo (*Brya Ebanus*); many varieties of Palms; Zapote (*Sapote Mammosa*), etc., etc.

Apart from the lime, lemon, orange, and palm trees, there is a great variety of trees bearing fruits which are indigenous in the country. The cacao is one of these, and is remarkably abundant on the northern alluvions, where the natives draw their entire supplies from the forests. It is known there as the *Cacao Mico*, monkey or wild cacao, and is distinguished from the cultivated variety by having larger nuts, and, it is claimed, a finer flavor. The pimiento-tree, closely resembling the Jamaica "allspice" (*Myrtus Pimenta*), is also indigenous. Its berry is somewhat larger than the variety found in the islands, but weaker in its aroma, and has not yet entered into the commerce of the country.

The Anona, of several varieties, is also indigenous; the Aguacate, or Alligator Pear (*Persea Gratimima*); Citron (*Citrus Tuberosa*); Tamarind (*Tamarindus Occidentalis*); Guava (*Psidium Guajavas*); Pines (*Bromelia Ananas*); Mango (*Mangofera Domestica*); Papaya (*Carica Papaya*); Zapote; Granado (*Punica Granatum*); Mamay (*Lucuma Bomplandi*); Nance; Jocote, or wild Plum; Manzanilla, etc., etc.

The sarsaparilla (*Smilax Medicinal*) is probably produced nowhere in the world of better quality or in greater abundance than in Honduras, but more particularly on its northern and eastern coasts. It is wholly collected by the Indians, but never in greater quantities than may be necessary to procure, by exchange, such articles of European manufacture as they may happen to require. It might be systematically obtained in quantities to meet every demand of commerce.

The vanilla (*Epidendrum Vanilla*) occurs in the same district with the sarsaparilla, and is remarkable for its luxuriance and the size of its pods. It has not yet become an article of export, but the specimens which have been sent to the United States and Europe have already elicited orders beyond the capacity of the available labor of the coast to supply.

The *Pita*, called in Mexico *Ixtle*, is a variety of the agave, very prolific, and yielding fibres varying in quality from the coarsest hemp to the finest flax. It is used for the manufacture of thread, cordage, hammocks, paper, etc., and, being hardy and easily cultivated, may be made an important article of export as well as of domestic use.

I have already said that Honduras produces freely all the great staples of the tropics. The lands upon both coasts are well adapted for cotton, which, however, is not now produced, except in small quantities at a few points by the Indians, for their own peculiar manufactures. The experiments which have been made in the production of this staple, both in San Salvador and Nicaragua, have been in every way satisfactory, so far as the quality of the article itself is concerned; but the difficulty of procuring skilled, and, above all, steady labor, proved insuperable, and led to the abandonment of the projected plantations. Nevertheless, during one year, fifty thousand bales of three hundred pounds each were exported from the western ports of Nicaragua. According to Mr. Baily, "it took a high standard in the Manchester market," where it would always have commanded a ready sale.

The sugar-cane of Honduras, as indeed of all Central America, is indigenous, and widely different from the Asiatic variety cultivated in the West Indies and the United States, being softer and slenderer, and containing a proportionately greater quantity of stronger juice. It grows luxuriantly, alike on the plains and among the mountains, at elevations of between three thousand and four thousand feet. Two crops, and, under very favorable circumstances, three crops a year are taken annually, and the cane does not require replanting but once in ten or twelve years. The crystals of the sugar produced from this cane are large and hard, and, with care in the manufacture, nearly as white as the refined sugar of commerce. There are no extensive establishments for its production, but innumerable little *trapiches*, or mills, driven generally by oxen, are scattered all over the state, to supply the local wants of the people. The greater part of the supply for ordinary consumption is in the form of "*chancaca*," or crude sugar, made into cakes of about two pounds each, and wrapped in plantain-leaves. In this form it is eaten with the native *tortillas*, and constitutes an article of daily food among the lower classes.

Coffee of excellent quality flourishes freely in Honduras, although it has never been adopted as an article of general production, not even to the extent of supplying the consumption of the state. I saw neglected patches at various places in the Department of Gracias, in all of which the bushes were heavily laden with the berries. In Costa Rica the cultivation of coffee has been introduced with the best success. In 1851, the product of that little state was upward of 20,000,000 lbs., bringing in the English market an average price of $12 50 per cwt., equal to $2,500,000 in value. There is every reason for believing that coffee of equally good quality with that of Costa Rica may be produced in Honduras, which has every requisite variety of soil and climate.

Cochineal seems to have been anciently cultivated, to a small extent, in Honduras, but the production is now entirely confined to Guatemala, of which state it constitutes the chief staple. The *Nopal* is abundant and indigenous in the plain of Comayagua, where its leaves are silvered with the webs of the *Cochineal Silvéstre*, or wild cochineal.

The tobacco of Honduras has a deserved celebrity throughout Central America; that of the Llanos de Sta. Rosa, Department of Gracias, is regarded as second to none in the world. It was, in fact, the discovery of the peculiar advantages of that locality for the cultivation of this staple which led to the foundation of the flourishing city of Sta. Rosa, which is now the most important place in the department, completely overshadowing the ancient city of Gracias. The cultivation of tobacco was commenced on the plains of Sta. Rosa near the close of the last century, and increased so rapidly that, in 1795, a royal factory was established there, and a factor appointed by the crown. From this time the tobacco produced here grew in importance and reputation, until it came to be sent not only throughout the old kingdom of Guatemala, but to Mexico, Peru, and even to Spain itself. The population of Sta. Rosa increased in proportion, and in 1823 the Constituent Assembly gave it the name of Villa. The political convulsions which have agitated the country since have been severely felt at Sta. Rosa, in the falling off in the production of its great staple, and in a corresponding decrease in population; still, the amount annually produced is considerable, of which a large part is exported to Cuba, where it is manufactured and sold as the production of that island. The plains of Olancho, as also the valley of Sonaguera, are said to produce a superior quality of tobacco. Some of the tobacco of Honduras finds its way to the other states, and considerable quantities have been exported from the Pacific ports to Hamburg and other ports of Germany. The attempts which have been made to export cigars have not been successful, chiefly from deficiency of skill in the preparation and manufacture of the tobacco. With increased experience and knowledge in these respects, there is no doubt that tobacco will become a principal article of production and commerce.

Indigo is not produced to any large extent in Honduras. Its cultivation has nevertheless been recently introduced in the valley of the Chamelicon, Department of Gracias, with the most satisfactory results. The quality of the article is found to equal that of Nicaragua and San Salvador, which is regarded as superior to the indigo of India. There is every reason to believe that the production might be extended with ease and profit throughout the valley of the Chamelicon, and the valleys of the other streams falling into the Bay of Honduras.

Maize flourishes luxuriantly, and two crops a year may be raised on the same ground wherever the soil is sufficiently moist, or may be made so by irrigation. In the interior, among the mountains, it is not customary to plant the fields a second time in the course of the year, except for the purpose of growing the stalks, to be cut down as *sacate* or fodder for cattle. The variety of maize in general use more resembles that of New England than of the Mississippi Valley. The grain is remarkably full and hard, and the ears relatively small, but numerous. Here, as in nearly every part of tropical America, maize is essentially the "staff of life;" and, made into *tortillas*, *tamales*, *atole*, *tiste*, and other forms of food, constitutes the chief support of the people. It is generally cheap, but occasionally suffers from the *chapulin* or *langosta*, a species of locust or flying grasshopper, which comes in such clouds as completely to destroy the largest *milpa* in the course of a few hours. As the pest of *langosta* is usually general, the visitation sometimes results in a great scarcity, bordering on famine; in which cases maize advances to as high as four and five, and even ten dollars per bushel. Fortunately, the insect seldom attacks the fields which are planted high up on the slopes of the mountains, where the people make their *milpas* during the periodical visitations of the *chapulin*.

Wheat and the other cereal grains of the temperate zone are produced in all the more elevated districts of Honduras. Little, if any, foreign flour enters the state, and the total consumption may be regarded as supplied at home. I found the wheat-fields in the vicinity of the Indian towns, to the southwest of Camayagua, on the terraces of the mountains, at an elevation of four thousand feet above the sea; but this grain will grow at lower altitudes. The stalk is short but firm, and the grain not so plump as that produced in northern latitudes. This may be the result of the poor quality of the variety in use, and to the circumstance that the seed is never changed. The flour is white and well-flavored, and in all respects equal to that produced in Chili and the United States.

Rice is largely used, particularly near the coasts, where it is produced with little labor and of the best quality.

Potatoes, as I have said, are cultivated to a limited extent on the higher plateaus of the mountains, but chiefly by the Indians, who carry them to the large towns, to which their consumption is chiefly confined. Elsewhere, and in all parts of the state, the *yam* and the *manioc* or *cassava* are abundant, and in general use. The yams produced near Omoa, Puerto Caballos, and Truxillo are remarkable alike for their excellent quality and great size, a single root sometimes weighing from fifty to sixty pounds! In conjunction with plantains, bananas, and the varieties of beans, which, under the denomination of *frijoles*, are of universal use, these constitute the principal vegetable supplies of the country. The plantain is wonderfully luxuriant on the northern coast. Next to the maize, or perhaps deserving the first place, it is the principal reliance of the people of the tropics as an article of food. It is easily propagated, and requires but little care after planting. Its yield is enormous, and from a single acre it is estimated by Humboldt to equal the crop of one hundred and thirty-three acres of wheat, and of forty-four acres of potatoes! It must therefore enter as an important element in all calculations on the subject of provisioning the laborers who may be engaged in the construction of the proposed public works in Honduras.

The fauna of Central America corresponds with its intermediate geographical position, partaking of the character of that of the equatorial regions of South America upon the one hand, and the semi-tropical districts of Mexico on the other. Thus we find several varieties of the ant-eater, corresponding with those of the valley of the Orinoco, on the northern and eastern coasts of Honduras, while the gray squirrel of our latitudes greets us with his familiar bark among the forests of the interior.

Among domestic animals, we find the horse, the ass, the ox, sheep, goats, hogs, dogs, and cats, all of foreign origin except one variety of the dog, which is indigenous.

The Horse is found in all parts of Central America, although not used, except at a few of the ports, for purposes of draught. The savannas afford him an abundance of pasturage, and sustain him in good condition. Over these he roves in nearly a wild state, and is seldom caught except with the aid of the lasso. Introduced by the Spaniards, he retains many of the peculiarities of the Arab stock. He is small, of good build, firm in the joints, and distinguished for the extreme smallness and beauty of his ears. He suffers much from insects, which frequently enter the ears, causing them to lop, and otherwise disfiguring the animal. He is also often attacked by bats (*vampiros*), and by a species of spider (*araña*), which attacks the feet, and causes the hoof to separate.

The Ox finds ample pasturage and congenial roving ground in the vast savannas and open forests of Honduras. With the horse, he gives evidence of his Spanish origin. He grows above what in this country is regarded as average size, is of great beauty and strength of form, powerful neck, short head, and compact, but relatively short limbs. He suffers much less than the horse from insects, and nearly always looks smooth and sleek. The cows do not yield a large quantity of milk, but it is of good quality. Vast herds of cattle are raised in various districts of the state, and constitute a principal part of the property of the people. Large numbers of oxen, broken to the yoke, are supplied to the mahogany-works on the coast and at Belize at from ten to fifteen dollars the pair. Ordinary cows sell at from four to five dollars.

The Hog is smaller than the European varieties, almost black in color, with thin bristles, long snout, short legs, and stout body. He is sometimes kept up and fattened, but is generally allowed to run at large and find his own food. The Chinese or East Indian variety has been successfully introduced by some enterprising citizens of Sta. Rosa, Department of Gracias.

Goats are not numerous, but breed rapidly, keep in good condition, and might be introduced to any desirable extent, especially in the more elevated districts. Since, from the abundance of cattle, they are not required for food, they exist in the country rather as domestic pets than for economic purposes.

Sheep are found in greater or less numbers, but are only raised systematically in Quesaltenango and the other departments of Guatemala, constituting what are called *Los Altos*, the Highlands, where their wool is extensively manufactured by the natives in a variety of thick cloth, much prized throughout all Central America. The wool seems to be long and coarse, and the flesh is but little used for food. There is good reason to believe that this animal might be introduced successfully in all of the elevated districts of Honduras.

The Ass is nowhere used for burden, and is kept simply for the purpose of crossing with the horse, and for the production of mules. The latter are in universal use, and are highly valued. They are chiefly raised in the mountain districts, and afterward transferred to the plains. Great pains have been taken to produce fine breeds, and with considerable success. Taken generally, they are rather small in size, but hardy to a wonderful degree. Some of large size, and well broken, command high prices, ranging from $70 to $300. The prices of ordinary cargo mules vary from $15 to $35. They are not shod, except in parts of Guatemala, but their hoofs are hardened by the application of hot lime-juice. Eight *arobas* (200 lbs.) constitute an ordinary load for a pack-mule in Honduras, while ten, and even twelve *arobas* are regarded as a cargo in the level districts of Nicaragua and San Salvador.

Among wild animals, Wright, in his Memoirs on the

Mosquito Shore, quoted by Strangeways, mentions the *buffalo*, but he probably mistook the *cimarrones*, or wild cattle of the coast, for the bison.

The Deer (*Cervus Mexicanus* and *Cervus Rufus*) is abundant in the woods and savannas. The variety first named resembles the European deer in color, but is somewhat less in size, and provided with large antlers. The second is more numerous, of lighter and browner tint, with short, smooth-pointed horns of, at most, two indentations. The young of this variety is very pale in color, almost white, and is highly valued for food. Captain Henderson may have confounded this variety with the antelope, which, he affirms, is found in Honduras. He says, "If this animal, which in this country is known by no other name than that of antelope, be not such in fact, it is difficult to designate to what class it should belong. The resemblance, so far as description can be relied on, is in every respect essentially the same." It is described as about half the size of the fallow deer, short tail, knees furnished with tufts of hair, body reddish brown, under part of buttocks white, horns about twelve inches long, and bent in the form of a lyre. It is said to go in large flocks.

The Peccary (*Sus Tajassu*, L.) is common in Honduras, in the valleys of the rivers, and in the neighborhood of the coasts.

The Waree (*Sus Americensis*) is also found in large droves in portions of Honduras, Nicaragua, and Costa Rica. Henderson supposes it to be the ordinary hog run wild.

The Tapir, or mountain-cow (*Tapir Americanus*, L.), is found upon the northern and southern coasts, but rarely in the interior country. It is sometimes partially tamed.

The Manatus, or Sea-cow (*Manatus Americanus*, L.), is found in all the creeks and lagoons of the northern coast. I have never heard of its existence on the side of the Pacific. It is well known to belong to the mammalia. It grows to the length of ten feet, and attains a weight of from seven hundred to one thousand pounds. The Caribs of the coast hunt it for the sake of its flesh, skin, and fat. It is taken with the harpoon, and its capture requires a great deal of judgment and skill.

Monkeys (*Simia*) are numerous, and of many varieties, including those known as the horned (*Simia Fatuellus*, L.), brown (*S. Apella*), and capuchin (*S. Capuchina*). The last-named variety is abundant, and is a very playful little animal. There is another variety, mentioned by Captain Henderson, which is common in Honduras, and which he thinks has escaped particular notice. "In form and size it resembles the *Apella*; and the female, in which the characteristic difference appears most strongly to exist, is particularly denoted by a loose, fleshy, appendant membrane, which frequently occasions its sex to be mistaken."*

The Raccoon (*Procyon Lotor* or *Ursus Lotor*, L.), is common, of medium size, living chiefly upon animal food, and is of thieving propensities. Individuals frequently live apart, and are called "*Pisotes solos*" by the Spaniards. These grow very fat, and of extraordinary size.

The Opossum (*Didelphys Opossum*) attains a length of ten inches, color gray, powerful head, long and very flexible tail, and the feet provided with sharp claws. The female has a cavity or sack in the belly for the reception of her undeveloped young. When they leave

* Henderson's Honduras, p. 130.

it they are generally carried on the back of the mother. Food, small birds, lizards, etc.

The Squirrel. There are two kinds of squirrels found in Honduras, the gray (*Sciurus Cinereus*, L.), and the small red squirrel (*S. Guajanensis*).

The Ant-eater is also found of several varieties, known as the striped ant-eater (*Myrmecophaga Pentadactyla*), and the little ant-eater (*M. Didactyla*). Among the other lesser animals may be enumerated the Quash (*Viverra Quasje*), which resembles the ichneumon, fetid in smell, with powerful lacerating teeth.

The Armadillo of three bands (*Dasypus Tricinctus*, L.), the eight-banded (*D. Octocinctus*), and the nine-banded (*D. Novencinctus*). The Gibeonite (*Cavia Paca* or *Mus Paca*, L.) is most plentiful, and is easily domesticated. It grows to the length of two feet, thick and clumsy in form, and of a dusky brown color, with four longitudinal series of spots on each side of the body. Its flesh is extolled as a great delicacy. The Indian Coney, or Rabbit (*Cavia Aguti*) is similar to the Gibeonite, and is about the size of the ordinary hare. It does not run, but leaps; is easily tamed, and largely hunted by the Indians for food and for its skin, which is of a durable quality. It swarms in the islands belonging to Honduras, in the bay of the same name.

Among the ferine animals found in Honduras is the Jaguar (*Felis Onca*, L.). It is of a bright tawny color, upper part of head striped with black, sides beautifully variegated with irregular black spots, breast and belly of a whitish color, seldom attacks men, and inhabits places almost inaccessible to human feet. Besides the jaguar we occasionally find also the Black Tiger (*Felis Discolor*), which is much the fiercest animal of Honduras. It grows of large size, and is remarkable for its strength. It often kills full-grown cattle, dragging them far in the woods; and it does not hesitate, if irritated, to attack men. The Ocelot, or Tiger-cat (*F. Pardalis*) resembles the common cat, but is much larger. It is timid, and seldom ventures from its hiding-places. It is valued for its skin. The Cougar, or Puma (*F. Concolor*) is also abundant, and is slender and graceful in form. It is usually called *Leon* (lion) by the natives. It is neither as powerful nor as fierce as the ounce or jaguar, and flies from the face of man. The *Coyote*, or indigenous wolf, is not uncommon.

The interior of Honduras is rather deficient in birds, but they abound on the coasts and in the valleys of the principal rivers. The most celebrated is the *Quetzal*, which was the imperial bird of the Quichés. It is best known in the museums as the *Trogan Resplendens*, and is found only in the Mountains of Merendon, in Honduras, and the Department of Quezaltenango, in Guatemala. The Parrot abounds every where, of numerous varieties, and of the most vivid colors. The *Guacamaya*, or Macaw, red and blue, are numerous on both coasts, as is also the Toucan. The Yellow-tail (*Cassicus Montezuma*) soon becomes familiar to all voyagers on the rivers of Honduras. It is remarkable not less for its bright colors than its pendent nests, of which forty or fifty sometimes hang from the branches of a single tree.

Among the *Raptores*, or birds of prey, are a variety of Hawks, Vultures (including the common Buzzard or *Zopilote*), Owls and Sea-eagles. The Crow, Blackbird, Mexican Jay, Rice-bird, Swallow, Rain-bird, Humming-bird (of numerous varieties), are also common. Of water-birds, the Pelican, Muscovy Duck, Black Duck, Curlew, Plover, Spoonbill, Teal, Darters, Herons, Ibises,

Cranes, etc., are all found abundantly on the shores of the lagoons and rivers. The Wild Turkey, Curassow, Quam (*Penelope Cristana*), *Chachalaca*, or indigenous hen, Mexican Partridge, Quail (in abundance), Snipe, and several varieties of Wood Pigeons and Doves, are most numerous in the interior country.

The Alligator is found in all the lagoons and rivers on both coasts. It attains the size of fifteen feet in length. It avoids the neighborhood of man, and generally abandons the streams as their banks become inhabited. Of the Lizard tribe there are infinite varieties. The most remarkable is the Iguana, which sometimes attains three and four feet in length. It is bluish gray in color, and lives almost exclusively on the blossoms of trees. Its bite is painful, but not dangerous. The flesh is delicate and much valued.

Serpents of several kinds are found both in Honduras and San Salvador, but they are chiefly confined to the coasts. The common practice of burning the dry grass and withered vegetation of the interior during the dry season has almost had the effect of annihilating this species of reptile. During a year spent in the state, and almost constantly occupied in the field, I do not remember to have seen more than four serpents, and only one of these (a *corral*) of a poisonous character. As we approach the coast, however, they become more numerous, but they are generally of harmless varieties. In respect to serpents of the coast, Messrs. Müller and Hesse observe:

"For the most part they are harmless, and they are seen by the natives in their houses rather with pleasure than alarm or disgust, since they are useful in the destruction of vermin. The harmless snakes have generally rounded spots on the head, angular marks under the tail and belly, while the body is covered with oval scales. The upper jaw, as in mammalia, is set for its entire length with sharp, wedge-shaped, solid teeth, and from the junction of the jaws springs another row. The under jaw is furnished in the same manner, so that, in opening the mouth, four rows of teeth are seen. The harmless snakes are, in general, long and slender in body, the head is handsomer, and the scales are smoother. In our journeys through the forests we observed several of these, and especially one large kind of bluish-white color, which we were unable to catch, as it disappeared rapidly when we approached it. This kind is named by the Indians *woulah*, and they say that, though it steals fowls, it destroys the smaller varieties of poisonous snakes. The venomous serpents are distinguished by a thicker body and shorter tail, a broad head covered with scales, and more especially by the poison-fangs, which are sharp, provided with a channel and an opening at the upper end, not at the top but at the side, for the exit of the poison. Behind these fangs lie several smaller teeth, but they are concealed in a fold of muscle. As we had no opportunity to see or investigate any such specimens, although the Indians, in hopes of reward, hunted several times in vain for us, we must content ourselves with repeating the ordinary names in use there. There is the golden snake, the whip-snake, tamagas, and barber's pole. The two latter are the most dangerous, and their bite destroys life. According to experience, the root of the guaco is a reliable remedy for the bite of a snake. It is found almost every where, especially on the island of Roatan. The number of serpents is perceptibly diminished by the advance of cultivation."

In addition to the snakes mentioned in this extract may be enumerated the rattlesnake, the ordinary black-snake, and the *corral*, the last ranking with the *tamagasa* in the deadly nature of its bite. It is of the most brilliant colors, covered with alternate rings of green, black, and red. It does not grow of large size, nor is it common.

The Tortoise and Turtle are every where numerous,

and of several kinds. The land turtle, chiefly of the species *Tubulata*, attains a foot in length. It has a dark shell, and is eaten in common with the sea tortoise, but is not regarded as of so good quality. The rivers abound in a species of turtle generally called *Hicatee.* It is smaller than the sea turtle, but inferior in no other respect. It attains a length of eighteen or twenty inches, and is remarkable for the depth of its shell. The varieties of sea turtle familiarly known as green turtle (*Chelonia Midas*) and hawk's-bill turtle (*C. Caretta*) are abundant on both coasts, and furnish a large supply of food, and a principal source of wealth to the Indians. From the variety known as hawk's-bill is taken the best tortoise-shell of commerce. There is still another species, which grows to larger size than either of those already enumerated, called the trunk turtle. Its flesh is not used, nor is its shell of good quality. A kind of oil, which is much valued, is extracted from this turtle, and, it is supposed, might be made a considerable article of trade.

Oysters, of two varieties, are plentiful, viz., what is called the bank oyster, found in beds, and growing in clusters of ten or twelve each, and the small or mangrove oyster, which is generally found attached to the roots of the mangrove-trees which line the shores of all the creeks and lagoons. Both varieties are esteemed for food. Vast beds of the first-named species exist in the Bay of Fonseca (*ante*, p. 98).

Crustacea of various kinds and sizes, from the largest lobster to the smallest crab, are most abundant. In particular, the mangrove crab (*Grapsus Cruentatus*), and the white and black land-crab (*Gecarcinus*), are very numerous in the lagoons and around the mouths of rivers. They constitute a very savory and nourishing food. Every half-rotten tree near the water is inhabited by countless thousands of soldier-crabs, which, at certain times of the year, migrate inland, and afterward return to the sea. Conchs are numerous in all the cays off the northern coast, and especially on those around the islands of Roatan and Guanaja.

Not only do all the lagoons and creeks of the coast abound in endless varieties of fish, but these swarm in all the rivers and lakes of the interior. In the sea may be found the Rock-fish (*Labrax Lineatus*), Hog-fish (*Helops*), King-fish (*Umbrina Alburnus*), Baracouta (*Sphyræna Baracuda*), Parrot-fish (*Tetrodon?*), Grouper (*Serranus*), red and black Snapper (*Coracinus*), Porgee (*Sargus*), Shad (*Alosa*), Gar-fish, Sword-fish, Porpoise, Flounder, etc. In the lagoons, the Jew-fish, Sheep's-head, Snook (*Macrocephalus*), Mud-fish, Mullet, Calapaver (*Mugil*), Mackerel, Drummer, Grunt, Eel, Cat-fish, etc. In the rivers the Mountain Mullet and Cat-fish are most numerous. The Shark abounds on both coasts.

A species of vine (*Sapindus Saponaria*) grows abundantly in the river valleys, which is often used by the natives for poisoning, or, rather, stupefying the fish of the streams. It is pounded, infused in water, and then poured in the stream, causing the fish to rise helplessly to the surface, when they are easily taken by hand. If allowed to remain in the water, they soon recover from the effects of the intoxication.

Honey-bees exist in Honduras of several varieties. One (*Apis Pallida*) is small, light-colored, and stingless. There is another species, found in the mountain districts, which is indistinguishable from the common honey-bee of the United States. The honey is largely used by the natives, who draw a principal part of the wax used in the ceremonies of the Roman Church from the natural bee-hives of the forests.

The absence of mosquitoes throughout Honduras and San Salvador generally is worthy of remark, since it is commonly supposed that this insect is one of the principal pests of the country. It is almost unknown in the interior districts, and only found at a few points on the coasts. Their almost total absence around the Bay of Fonseca is one of the best evidences of the absence of pestilential marshes and lagoons in its vicinity. The flea is common every where, and a source of infinite annoyance. The *agarrapata*, or wood-tick, is abundant on the low grounds, and particularly in sections frequented by herds of cattle. They are readily removed from the person by balls of soft wax, which every traveler carries for that purpose. The *chigoe*, *niqua*, or *jigger*, a small black flea, which attacks the feet and burrows under the skin, causing irritating sores, is scarcely known upon the Pacific coast. It is nevertheless found upon the northern coast, but rarely attacks persons who preserve proper cleanliness of person. Among spiders the tarantula may be enumerated, but it is not often seen. A species called *araña de cavallo* I have already mentioned as sometimes attacking the feet of horses. Among beetles, the elephant beetle is remarkable for its size. At night the neighborhood of the coasts is sprinkled with fire-fly stars of great brilliance and beauty. Scorpions are found every where, in greater or less abundance; but it is only the sting of the *alacran del monte*, wild, or forest scorpion, which is to be greatly dreaded. The house scorpion is largest, but pale in color, and its sting is far less virulent, corresponding nearly with that of the common wasp. The centipede (*Scolopendra Morsi-*

tans) attains, on the north coast, a length of six or seven inches. Its head bears a pair of strong nippers, and it moves upon twenty divisions of the body, to each of which are attached two feet. It is often found in dwelling-houses, but is not to be feared.

The insect, however, which is most dreaded in Honduras, as indeed in all Central America, is the *Langosta* or *Chapulin*, a species of grasshopper or locust, which at intervals afflicts the entire country, passing from one end to the other in vast columns of many millions, literally darkening the air, and destroying every green thing in their course. I once rode through one of these columns which was fully ten miles in width. Not only did the insects cover the ground, rising in clouds on each side of the mule-path as I advanced, but the open pine forest was brown with their myriad bodies, as if the trees had been seared with fire, while the air was filled with them, as it is with falling flakes in a snow-storm. Their course is always from south to north. They make their first appearance as *saltones*, of diminutive size, red bodies, and wingless, when they swarm over the ground like ants. At this time vast numbers of them are killed by the natives, who dig long trenches, two or three feet deep, and drive the *saltones* into them. Unable to leap out, the trench soon becomes half filled with the young insects, when the earth is shoveled back, and they are thus buried and destroyed. They are often driven, in this way, into the rivers and drowned. Various expedients are resorted to by the owners of plantations to prevent the passing columns from alighting. Sulphur is burned in the fields, guns are fired, drums beaten, and every mode of making a noise put in requisition for the purpose. In this mode detached plantations are often saved. But when the columns once alight, no device can avail to rescue them from speedy desolation. In a single hour, the largest maize-fields are stripped of their leaves, and only the stems are left to indicate that they once existed.

It is said that the *Chapulin* makes its appearance at the end of periods of about fifty years, and that it then prevails for from five to seven years, when it entirely disappears. But its habits have never been studied with care, and I am unprepared to affirm any thing in these respects. Its ordinary size is from two and a half to four inches in length, but it sometimes grows to the length of five inches.

CHAPTER XII.

EXISTING ABORIGINAL INHABITANTS—THE XICAQUES, PAYAS, SAMBOS, AND CARIBS.

I HAVE elsewhere said that the Indian or aboriginal element predominates in the population of Central America. The population of Honduras forms no exception to this remark; and in some districts of the state it is difficult to say if the whites have assimilated most to the Indians in habits of life, or the Indians most to the whites. In the eastern portion of the state, within the district which lies between the Rio Roman and the Cape or Segovia River, an area of not less than 15,000 square miles, the country is almost exclusively occupied by native tribes, known under the general names of Xicaques and Payas. Portions of all these tribes have accepted the Catholic religion, and live in peaceable neighborhood and good understanding with the white inhabitants. The large town of Catacamas, and some other towns of less note in the vicinity of Juticalpa, in Olancho, are exclusively inhabited by Christianized Payas and Xicaque Indians. But, apart from these, there are considerable numbers who live among the mountains, and who conform more closely to their original modes of life. Yet they also are peaceful, and their relationship with the Spaniards is entirely friendly. They bring down sarsaparilla, deer-skins, dragon's-blood, and other articles, including a little gold washed from the sands of the mountain streams, and exchange them for such articles of civilized manufacture as their wants require. They tacitly recognize the authority of the government, which, however, does not interfere with the simple patriarchal system which they keep up for their organization. Occasionally small parties come down to the coast to work in the mahogany establishments. When their engagements are completed, they quickly return to their homes.

At the time of the discovery, these Indians were found to be, in respect of civilization, far below the Quichés, Kachiquels, and Nahuals, who occupied the plateaus of Guatemala, San Salvador, and the western part of Honduras. But they were, at the same time, greatly in advance of the roving fisher-tribes who dwelt on the low shores of the Caribbean, now called the Mosquito Coast. They were at first intractable, and, favored by the physical conditions of their country, for a long time obstinately resisted the attempts of the Spaniards to reduce them to their sway; but subsequently, when the general settlement of the country to the westward had been effected, and the power of the Spaniards came to be better appreciated, a friendly understanding sprung up, which has not been disturbed for many years.

The names Xicaques and Payas may be regarded as general designations. The *Toacas* or *Towkas*, some of whom live on the banks of the Rio Patuca, and the *Secos*, found on Rio Tinto, or Black River, probably belong to the Payas. They are described by Young, who visited them, as having "long black hair hanging over their shoulders, very broad faces, small eyes, with a peculiar expression of sadness and docility, which prepossesses the beholder in their favor."

"They are short," he continues, "but remarkably strong, and

capable of carrying heavy burdens over the rocky passes of their steep mountains without appearing to suffer much fatigue. Their character for faith and honesty stands high; but, like all other savage tribes, they have a great fondness for spirituous liquors. They bring for sale sarsaparilla, cacao, pimiento, *kinkooras*, several sorts of bread kind, fowls, turkeys, ducks, etc., and receive in return iron pots, knives, *machetes*, powder, shot, beads, and similar articles of use and ornament. * * In character they are mild and inoffensive. They are industrious, and skillful in manufacturing from their wild cotton a sort of cloak called *kinkoora*, which, being dyed according to some device, and the down of birds interwoven in the fabric, has a very pleasing appearance. * * At the present day, the grossest superstitions exist among the Poyers, and their idolatrous feasts are as common as ever; but their savage character has disappeared, for they are now a mild and peaceable race, having tact and ingenuity in their little manufactures which would puzzle a machine-loving European. * * There is another class of Poyer Indians much lower in civilization. They are termed wild Indians, for, like the Arabs, they wander to and fro as they list, making plantations which, in the course of a certain number of moons, they revisit to gather the fruit. They collect honey, vegetable dyes, sarsaparilla, etc., which they sell to their more civilized brethren for hooks, harpoons, lance-heads, knives, and other articles. They have no intercourse with the Sambos on the coast, and it is only because they can not do without such things as I have enumerated that they visit the Poyer villages. * * The Indians living on the banks of the Seco River, and called *Secos*, have much the same character as the Poyers.

"The *Towcas* [*Toacas*, *Thuacos*, or *Juacos*] are remarkable for their industry and inoffensive character. They are generally a finer race of men than either the Poyers or Secos. They speak at all times low and with great ease, and have an air of gentleness and melancholy. They sound the letter *s* in almost every word. They are celebrated for their skill in making *dorys* and *pitpans*. Their principal residence is near the head of Patook (Patuca) River. * * The Towcas, like the other tribes, have a great character for faith and probity, and are equally famed for carrying heavy burdens. They are very dexterous in shooting birds on the wing with their bows and arrows, and are well suited for any thing requiring sagacity and endurance. It is astonishing to observe how little value they put on their labor. For instance, they will sell a dory or pitpan for one axe and a machete, or two iron pots, and so on, notwithstanding the immense time which they expend in making them."

Young visited a Poyer or Payas village on one of the tributaries of Black River, of which he has given us the subjoined account. It illustrates the condition and mode of life of these Indians in general.

"The Indian town, to my astonishment, was comprised in one large house of an oval form, about 85 feet in length and 35 feet wide, in which all the natives resided truly in the patriarchal style. Crickeries were erected all around, close to each other, separated by two or three cabbage boards, each family having one of these compartments. At one side of the house a place was divided off, about sixteen feet by ten feet, and hidden from view by green leaves, which were replenished as fast as they faded. In this place the women are kept during their confinement, and, after a few days, they are again able to attend to their multifarious duties. On our entrance, the women were busily occupied, some pounding cassada and Indian corn together, boiling it, and making it into a beverage called oulung; some preparing cassada for bread in the morning; others making tournous; others, again, rubbing cacao and squeezing sugar-cane; in truth, the whole body of them were most busily employed, under the management of the chief's wife, the chief, who is called by the English name of officer, being absent. We were looked upon with a quiet sort of wonder, the women merely gazing for a few minutes upon the white men, of whom, perhaps, they had heard much, and then they resumed their pounding, boiling, and beating. The oulung is a beverage not to be despised on a warm day by those who do not mind a particularly sour taste. After the second time of tasting it, I sought it with pleasure. Their bread, too, is sour, but even that I relished. It is made

of pounded cassada into rolls about fifteen or sixteen inches in length, and about the thickness of a man's wrist. It is then wrapped round with several layers of leaves, and slowly barbacued until done. When eaten fresh, it is good, the sour taste being acquired by keeping. The house is thatched in a very neat manner with swallow-tail leaf to about four feet from the ground, so that the rain, however violent, does not trouble them. They are noted for cleanliness. The situation was well chosen, and a few yards from the house, down a steep pass, was a stream of water, forming innumerable cascades as it ran leaping and dashing over the huge blocks of stone with which it abounded. Here, as we sat, our ears drank in delight at the soothing sound of the water, and we beheld with extreme gratification the verdant hills, the rich plumage of birds as they flew by, and heard the chattering monkeys filling the wood with their noise. I observed around the house numerous fowls, a few Muscovy ducks, turkeys, and pigs; and they can, in general, obtain game by a little exertion in hunting. The peccary, which inhabits high and dry places, often falls here before the superior dexterity and cunning of man. Waree are not found on the Poyer Mountains, so that the Indians sometimes form a party, and descend to one of the hunting passes in the Black River, or such places as they are known to frequent. Very few of them have guns; they merely go armed with a lance and bow and arrow, and they rarely return without a noble supply of barbacued meat. After partaking of a couple of fowls, some cassada and plantains, cacao, and boiled cane-juice, prepared for us by these kind people, we betook ourselves to repose. Early in the morning, while in my hammock, an Indian woman timidly touched me, saying 'Englis,' at the same time presenting me with a hot roll of bread, nicely done up in fresh leaves; another soon came to me with a bundle of oulung, and so it continued until I had three or four bundles of oulung, and nine large rolls of bread. In return, I presented them with a little tobacco, some needles, and salt, and gave a clasp knife to the officer's wife. Soon after, I was agreeably surprised by several of the men arriving from the plantations loaded with sugar-cane, plantains, cacao, etc., which we very willingly received in exchange for a few hooks, needles, etc.

On inquiry, I learned that there was another town about fifteen miles off, judging from the rate they travel in an hour, and in the route to the Spanish country. Before our departure, a number of Indians came from the neighboring town, having been apprised of our arrival, bringing sarsaparilla to trade with for Osnaburg; but we not having that, or cloth of any kind, they were compelled to carry their heavy burdens back."

The coast around Carataska Lagoon, and as far to the westward as Brewer's or Brus Lagoon, was for many years occupied by Sambos, corresponding generally in character with those of the Mosquito Shore. But the Caribs, spreading rapidly eastward from Truxillo and Black River, have now nearly displaced them, and driven them to the southward of Cape Gracias á Dios, into what is called the Mosquito Territory.

These Sambos or Mosquitos are a mixed race of negroes and Indians. It seems that early in the seventeenth century a large slaver was driven ashore not far from Cape Gracias. The negroes escaped, and although at first they encountered hostility from the Indians, they finally made peace, and intermixed with them. The buccaneers had their haunts among them during the period of their domination in the Caribbean Sea, and bequeathed to them a code of morality, which subsequent relations with smugglers and traders have not contributed to improve. The negro element was augmented from time to time by runaway slaves (*cimarrones*) from the Spanish settlement, and by the slaves brought from Jamaica by the planters who attempted to establish themselves on the coast during the early part of the last century.

The Sambos were fostered by the royal governors of Jamaica during the wars with Spain as a means of annoyance to the Spaniards, and with the ultimate purpose of obtaining possession of their country. Governor Trelawney, in 1740, procured from some of the chiefs a cession of the entire shore to the British crown, which act was followed up by the appointment of a governor or superintendent, the erection of forts, and other evidences and acts of occupation and sovereignty. The pretensions thus set up were nevertheless formally and fully relinquished by subsequent treaties with Spain, which provided for the destruction of the English forts, and the unqualified abandonment of the shore. Nor were these pretensions renewed so long as Spain retained her power in America. It was not until her dominion was succeeded by the feeble sovereignty of the Spanish American republics that the traditionary policy of Great Britain on the Mosquito Shore was revived. Its revival has led to that singular complication which is now familiar to the public as "the Mosquito question."

The relations of the Sambos, first with the buccaneers, and subsequently with the English, by supplying them with fire-arms and other means of aggression, made them formidable to the neighboring Indian tribes. They often left the creeks and lagoons of the shore, and, going up the various rivers, made descents on the Indian towns on their banks, carrying off the inhabitants to be sold as slaves. For many years an active traffic was thus kept up with Jamaica. As a consequence, the Indian towns nearest the coast, and most exposed to these incursions, were either abandoned entirely, or their inhabitants purchased security from attack by annual presents of boats, skins, and other products of their country to the piratical Sambos.

But with the decline and final suppression of the traffic in Indian slaves, the Mosquito Sambos have lost much of their activity, and have surrendered themselves more and more to their besetting vice of drunkenness, which, operating on constitutions radically tainted and weakened by unrestrained licentiousness, is hastening their utter extinction.

As I have said, the increase and expansion of the Caribs have already driven most of the Sambos, who were established to the northward and westward of Cape Gracias á Dios, into the territory of Nicaragua, southward of the Cape. As the whole Mosquito population does not probably exceed six or seven thousand, it follows that the proportion which remains in Honduras is insignificant. All accounts concur in drawing a wide distinction between the Sambos and Indians proper, which is little to the advantage of the former.

"The difference between the Sambos and Indians," says Young, "is very striking. The former are of all shades of color, from the copper of the Indian to the dark hue of the negro, their hair being more or less woolly as they approximate to the latter. They are, in general, well proportioned and active, but more capable of undergoing privations than the fatigue of hard labor. * * They ornament their faces by laying on large daubs of red and black paint. * * Their fondness for liquor is excessive, and from this they suffer great calamities, for, having once commenced to drink, they go on till they fall down in a helpless state of intoxication, and lie exposed to the heavy dews or pouring rain. Their bodies are wasted by fearful disorders, which eventually carry them off: this is one cause of the gradual decrease of population. * * They do not appear to have any idea of a Supreme Being, but many who have at various times been at Belize know the meaning of God, and often say, 'Please God' so and so; or, if they wish to be implicitly believed, they will gravely say, 'God swears.' They have an implicit belief in an Evil Spirit, whom they call Oulasser, and of whom they are in much fear, and after sunset a Sambo will not go out alone, lest

ward granted, since which time most of the fugitives have returned to their former seats.

When San Vincent was first visited by Europeans, it was found in possession of two distinct families of natives, who had a common language, but differed widely in color and in modes of life. These were respectively called the Black and Yellow Caribs, and the natural jealousies between them were often fomented by the whites into open and exterminating hostilities. When, however, the deportation took place in 1796, the feeble remnants on both sides had been forced into friendly relationship by the weight of common misfortunes. The fusion of blood, nevertheless, had not been sufficiently great to obliterate the original distinctions of color, which are to be observed to this day. It has been supposed that these distinctions were produced, in the same manner that corresponding changes were caused on the Mosquito Shore, by the infusion of negro blood. It is said that some time about 1675, a Guinea slaver was foundered on one of the small islands in the neighborhood of San Vincent, and that the negroes who escaped mingled with the natives, originating what were afterward called the Black Caribs. Subsequent differences arose between these and the pure Caribs, which led to a division of the island, in which relation they were found by the Europeans. This explanation seems probable, for the presence of negro blood in the Black Caribs is evident and palpable. They are taller and stouter than the pure Caribs, and more mercurial and vehement. The latter are short, but powerfully built. Both are active, industrious, and provident, exhibiting in these, as, indeed, in most other respects, decided contrasts with the Sambos of the Mosquito Shore. They are far more civilized in their habits, living in well-constructed huts, which are kept clean and comfortable. They still retain their original language, which is the true Carib of the islands, although most, if not all of them, speak Spanish, as well as a little English.

They profess and practice the Catholic religion, yet preserve many of their native rites and superstitions. Altogether, they constitute a good and useful laboring population, and form the chief reliance of the mahogany-cutters on the coast. They supply Omoa and Truxillo, as also Belize in part, with vegetables and fresh provisions, and are the chief collectors of skins, sarsaparilla, and other articles exported from Honduras. Intelligent, faithful, inured to the climate, and, moreover, expert in the use of the axe, and with some knowledge of the building of roads and bridges, they must prove of the greatest service in the future development of the vast resources of that country, and of the utmost importance in the construction of the proposed railway between the seas. It is calculated that there are among them fully three thousand men more or less instructed in precisely the kind of work required in the prosecution of the enterprise referred to, and whose labor may be procured for a reasonable compensation.

All travelers concur in awarding high praise to the Caribs (called Kharibees by Roberts) of Honduras. Young says of them:

"They are peaceable, friendly, ingenious, and industrious. They are noted for their fondness for dress, wearing red bands around their waists to imitate sashes, straw hats knowingly turned up, clean white shirts and frocks, long and tight trowsers, and, with an umbrella or cane in hand, have an air of great satisfaction with themselves. The Carib women are fond of ornamenting their persons with colored beads strung in various forms. When bringing the products of their plantations for sale, they appear dressed in calico bodices and lively-patterned skirts, with handkerchiefs tied around their heads, and suffered to fall negligently behind. * * The Caribs can not be considered a handsome race, but they are hardy and athletic. The difference in their color is remarkable, some being coal-black, and others nearly as yellow as saffron. They are scrupulously clean, and have a great aptitude for acquiring languages, most of them being able to talk in Carib, Spanish, and English; some even add Creole-French and Mosquito. * * * Polygamy is general among them, some of them having as many as three or four wives; but the husband is compelled to have a separate house and plantation for each, and, if he make one a present, he must make the others one of the same value; and he must also divide his time equally among them—a week with one, a week with another, and so on. When a Carib takes a wife, he fells a plantation and builds a house; the wife then takes the management, and he becomes gentleman at large until the following year, when another plantation has to be cleared. The wife attends these plantations with great care, perseverance, and skill, and, in the course of twelve or fifteen months, has every description of bread-kind in use among them; and, as the products are entirely her own, she only keeps sufficient at home for her husband and family, and disposes of the rest to purchase clothes and other necessaries. Just before Christmas, the women engage several creers, freight them with rice, beans, yams, plantains, etc., for Truxillo and Belize, and hire their husbands and others as sailors. It is the custom, when a woman can not do all the work required on the plantation, for her to hire her husband, and pay him two dollars per week. The women travel considerable distances to their plantations, and carry their productions in a kind of wicker-basket. I have known them walk from far beyond Monkey-apple town to Fort Wellington, a distance of forty miles, to exchange their baskets of provisions for salt, calico, etc. Men accompany them on their trading excursions, but never, by any chance, carry the burdens, thinking it far beneath them. In the dry seasons, the women collect firewood, which they stack in sheltered places, to be ready for the wet norths. Industry and forethought are peculiar traits of character in Carib women, consequently they easily surround themselves with necessaries and comforts. The men can hew and plant, hunt and fish, erect a comfortable house, build a good boat, make the sails, etc. Some are capital tailors, and others are good carpenters; altogether, there can not be a more useful body of men. They often go to the various mahogany-works around Roman River, Limas River, Truxillo, or Belize, and hire themselves as mahogany-cutters, for which, by their strength and activity, they are well fitted. They hire for five or six months, sometimes longer, for eight to twelve dollars per month and rations. I have known some Caribs of superior manual power, and who understood the whole routine of mahogany-cutting, obtain as much as fifteen and sixteen dollars a month. On the expiration of their engagement they return to their homes, laden with useful articles, and invariably well dressed. I saw a Carib belonging to Cape Town that had just returned from Belize, who sported a pair of cloth boots, a white hat, black coat, white trowsers, a fancy-colored shirt, a pair of splendid braces, and an umbrella. His coat happened to be an extremely tight fit, and, as he appeared to be very uncomfortable, we asked him to cut up a pine-apple, which, after several vigorous efforts, he succeeded in accomplishing.

"The Caribs grow the Bourbon sugar-cane, and they declare that the soil is well adapted for its cultivation; I have myself seen it sixteen feet in height, and thick in proportion, from the plantation of Captain Samboler, at Zachary Lyon River. Tobacco is now grown in small quantities by the Caribs, and also by the Mosquitians at Patook, but they have not yet discovered the proper method of drying; the tobacco of the one tribe tastes like dried hay, and that of the other is so strong as to occasion bad symptoms to those unaccustomed to its use. If the proper method of preparing tobacco were practiced, it might become an article of exportation. In the interior, among the Spaniards, a large quantity is produced, and conveyed on the backs of mules to Truxillo for sale. Some of the superior sort is made into "puros," twelve of which can be had for fivepence currency; and three dozen cigaritos for the same price. Their best tobacco is not to be compared in flavor to that from Havana, in consequence of the mode of damping and drying practiced by the Central Americans, but it is equal in point of quality and size. The Carib houses are all exceedingly well built, the posts being of iron-wood, subah, etc.; the rafters and beams of Santa Maria; the thatch, swallow-tail or cahoon, and wattled with cabbage boards; they have apertures made for windows with shutters, which are closed in the evening with much care, to prevent the admission of the land wind. The Carib houses being open to the sea-breeze, and always closed against the land wind, is no doubt the main reason of the healthiness of their towns; much, however, is attributable to their cleanliness, and the plenty in which they live.

"The old people are supported by their sons or other relatives, and are treated and spoken of with much respect, the children seeming to vie with each other in testifying their affection. At every Carib town numerous pigs and fowls, belonging to the women, are indiscriminately running about, for the people prefer making plantations, sometimes as far as five miles from the town, to stying up the hogs, which they would be obliged to do if their plantations were close at hand, as the pigs, in their perambulations, would find them out, and do much mischief. These hogs, when fattened, are sent to Truxillo and other places for sale."

In the departments of Gracias, Comayagua, and Choluteca there are a number of purely Indian towns, in which the inhabitants retain their ancient language and many of their primitive habits. The cluster of villages in the Mountains of San Juan, to the southwest of Comayagua, viz., Guajiquero, Opotero, Similiton, Cacauterique, etc., as also a number of others among the Mountains of Lepaterique, viz., Aguanqueterique, Lauterique, Cururu, Texiguat, etc., are all purely Indian towns. Their population is industrious, provident, and peaceable. The elevated districts which they occupy enable them to cultivate wheat, potatoes, and other products of higher latitudes, which they carry for sale to large distances. The traveler meets them in the most secluded and difficult passes, patiently pursuing their journeys, and never speaking unless first addressed. They almost invariably carry their bows with them, but only for protection against wild beasts. Their present abodes among the mountains do not appear to have been their original seats, but to have been forced upon them by the gradual usurpation of their lands by the whites, or chosen to avoid a contact which they disliked. They are, nevertheless, exceedingly jealous of their rugged retreats, and are never excited except by some encroachment, real or fancied, upon the limits of the lands pertaining to their respective towns. They all profess the Catholic religion, but their forms of worship, and especially their music, are strongly impressed with aboriginal characteristics.

The existing Indian element in Honduras, left to itself, promises little or nothing for the development of the country; yet, with the introduction of an intelligent and enterprising people, their industry may probably be turned to good account. Frugal, patient, and docile, they have many of the best qualities of a valuable laboring population, and only lack direction to become an important means in the physical regeneration of the country. The Caribs certainly have shown great capacity for improvement, and at their present rate of increase must always be able to supply every industrial demand which may be created on the northern coast, where the climate is least favorable for the introduction of foreign labor.

CHAPTER XIII.

POLITICAL ORGANIZATION—CONSTITUTION—RELIGION—EDUCATION—INDUSTRY—REVENUES—CURRENCY—FUTURE PROSPECTS.

THE dissolution of the Federal Republic of Central America in 1838 left the various states which had composed it in a singular and anomalous position. Some of them, including Honduras, still adhered to the idea of nationality, and while, in fact, exercising all the powers of distinct sovereignties, they carefully avoided taking the title. They called themselves *States*, and named their highest executive officers "chiefs" or "directors." They supplied the want of a common or national constitution by means of treaties of alliance and friendship, which, in certain contingencies, bound them to support each other by force of arms.

The three central or liberal states, Honduras, San Salvador, and Nicaragua, nevertheless cherished the hope of reconstructing the confederation, and exerted themselves to procure the concurrence of Guatemala and Costa Rica. To this end a national convention was called in 1842, and subsequently another in 1847; but, from the neglect or refusal of the states last named to send delegates, as also from the difficulty of defining satisfactorily the relative powers of the allied states themselves, the attempts at union failed.

Finally, abandoning the hope of inducing Guatemala and Costa Rica to enter into the proposed new federal republic, the central states, in 1849, sent commissioners to Leon, in Nicaragua, where they agreed upon a basis of union or pact, under the title of the "National Representation of Central America." This pact was unanimously ratified by the people of the several states in their primary capacity, and delegates were chosen, in accordance with its provisions, to frame a national constitution on the principles laid down in its articles. This constituent assembly met in the city of Tegucigalpa, in Honduras, in the autumn of 1852, and proceeded to the discharge of its duties. But, meantime, the reactionary element in Guatemala had brought such influences to bear upon the government of San Salvador as to induce it to withdraw its delegates from the convention. This example was soon after followed by the government of Nicaragua, and, as a consequence, the assembly was broken up.* To Honduras, therefore, remains the honor of having adhered to the principle of union and nationality to the last moment:

"Faithful among the faithless found!"

Since that event, both Nicaragua and San Salvador have assumed the name of republics; and although this step has not been taken by Honduras, that state may nevertheless be regarded as a distinct nationality. Its constitution, framed in 1848, "in the name of the Eternal Being, the Omnipotent Author and Supreme Legislator of the Universe," is thoroughly republican in its provisions. The Declaration of the Rights and Duties of the People sets forth that

Sovereignty is inalienable and imprescriptible, limited to the welfare and convenience of society, and no

* For an "*Outline of the Political History of Central America.*" including the history of Honduras, see my work, "Nicaragua, its People, etc.," vol. ii., p. 365–452.

fraction of the people, nor can individuals exercise it, except in conformity with laws established by the general consent. All power emanates from the people, and all public functionaries are their delegates and agents, but only to the extent defined by written constitutions, or decreed by laws framed in conformity with them. Such functionaries are furthermore amenable, even with their lives, to the people, who have intrusted them with power, for its faithful discharge. All the inhabitants of the state have the indisputable right of life, liberty, the pursuit of happiness, and the acquirement and disposition of property, in modes not detrimental to the rights and well-being of others. They are, at the same time, obliged to respect and obey the laws, and to contribute, to the just proportion of their means, in support of the expenses of government, not less than with their lives, if necessary to the service and defense of their country. Armies can only exist for the public protection and defense of the state, and no member of the army, while in active service, is eligible to the office of president, senator, or deputy. The press is free, and every citizen may write and publish, without censorship or hinderance, amenable only to the laws for the abuse of his privileges. No citizen can be tried by military tribunals except for offenses committed while in actual service in the army. Every citizen has the right of expatriation. Epistolary correspondence is inviolable; nor can stolen or intercepted letters be used in evidence against their writers. All causes of difference between citizens may be decided by arbitration, and the parties may at any time withdraw their suits from the jurisdiction of the courts, and submit them to arbitrators, whose decision in all cases shall be final.

The general organization and powers of the government, as set forth in the Constitution, may be summed up as follows:

Citizenship.—All persons born in the state, or in the other states of Central America, and resident in the territories of Honduras, are recognized as citizens. Foreigners may acquire the rights of citizens by legislative act, but nevertheless shall be entitled to the same protection with citizens from the moment they have declared their intentions to become such before the competent authorities.

The right of suffrage belongs to all citizens over twenty-one years of age, "*but after* 1870 *it shall be limited to such only as may then be able to read and write.*" This right, as well as the title of citizen, is lost by entering foreign employ or by criminal conviction. It is suspended during criminal processes against the person by conviction of fraudulent indebtedness, by notoriously vicious conduct, moral incapacity legally declared, *and by entering domestic service near the person.*

Foreigners become naturalized by holding real estate of a fixed value, by residence of four years, and by marrying in the state. They are obliged to pay taxes in common with the citizens at large, and have the same right to appeal to the courts.

Government and Religion.—The government is popular and representative, and composed of three distinct powers, viz., legislative, executive, and judicial; the first residing in the General Assembly, the second in the President, and the third in the courts. The state recognizes the Apostolic Roman Catholic religion, to the exclusion of the public exercise of all others; but no laws can interfere with the private exercise of other forms of worship, nor with the fullest liberty of conscience.

Elections.—The state is divided into election districts of fifteen thousand inhabitants, each entitled to one deputy; but, pending a census (not yet made), the several departments each elect one senator and two deputies. As there are seven departments, it follows that the legislative body is composed of fourteen deputies, half of whom are elected annually. A deputy must be at least twenty-five years of age, a citizen of the department which elects him, a proprietor to the value of $500, or in the exercise of some profession or art which yields that annual return. The senators are seven in number; they must not be less than thirty years of age, proprietors each to the value of $1000, or licentiates in some of the liberal professions. Three of the seven are elected annually. Eight deputies and five senators constitute a quorum of the Legislature, of which the ordinary sessions are limited to forty days. The Legislature imposes taxes; names, in joint session, the magistrates of the Supreme Court of Justice; grants the annual appropriations; fixes the military contingent; controls the educational system; makes war or peace; ratifies treaties; and has the power of impeaching and trying the executive officers of the state, etc.

The Executive.—The executive power is vested in a President, who must be a native of Central America, a citizen of the state for five years, thirty-two years of age, and a proprietor of real estate to the value of $5000. He must receive an absolute majority of votes; or, in case no candidate receives such majority, the Legislature elects one of the two having the highest number of votes. The President holds his office for four years, and is incapable of being elected to serve for two consecutive terms. He may select his ministers for the various departments of government, who have, *ex officio*, a seat in the Legislature, but are not entitled to vote. His remaining duties and powers are such as usually pertain to a republican executive, including the power of the veto. He is especially empowered to make contracts for colonization, and for the general development of the resources of the state, which are subject to the legislative sanction.

Council of State.—This council is composed of one senator, elected by the General Assembly; one magistrate of the Supreme Court, selected by his associates; the Minister of Domestic Relations; the Treasurer of State; and two citizens, distinguished for their services, who are named by the General Assembly. Their duties are, for the most part, advisatory, but in cases of emergency they may exercise extraordinary powers, subject to the subsequent entire revision of the General Assembly. The necessity of the council results from the difficulties in the way of convening the Legislature in cases requiring prompt action, owing to the delays in communication, and the diffusion of the people over a wide territory.

Judiciary. — The judiciary consists of a Supreme Court of Justice, divided into two sections of three magistrates each, one of which is established in the city of Comayagua, and the other in that of Tegucigalpa. They must be composed of advocates of established reputation, twenty-five years of age, and proprietors to the value of $1000. They are elected, on recommendation of the executive, by the General Assembly, and hold their offices during good behavior. They take cognizance of all causes of a general character, or which may be brought up to them from the inferior or district courts, the attributes of which are set forth with great minuteness and care. All persons accused of crime must be examined within forty-eight hours after their arrest, and the judge must decide upon their detention or liberation within the next twenty-four hours.

No person can be called upon to testify against himself, nor against any of his relatives within four degrees of consanguinity. Capital punishment is abolished.

Departments.—Each department has a chief officer, called "Jefe Politico," named by the executive, who must be twenty-five years of age, and a proprietor in the department where he is named. He is the organ of communication between the central government and the people of the departments for the promulgation and execution of the laws. The officers of every municipality must be able to read and write, and must act in concert with the political chief of the department.

Such are the outlines of the Constitution, under which the internal affairs of the country seem to be well administered. Few cases of importance come before the courts, since all offenses of a petty nature are summarily disposed of by the municipal authorities.

Although the Catholic religion is the only one recognized by the Constitution, it is not to be inferred that the government and people of Honduras are intolerant and bigoted. There is probably no state of Central America in which there prevails so great a degree of liberality in respect of religion. This has resulted from a variety of causes and circumstances connected with the history of the country. Both at the time of the separation from Spain and subsequently, during the struggles attendant on the organization of Central America as a republic, the Church, as represented by the great body of the priesthood, took an active part with the aristocracy and Monarchists against the Liberal or Republican party. The struggle was so protracted and bitter as not only to estrange the great mass of the people from the Church, but to lead them to limit its power and influence by the most decisive measures, when their own success enabled them to do so with safety. The first blow fell upon the Archbishop of Guatemala, who was banished from the republic. The members of all the monkish orders were next expelled; the convents were suppressed, and the estates and revenues pertaining to them confiscated for educational purposes. The sale of indulgences and the promulgation of papal bulls were also prohibited; and finally, in 1832, the laws recognizing the Catholic creed as the faith of the country were not only abrogated, but religious freedom unconditionally decreed by the general Congress. The State of Honduras distinguished itself by action still more decided. It passed a law legitimatizing all the children of priests, entitling them to bear the names and inherit the property of their fathers, and declaring the cohabitation of priests with women to be an evidence of marriage in every legal sense, and subjecting them to all of its responsibilities. It was in vain that bishops and popes rained their bulls of excommunication and malediction upon the republic. A special excommunication, directed against the president, Morazan, was put into a cannon by a common soldier, and fired off in the direction of Rome, in token of contempt and defiance; and, although these extreme measures were naturally followed by a degree of reaction, and in Guatemala, the seat of the old viceregal court and centre of monarchical influences, by the re-establishment of the conventsand priestly censorship of books, still, in the remaining states, the power and prestige of the Church remained permanently broken down; and while it may be conceded that there is much of ignorance and superstition among the people at large, it may at the same time be doubted if, under the general deference to religion among the better classes, there really exists a faith in papal infallibility or a real devotion to the dogmas of the Church; and although the people of Honduras, in common with those of Central America in general, are nominally Catholics, yet, among those capable of reflection or possessed of education, there are more who are destitute of any fixed creed, Rationalists, or, as they are sometimes called, Free-thinkers, than adherents of any form of religion.

Honduras was early established as a bishopric, with its episcopal seat at Truxillo, whence it was removed to Comayagua, where a cathedral was built, and where it still remains. For many years the see had remained vacant, until 1854, when it was filled by the consecration of Señor Don Hippolito Casiano Flores, the present incumbent. Finally, it may be observed that the Church in Honduras is supported only by voluntary contributions and a small annual appropriation on the part of the state. It is without rents or revenues of any kind.

Honduras has two universities; one established in the city of Comayagua, and another in Tegucigalpa. They have nominally professorships of law, medicine, and theology, but, in fact, their course of instruction is little in advance of that of the common schools of the United States, except, perhaps, in the department of languages. In the department of natural sciences, and in those studies of greatest practical importance to the development of the resources of the country, chemistry, engineering, the higher mathematics, they are entirely deficient, and much behind those of Nicaragua, San Salvador, and Guatemala. Indeed, most of what are called educated men in the state have received their instruction in foreign countries or at the institutions just named. Efforts have been made to elevate the character and efficiency of these establishments in Honduras, but they have been too feeble to produce any important change. Still, the fact that they have been rescued from a state of entire suspension, and are not deficient in pupils in the elementary branches of knowledge, gives encouragement for the future, and, with the restoration of peace and the return of national prosperity, there is reason to believe they may become an honor to the country.

The Lancasterian system of education was introduced in Central America during the existence of the Federation, and has been continued, with some modifications, in the various states. The requisite data for estimating the public or common schools of Honduras do not exist, since such few returns from the departments as have been incidentally published in the official paper are confessedly imperfect. On a very liberal estimate, there may be four hundred schools in the state, with an average attendance of twenty-five scholars each, or an aggregate of ten thousand pupils of all classes in a total population of three hundred and fifty thousand. There are no libraries in the state worthy of mention, and, besides the government Gazette, no newspapers. There are several presses, but they throw off little except acrimonious political pamphlets, or hand-bills of a personal character. It follows from these facts that the ignorance of the people at large is profound and melancholy.

There exist no data for calculating either the amount or value of the industrial products of Honduras; none of an authentic character in respect to its commerce, or the revenues derived from duties on imports or from taxes. Upon all these points little can be said which is not purely conjectural. The amount of foreign products consumed in the state is nevertheless considerable, and the exports commensurate in value.

The leading articles of export may be enumerated as follows; but, as I have said, the values are in all cases conjectural, and at best approximate:

Bullion	$400,000
Mahogany and other woods . .	200,000
Cattle	125,000
Hides, sarsaparilla, tobacco, indigo, etc.	400,000
	$1,125,000

The revenues of the state from all sources may be roughly estimated at $250,000. The sale of *aguardiente*, or native rum, is a government *estanca* or monopoly, and yields a considerable annual income to the state.

The currency of Honduras has been much vitiated by the large issue of what is called "*moneda provisional*," or, familiarly, "*cobre*," *i. e.*, copper coin slightly alloyed with silver, and of the denomination of quarter and half dollars. The issue has not at any time been limited by law, and has been going on since 1839, with a corresponding depreciation of value, until now it passes at the rate of twelve dollars of "cobre" for one of "*plata*" or silver. But, notwithstanding the laws upon the subject, made originally with the view of forcing this provisional money into circulation, it has always been rigidly excluded from the northern departments of Gracias, Yoro, and parts of Sta. Barbara and

Olancho, where the people utterly refuse to receive it. It is difficult to say how much of this coin is in circulation, but it may be estimated at $1,000,000 in nominal value, equal to $100,000 in silver. It is but just to observe that the actual government of Honduras is making laudable efforts, by stopping the farther issue of this debased coin, and by a gradual annual redemption, to withdraw it from circulation, and to supply its place by an issue in denomination and standard conforming to that of the United States.

Apart from the "moneda provisional," the *macaco*, or cut money of the old kingdom, a portion of its coinage and that of the Federal Republic, together with American and English coin, make up the bulk of money in circulation. The foreign coins pass at their true valuation, and not, as in New Granada, Nicaragua, and in some other of the South American States, at a nominal advance. As the exports of the state are fully equal to its imports, the little money which is in circulation remains in the state, to answer the limited requirements of its interior trade.

The cattle of Honduras constitute at present its most obvious source of wealth. The comparatively open character of the interior country, and its vast savannas, covered with natural and unfailing meadows, are circumstances eminently favorable for the increase of this kind of property to an indefinite extent; but, for obvious reasons, cattle do not now afford any considerable revenue to the proprietors, since the domestic consumption is small, and the demand in the neighboring states limited in amount. Mr. Baily has suggested the possibility of salting beef in the state, and making it an article of export to the West Indies and other markets, and there seems to be much reason in the suggestion. It may be objected that the high temperature of the country must prove an insuperable difficulty to the success of the experiment; but there are certainly many portions of the interior where the elevation, and consequently cool climate, must obviate this objection, even if it were well founded.

The entire industry of Honduras, it must be confessed, is at a very low ebb. This has been the natural consequence of the condition of the country, both before and after its independence, not less than of the composition of its people.

The narrow colonial system of Spain had the effect to keep many of her American possessions, and especially Central America, entirely excluded from intercourse with the rest of the world. None of the improvements in the arts or in agriculture, which elsewhere were effecting gradual but total revolutions in the industry of nations, were permitted to reach that country. Trade was monopolized by the crown, which equally undertook to regulate the amount of production of the various articles for which these colonies were distinguished. A single example will illustrate the extent to which this jealous and oppressive policy was carried. Early in the eighteenth century, the cultivation of the grape had been introduced upon the northern coast of Honduras with so much success and promise as to attract the attention of the government of Spain, and lead it to fear that the colony might ultimately come to rival the mother country in the production of wine. Orders were consequently issued to the officers of the crown to destroy the vines, which orders were carried into execution. Since that period no farther attempts have been made to introduce the grape, but no doubt exists of the fact that it might be produced in the greatest abundance, and become an element of wealth to the state.

The internal troubles which followed the independence have left the country no opportunity to repair the errors of the previous colonial system, which had so effectually suppressed its industry, and prevented the development of its resources. These commotions deterred foreign enterprise from taking that direction, while they equally debarred the people themselves from making an effective use of the limited means at their own command for their own improvement.

A great and, until remedied, an insuperable obstacle to the development of Honduras, is the want of adequate means of internal communication. The roads, so called, are mere mule-paths, often conducted, to avoid large and rapid streams, over the steepest and roughest mountains, where in places they are so narrow, abrupt, and obstructed, that the stranger recoils in despair of effecting a passage. The loads carried by mules are necessarily light, and the expense of transportation becomes so great as effectually to prohibit the exportation of the more bulky products of the state, except from places near the coast. All articles of importation, also, which can not be packed on mules, require to be transported on the shoulders of men; and the pianos, mirrors, and other foreign articles of bulk and value in use in the larger towns of the interior have all been carried in this manner from the sea-ports—distances varying from sixty to one hundred miles! The requisite machinery for working the mines in a manner adequate to their importance is also excluded for the same reason. But with the opening of a single good road through the state, and especially in the event of the construction of the proposed railway between the seas, these difficulties will be, in a great degree, removed, and industry increase in proportion to the incentive which may be held out for its exercise. The importance of these material considerations is well understood by all the educated portions of the people, and it is but just to say that they are disposed to make use of every means in their power, alike by the encouragement of foreign enterprise, and by an active co-operation on their own part, to hasten the development and secure the prosperity of the state. Liberal in politics and religion, and repelling those prejudices which it has been the effort of demagogues in Mexico and Guatemala to inspire against the United States, they look toward the latter country as the direction from whence their cherished hopes for the future are to be realized. As an evidence of their admiration for its example, and with the view of opening new and more intimate relations with it, the government of Honduras last year commissioned Don José Francisco Barrundia, one of its ablest and most venerated citizens, as envoy and plenipotentiary in the United States—a man who, as one of the most active promoters of the independence of Central America, the author of its Constitution, and at one time its president, was eminently fitted to give weight and character to his mission. His sudden death, on the eve of entering on the discharge of his duties, has justly been regarded in Honduras as a national calamity. There is, nevertheless, good reason to believe that the sentiments and principles which dictated his nomination are still cherished and active, and that the grand objects had in view in his appointment will ultimately be accomplished.

Civilization is harmonious; and there can be no great intellectual, political, or social advancement which is not preceded by a corresponding material progress. This truth has gradually forced itself upon the minds of the reflecting portion of the people of Central America, and they have come to understand that political permutations are powerless to effect the regeneration of the country. They distinctly perceive that the existing elements of population, however important in the aids which they may afford, are yet inadequate to that great end.

It has not always been prudent for them to avow their own convictions in the face of prejudices which are diligently fostered by demagogues for sinister and selfish purposes. The special power conferred upon the President by the Constitution of Honduras, "to conclude contracts for colonization," nevertheless indicates the direction in which the framers of that instrument looked for relief from the difficulties and dangers of their condition. As I have elsewhere intimated, it is only by a judicious system of colonization, which shall ultimately secure the predominance of white blood, at the same time that it shall introduce intelligence, industry, and skill, that the country can hope to achieve peace, prosperity, and greatness. With vast resources, a climate adapted to every caprice, not less than to the products of every zone, and an unrivaled position, it would be a practical denial of the evidences of high design, to doubt the future power and greatness of the hitherto little known, the long-distracted, and, as yet, utterly undeveloped Republic of Honduras.

INTER-OCEANIC RAILWAY.

CHAPTER XIV.

PROPOSED INTER-OCEANIC RAILWAY THROUGH HONDURAS.

"A SHORT and easy passage" between the Atlantic and Pacific Oceans, across the isthmus which connects North with South America, has, for more than three centuries, been a leading object of human ambition and enterprise. It was the hope of finding "el secreto del estrecho," the secret of the strait, which led Columbus to coast along the continent from Honduras to the Orinoco, which carried Magellan to the straits which bear his name, and which animated and sustained Cortez when, followed only by a handful of soldiers, he advanced into the heart of the hostile empire of Mexico, and sent his exploring squadrons into the unknown waters of the great South Sea.*

From the moment, however, when the fact that no natural connection existed between the two oceans became established, the idea of opening an artificial communication began to occupy the minds of men. As early as 1551, three points had been indicated as favorable for this purpose.

* The Emperor Charles V., in 1523, in a letter from Valladolid, enjoins Cortez to search carefully for "the secret of the strait," which should connect the eastern and western shores of New Spain, and shorten, as was then supposed, by two thirds, the voyage from Cadiz to "the land of spices" and the shores of Cathay. In his reply to this letter, Cortez indulges in sanguine hopes of making this grand discovery, "which," he adds, "would make the King of Spain master of so many kingdoms that he might consider himself lord of the world."

I. The Isthmus of Tehuantepec.
II. The Isthmus of Nicaragua.
III. That of Panama and Darien.

Since then, two other lines have been suggested, viz., one from Chiriqui Lagoon, on the Caribbean Sea, to the Gulf of Dulce, on the Pacific, and a second, falling properly within the continent of South America, from the River Atrato, flowing into the Atlantic, to the River Choco, falling into the Pacific.

Of all these, three have been claimed to be fit places for opening a canal between the seas, viz., Nicaragua, Darien, and Atrato. It was once supposed canals might be opened at Tehuantepec and Panama, but since the proper surveys have been made at these points, this idea has been relinquished. The survey recently made at Nicaragua has also shown that the construction of a canal there, although possible, will be attended with unexpectedly great difficulties, and a cost so heavy as to preclude any adequate return on the capital invested. A reconnaisance at Darien, just concluded, has proved the utter impracticability of that line for a canal. The Atrato line remains to be brought to the test of a survey—a test which has proved fatal to many plausible speculations in other instances. But, even if it should be shown that a canal is feasible at that place, its extreme southern position will always be a great obstacle to its success, inasmuch as the principal points in the Pacific with which it is most important to have a means of speedy communication lie in high northern latitudes.

In fact, so far as the United States are concerned, the great desideratum is a route as far to the northward as possible; and whether it be by water or railway, adequate ports on both seas are indispensable requisites. Without these, there can be neither facility nor security of communication; and every mile to the southward of the latitude of New Orleans which any route may lie, adds two miles to the aggregate distance between the Atlantic States and California, Oregon, the Sandwich Islands, and the great centres of Oriental trade which are now opening to our enterprise.

Any route, therefore, which shall best conform to these conditions, viz., a high latitude and good ports, has not only the first claim on the public attention and support, but will, in the end, supersede all others.

And here it may be observed, that when the project of opening an inter-oceanic communication across the Central American Isthmus first began to attract the attention of the world, steam-boats and railways were unknown. Accordingly, no lines were indicated except such as were supposed to have an adaptability for canals; and hence also resulted that predilection, almost amounting to prejudice, with which certain particular lines have continued to be regarded, even since modern discovery has altered the entire nature of the question. The Spaniard designated the Isthmus of Panama and Tehuantepec as probably the only places where a canal could be dug. He was governed in this selection wholly by the consideration which I have named, and to which all other considerations were necessarily subordinate. Had he been acquainted with steam in its application to land-carriage and to navigation, he would never have given those isthmuses a second thought, but would have selected other lines which should combine the great and indispensable conditions to a good and permanent route of transit, viz., good ports, salubrious climate, and advantageous commercial position.

But now, however desirable a water communication

between the seas may be esteemed, it is well known that many of the requirements of trade, and all those of travel and the transmission of intelligence, can be met by railways better than by canals. Their greater adaptation to natural conditions, facility of overcoming physical obstacles, and greater cheapness of construction, also commend them more directly to practical attention.

To the list of proposed routes of inter-oceanic communication already presented, I have now to add another, which has peculiar advantages, and such as must give it a permanent superiority over all others as a means of transit between the seas, and of safe, rapid, and easy communication with the more important commercial centres on the Pacific Ocean. This route lies wholly within the State of Honduras, and has already undergone a close *reconnaisance*, with the results herewith presented.

The proposed line commences at Puerto Caballos, on the Bay of Honduras, in lat. 15° 49′ N., and long. 87° 57′ W., and runs nearly due south, across the continent, to the Bay of Fonseca, on the Pacific, in lat. 13° 21′ N., and long. 87° 35′ W. Its total length from anchorage to anchorage, or from five fathoms of water in Puerto Caballos to five fathoms of water in the Bay of Fonseca, is one hundred and forty-eight geographical, equal to about one hundred and sixty statute miles. Starting at Puerto Caballos, the line pursues a course a little east of south, across the plain of Sula, until it strikes the Rio Ulua, near the town of Santiago. Thence it follows the valley of that river, now called the Humuya, to its very source, in the great plain of Comayagua, a distance of not far from one hundred miles from Puerto Caballos. At the southern extremity of this plain there is a slight elevation, which constitutes the "summit" between the Atlantic and Pacific. Here the sources of the Humuya interlock with those of the Rio Goascoran, which flows through its proper valley into the Gulf of Fonseca.

Two important facts are to be observed in tracing this line:

I. That the valleys of the Humuya and Goascoran, in conjunction with the central plain of Comayagua, *constitute a great transverse valley extending from sea to sea, completely cutting through the chain of the Cordilleras.*

II. That this great transverse valley or natural cut extends due north and south, and permits the location of the proposed road so that, in its whole course, it will scarcely deviate five miles from a right line.

These natural conditions, not less than capacious, safe, and altogether unexceptionable harbors at both extremities, and a country eminently salubrious, distinguish this line as combining the obvious and primary requisites for an adequate and permanent inter-oceanic communication to a degree which has no parallel in any project which has yet been presented to public consideration.

Commencing, then, at Puerto Caballos and proceeding southward, the leading facts connected with the line of the proposed road will appear in their just order.

I. PUERTO CABALLOS.

Puerto Caballos has already been described (*ante*, p. 100), and little need be said here except that it is secure, and that its capacities are adequate to all the requirements of existing or prospective commerce. It was surveyed in 1853 by Lieutenant Jeffers, U. S. N. (see *Chart*), who reported:

"Puerto Caballos is a good harbor, of great capacity, sufficient depth of water, and easy of entrance and exit. Situated at the base of the hills, there are neither marshes nor swamps to affect the healthfulness of the locality, which is sufficiently extensive for the formation of a large city. The lagoon, which is of salt water, and open to the sea, abounds in fish."*

* The evidence of Lieutenant Jeffers is conclusive; but, if confirmation were needed, it might be found in the concurrent testimony of Captain Theodore Lewis, who visited Puerto Caballos in the schooner "George Steers," April, 1854. The following extract is from the log-book of that vessel:

"*Wednesday, April 17th*, 1854. At 10 A.M. got under way with the sea-breeze, weather clear and very pleasant.

"Desirous of seeing the Bay of Puerto Caballos on our passage down the coast, I directed the pilot to steer for it, and at 1 P.M. we rounded the point and entered this capacious harbor. The mouth is about two miles wide from north to south, and the port is about the same depth from east to west. We rounded the point, within one hundred yards of the shore, with not less than ten fathoms of water, and sailed along the northern side of the bay, for the purpose of examining minutely its capacity and depth of water.

"To do full justice to this capacious anchorage, and preclude the possibility of a doubt on the subject, I went myself in the boat with lead and line, and ascertained by a regular chain of soundings the depth of water for over two thirds of the northern portion of the bay.

"In the middle of the bay, or nearly so, I had twelve fathoms at several casts, gradually shoaling as we neared the north shore to ten, nine, eight, seven, six fathoms, and when within about twenty yards of the beach, five fathoms, mud bottom, clear ground. At this time we had entered the bay for about two thirds of the distance from the point which forms its entrance to its head.

"From the most diligent inquiry of many of those who follow the coasting trade, I am informed that westerly gales on this coast at no season amount to any thing.

"Westerly winds on this coast, I am able to say from my own experience and that of others, begin rainy, with an easy breeze gradually veering to the northwest, increasing in strength, and by the time they arrive at N.N.W., blow with great force, at times for forty-eight hours, with but little intermission, and raise a considerable swell. But they quickly subside on the clearing up of the weather, and with the least easting, say one quarter of a point.

"By a reference to the chart, it will be seen that a vessel is completely sheltered, when in five fathoms of water, from any sea that may roll into the bay from the westward, and the sea from this quarter never amounts to any thing of consequence. As an instance: the 'George Steers' was anchored south about three hundred yards from the southeast point of the harbor of Omoa, in three fathoms of water, during several of the hardest westerly gales, and in no case did the water come over the bow or wet the deck of this sharp vessel, or prevent boats from landing on the beach, due east from the pl--- where she was anchored.

From Nature and on Stone by D. C. Hitchcock. Printed by Sarony & Co. N. Y.

PUERTO CABALLOS.

It may be added that the ground around the port is firm, and a considerable part of it cleared and under cultivation. In abundance of good water, and in fertility of soil, the neighborhood of Puerto Caballos offers every condition necessary for the building up and support of a large and flourishing town.

II. PUERTO CABALLOS TO SANTIAGO.

From Puerto Caballos, in order to reach the great and beautiful plain of Sula or Santiago, through which flow the large rivers Chamelicon and Ulua, it is necessary to make a circuit of nearly three miles to turn the eastern end or base of the high mountain chain of Merendon or Omoa, which is a branch of the Cordilleras, and which here finds an abrupt termination.

The plain of Sula forms a great triangle, its base resting on the sea, and extending for upward of fifty miles along the coast, from the outposts of the mountains of Omoa to those of Congrehoy, and its apex extending due south on the line of the proposed road in the direction of Comayagua. (See *ante*, p. 149.) A portion of this plain, to the right or eastward of the Rio Ulua, is flat, and, during high water, subject to overflow. Such, however, is not the case with the western portion of the plain, over which the road will be located. Here the ground is firm, and the streams have all sand or gravel beds. No bottomless marshes, such as those

"With the wind from the N.W. to N., the points from which the hardest gales blow, there is room for three hundred sail of vessels of all classes, from a ship of one hundred and forty guns down to a sloop or *dory*, to ride in perfect security.

"A gentleman resident on this coast, and of great experience in the winds and weather hereabouts, informed me that some time back he was voyaging in a *dory*, when the sky, swell, etc., gave unmistakable evidence of a norther, and compelled him to make Puerto Caballos for security. Here he rode out in perfect safety one of the most furious northers he had ever witnessed.

"THEODORE LEWIS."

which have obstructed the Panama road, are found here, nor, indeed, upon any part of the entire line.

In the opinion of Lieutenant Jeffers, the road, after turning the base of the hills back of Puerto Caballos, can be made perfectly straight to the town of Santiago, where the Ulua is formed by the junction of the rivers Santiago, Blanco, and Humuya. The latter, keeping the direction of the Ulua from north to south, should properly bear the same name. From Puerto Caballos to Santiago there formerly existed a graded road, which may still be followed, although much grown up since the abandonment of the port. The ascent to Santiago is so gentle as to be imperceptible, and the cutting and filling will be so slight as scarcely to deserve mention.

Santiago may be regarded as the head of steamboat navigation on the Ulua, although vessels of light draught, at favorable stages of the water, might ascend much farther. Lieutenant Jeffers, who examined the river minutely, reports that "steamers drawing seven feet may enter the Ulua at all times, and from June to January ascend as far as the junction of the Humuya. Light draught steamers can always ascend to the mouth of the Humuya, and by the Rio Blanco to a point near Yojoa." (For a consideration of the River Ulua and its branches in reference to their capacities and economic values, see *ante*, p. 73.)

III. FROM SANTIAGO, BY VALLEY OF RIO HUMUYA, TO PLAIN OF ESPINO.

From Santiago the line of the road is discretional. It may be located on either bank of the Humuya. A detailed and minute survey can alone determine which bank affords the greater facilities. Lieutenant Jeffers is of opinion that the left, or western bank, is the more favorable. In following the left bank, it will be necessary to bridge the Santiago or Venta, a large and broad stream, requiring a bridge of from five hundred to seven hundred feet in length, and afterward to bridge the Blanco, which is narrow, not exceeding sixty feet in width. If, on the other hand, the Ulua is crossed below the junction of the streams, but one bridge will be necessary. Crossing, however, a larger body of water, it would require to be of more considerable dimensions than that over the Venta.

Taking either bank, the road would pursue essentially the same direction. The plain continues for about ten miles beyond Santiago, where it is contracted by the hills and mountains which border the comparatively narrow valley of the Humuya. From this point the ascent becomes more rapid. The course of the River Humuya, up to the plain of Espino, is direct, and the valley, according to Lieutenant Jeffers, is "formed between hills of from fifty to five hundred feet of altitude, which, in general, come down to the banks of the river, but occasionally recede, and leave strips of level above the reach of inundations. The slopes of these hills are seldom abrupt, and no heavy work will be required at any point. The alternation of cut and fill," he continues, "for the entire distance, is very favorable. The country around is generally broken, but intersected with numerous fertile valleys. This portion is more valuable for grazing than for agricultural purposes. The hills are covered with the pine and oak, and on the borders of the streams exist vast quantities of mahogany, cedar, guanacaste (*Lignum Vitæ*), India-rubber, and other valuable trees."

About midway between Santiago and the plain of Espino, the River Sulaco, descending from the right, unites with the Humuya. This is a considerable stream, draining a broad and fertile valley, and extending in the direction of the rich department of Olancho. The construction of the proposed rail-road would lead not only to the development of the valley of the Sulaco by means of dependent wagon-roads through it, but also bring the rich district of Olancho in close communication with the coast at Puerto Caballos.

The plain of Espino may be said to commence at the town of Ojos de Agua. This town is fifty-five miles (approximately) from Puerto Caballos, and the valley is here elevated nine hundred and thirty-six feet above the sea. The average grade of the proposed road to this point will therefore be seventeen feet to the mile.

IV. PLAIN OF ESPINO TO PLAIN OF COMAYAGUA.

From Ojos de Agua to the point where a transverse range of hills separates the plain of Espino from that of Comayagua, there exist no difficulties whatever to the building of the road. A few bridges over small streams, none requiring to be more than thirty feet water-way, are about the only constructions which will be required. The plain of Espino slopes gently toward the north, and lends its aid in overcoming the summit, without involving any effort of engineering skill. From the upper or southern extremity of this plain there are two ways of reaching the plain of Comayagua, viz.: first, by following the valley of Humuya, which here makes a considerable bend to pass the intervening hills; or, second, by passing these hills on a direct line, over an intermediate summit of about one hundred and fifty feet.

The choice between these two lines will be determined, no doubt, by the choice of a pass over the general summit, at the southern extremity of the plain of Comayagua. If the pass of Guajoca be adopted, then the line of the river will be selected; if that of Rancho Chiquito be chosen, then the line of the road will be carried directly through the hills, and past the city of Comayagua, the capital of the state.

It may be observed that the plain of Espino, sometimes called Maniani, is about twelve miles long by eight broad, and exceedingly beautiful. It is stated that, under the crown, traffic was carried on between Maniani and Puerto Caballos in boats. In later times loaded canoes have descended, and Lieutenant Jeffers went down in a canoe from Ojos de Agua. The current of the stream, however, is rapid, and much obstructed by boulders and rocks, making the navigation both difficult and dangerous.

V. PLAIN OF COMAYAGUA.

The great plain of Comayagua constitutes precisely that feature in the general topography of the country which gives not only practicability, but eminent feasibility to the proposed railway. It is situated in the very centre of the state, midway between the seas, and is about forty miles in its greatest length, by from five to fifteen broad. Its greatest or largest axis is north and south, and nearly coincides with the line of the proposed road. These dimensions are exclusive of the lateral or dependent valleys of the streams, which concentrate themselves in this basin, and form the Rio Humuya. Like the plain of Espino, it slopes gradually to the north, and thus renders the grade of the proposed road to the summit gentle and easy. This plain is the only one in all Central America the longest axis of which coincides with the meridian—a feature which was early remarked by the Spaniards, and which led to the foundation of the city of Comayagua.

"It was intended," says Juarros, the historian of Guatemala, "by means of this place, to obtain *an easy communication between the Atlantic and Pacific;* its situation, being about half way between Puerto Caballos and the Bay of Fonseca, would render it a convenient intermediate depôt. The climate being healthy and the soil fertile, much of the sickness and waste of human life would be prevented, and many of the fatigues and privations avoided that were usually experienced in the journey from Nombre de Dios (Chagres) to Panama."*

The line of the road across the plain of Comayagua is, as I have said, discretional, and will depend upon the summit pass. Should the pass of Rancho Chiquito be fixed upon, the road would pass through the hills separating the plains of Comayagua and Espino, on a nearly right line, and emerge near the city of Comayagua; thence on the right bank of the Humuya to a point near the town of San Antonio, there cross the stream, and proceed on a direct course to the town of Lamani. The plain on the right bank of the Humuya is more broken than on the left, but not to a degree to embarrass the operations of the engineer or constructor.

On the other hand, should the pass of Guajoca be adopted, as I have already said, the road would follow the valley of the river through the hills, a distance of perhaps three miles, enter the plain of Comayagua on the left bank of the river, and traverse the western portion of the plain near, or through the small towns of Lajamini and Ajuterique, the large and flourishing town of Las Piedras, to the village of Tambla. This portion of the plain is wonderfully fertile and favorable

* *History of the Kingdom of Guatemala*, Baily's Translation, p. 331.

for the work. The streams, with a single exception, are small, and exhaustless quarries of blue marble border the line.

It was in the valley of the river, between the hills dividing the two plains, that the surveying party were led to believe, by the representations made to them, the great, if not only, difficulty between the summit and the Atlantic was to be found. There is, however, absolutely no difficulty in the way of a rail-road; in fact, there is room for a dozen roads, at slightly different grades. The hills are high, but not so steep as to preclude cultivation down to the edge of the water, which, in a country of rains, presupposes a declivity not inconvenient for our purposes.

From Ojos de Agua to Lamani and to Tambla is a distance of about forty miles. The elevation of Tambla is one thousand nine hundred and forty-four, and of Lamani two thousand and sixteen feet above the sea. The grade, therefore, from Ojos de Agua to Tambla, the elevation of the latter over the former being one thousand and eight feet, will be twenty-five feet two inches to the mile. To Lamani the distance would be somewhat greater, and the grade slightly heavier, in consequence of the intermediate summit of one hundred and fifty feet between the plains.

From Puerto Caballos to Tambla the distance may be set down at ninety miles, and the average grade twenty-one feet nine inches to the mile.

VI. THE SUMMIT.

By the summit I mean the section between Tambla or Lamani and Rancho Grande, a distance of nearly fifteen miles, the dividing point, or summit proper, being midway between these two places. It is within this section that the principal, I may almost say the only, engineering difficulties on the whole line are to be found. But these are not of a serious nature, nor are they greater than occur on nearly all roads of equal length in all countries. No tunnels nor deep cuttings are required to pass the summit; it may be reached from the north by side cuttings, in a friable sand rock, approaching chalk in appearance and texture, and which yields readily to the pick. It can be cut almost as easily as clay, with the advantage of admitting of vertical walls, and not washing.

The summit may be overcome at two passes, neither of which varies the route materially from a right line, viz., the pass of Rancho Chiquito, followed by the mule-path, and that of Guajoca.

The summit at the former pass is three hundred and ninety-two feet above Lamani, to be overcome in six miles, which gives a grade of sixty-five feet to the mile. From Rancho Chiquito to Rancho Grande the distance is eight miles, and the descent five hundred feet, involving a grade of sixty-two feet six inches to the mile. These are the *maximum* or heaviest grades on the entire road. Nowhere else do they exceed forty feet to the mile.

The pass of Rancho Chiquito is not a rocky summit, abruptly dividing the waters flowing into the great oceans, but a beautiful valley, a savanna or natural meadow, bounded on the east by a parallel range of high mountains, and on the west by a corresponding range of hills. In this meadow, dotted over with cattle, the traveler finds two bright streams, scarcely a hundred yards apart, flowing in opposite directions. One is a source of the Humuya flowing into the Atlantic, the other of the Goascoran falling into the Pacific.

An active spadesman could reverse their directions in a single day.

The pass of Guajoca is lower by one hundred feet than that of Rancho Chiquito. From the village of Tambla to the summit is about seven and a half miles. The grade necessary to reach it would therefore be but forty-seven feet four inches to the mile. From the summit to Rancho Grande is also between seven and eight miles, with a uniform descent of fifty-five feet to the mile.

Like that of Rancho Chiquito, the pass of Guajoca is a broad savanna, in which the sources of the Goascoran and Humuya almost mingle. Upon the north side rises abruptly a high continuous ridge, twelve or fifteen hundred feet in height, which extends exactly parallel to the line of the road, and permits, by means of a side cut, precisely such a grade, in approaching the summit from the north, as the locating engineer may find it best to adopt.

In my own judgment, the pass of Guajoca is greatly preferable, in all respects, to that of Rancho Chiquito. Not only is it one hundred feet lower to start with, but, with an average cutting of thirty feet for a mile, it may be reduced one hundred or one hundred and twenty-five feet more, so that the extreme rise from Tambla shall not exceed three hundred feet. The Valley of Cururu, which the line would follow, is bounded by parallel straight ridges, upon the slopes of which any grade may be selected which may be deemed advisable. That is to say, the grade may be carried over three or eight miles, and the road located with a rise of from forty to one hundred feet per mile, in the discretion of the engineer.

As I have said, the road will follow the Valley of

Cururu to the divide, and thence descend the valley of a small stream, the Carrizal, to Rancho Grande, where the streams descending from the two passes unite and form the Rio Rancho Grande. Should the cut above contemplated be made, the maximum grade *on the entire line of the road* will fall below sixty feet to the mile, and not exceed forty feet for a distance of more than six miles.

VII. VALLEY OF THE GOASCORAN.

After passing the summit, the line of the road will follow the valley of the Rio Goascoran to the plains surrounding the Bay of Fonseca. The grade will be very nearly uniform, although averaging higher than on the northern declivity. The character of the country, and the facilities for the construction of the road, are thus summed up by Lieutenant Jeffers:

"The country is in general of the most favorable character. The line of the road, being traced upon a table on the banks of the river, and beyond the reach of freshets, presents the character of an inclined plane from the summit to the harbor. The amount of cutting and filling will be very small, except in the division on each side of the summit; the curves will be good, and the grades not greater than are to be found upon successful roads. There will be no tunnels required, and very little excavation in rock.

"The elevation to be overcome, to pass the summit at Rancho Chiquito, is twenty-five hundred feet, but when it is considered that there are no descents, *and that it is the total of ascents, and not the elevation of the summit*, that constitutes the expense of working, it will be seen that this is by no means unfavorable.

"South of Goascoran the formations are of limestone, white sandstone, disintegrated quartz, gravel and sand, mixed with lavas and volcanic stones. No cutting of any extent will be necessary in these rocks. At Goascoran there are extensive beds of blue limestone, and in all the streams an immense quantity of large boulders of granite, gneiss, conglomerate, and sandstone. From this point the rock is a white sandstone, sufficiently soft to be quarried with the pick, but hardening and toughening by exposure. Its durability is sufficiently proved by the existence of engraved figures upon the rocks near Aramacina, which are in a good state of preservation, although of a date anterior to the conquest. Excavations can be made at an expense little or no greater than in earth, with the advantage of durability, and no liability to wash. Upon the whole line there is abundance of gravel, sand, lime, and brick-clay.

"At Aramacina the yellow pine appears on the hills, and at San Juan and Aguanqueterique it is to be found of good size and in inexhaustible quantities in the immediate vicinity of the road. The pine attains a size of thirty inches, and from fifty to seventy-five feet of altitude, differing in no respect from the best North Carolina. The oak is also to be found in considerable quantities, as well as many other useful and valuable woods in any desirable abundance.

"The width of the valley is so small, compared with its length, that there are no streams to be crossed between the terminus and the summit having a water-way to exceed thirty feet: the expense in this important item will consequently be exceedingly small. For the construction of bridges there is, nevertheless, abundance of timber on the ground.

"The smaller streams running into the Goascoran

afford a supply of water-power applicable to the running of saw-mills or other machinery."

VIII. BAY OF FONSECA.

The magnificent Bay of Fonseca (see *ante*, p. 92), the western terminus of the proposed road, is, beyond dispute, the finest port, or, rather, "constellation of ports," on the entire Pacific coast of America. It is fifty miles in length by about thirty in average width, perfectly protected, and contains two or three large islands, offering inner ports with ample water, and admirable sites for towns and commercial and manufacturing establishments of all kinds. The three states of San Salvador, Honduras, and Nicaragua touch upon it. Honduras, however, has far the largest front on the bay. The port of La Union, in the subordinate bay of the same name, is the principal port of San Salvador. Its trade last year amounted to something over $500,000, and the revenues to about $100,000. The principal port of Honduras is Amapala, on the island of Tigre. It is a free port, and is rapidly advancing in importance, its population and trade having doubled within the past two years. An American company has erected on the island a large steam saw, planing, and shingle-mill, which is now in active and effective operation. This company is ready to contract for supplying cross-ties and lumber of all kinds for the construction of the Pacific section of the road, and for its various dependent edifices, such as stations, dépôts, etc.

The precise point of termination on the bay will depend upon such considerations as may be disclosed from a careful examination by the engineers, and by other circumstances. The road may be carried to the port of San Lorenzo, at the head of the inner bay of that name, which possesses throughout not less than four fathoms of water. This line would run on dry, firm ground, but would involve a bridge of one hundred feet in length over the Rio Nacaome. By the construction of a short causeway, or one hundred and fifty yards of pile bridging, the road could be conducted upon the large island of Sacate Grande, to a point indicated in the chart, fronting upon a capacious and excellent anchorage. It might even, with some difficulty, be carried across the northern end of that island, and be made to terminate on the island of Tigre by means of a pile bridge a mile and a quarter long, over a strait having but six feet depth of water at low tide.

The road can also be brought, without serious difficulty, to a point on the main land fronting on the Bay of Chismuyo, but here it would be necessary to carry out a wharf of considerable length, while at San Lorenzo, Sacate Grande, and Tigre a wharf or dock of ordinary length would enable the largest steamers to "tie up" beside the dépôts of the company.

The road could readily be made to terminate at La Union; but as this would involve going into another state, without attaining any object beyond what would be equally secured at the other points named, the fact is not of importance beyond showing the great facilities which the bay affords for the work in question.

The chart of the Bay of Fonseca, from the survey made by Sir Edward Belcher, under the instructions of the British government, and published under the authority of the Admiralty, precludes the necessity for any farther account of this remarkable bay, which seems to have been marked out by the Creator as the ultimate centre of the commerce of the Pacific. Salubrious, surrounded by a country of illimitable agricultural resources, and with rich and exhaustless coal, gold, and silver mines inland; abounding in fine fish, including excellent oysters, etc., etc.; in short, possessing all the necessaries for sustaining a large and prosperous population, the Bay of Fonseca is unrivaled in its adaptation for a terminus of a great work of universal utility like the one proposed.

IX. GRADES.

In the construction, but to a still greater degree in the working of railways, the matter of grades is a most important consideration. From the preceding statements, it will be seen that the first fifty miles of the proposed road will have an average grade of seventeen feet to the mile, the next forty miles an average grade of twenty-five feet two inches to the mile. For the division of fifteen miles crossing the summit, the maximum grade, irrespective of probable lessening of grades by a summit cut, will be fifty-five feet to the mile, and that only for a short distance. From thence to the Pacific the maximum grade will not exceed forty-five feet to the mile. The sum total of ascents and descents, from sea to sea, is four thousand seven hundred feet, which gives an average grade of a little over twenty-eight feet to the mile. The results are highly favorable, as will be seen from the following comparison:

TABLE OF MAXIMUM GRADES.

Baltimore and Ohio Road, per mile	. .	116 feet.
Baltimore and Susquehanna,	"	90 "
Boston and Albany,	" . .	89 "
New York and Erie,	"	60 "
Panama (eastern slope),	" . .	53 "

Panama (Pacific slope),	per mile . .	60 feet.
*Tehuantepec (proposed road),	" . .	64 "
Honduras (proposed road),	" . . .	55 "

The one hundred and sixteen feet grade on the Baltimore and Ohio road is *eight and a half miles long;*† that is to say, nine hundred and eighty-six feet of altitude, or nearly one half of the sum total of ascents on the proposed Honduras road, are overcome in this short distance. The sum of ascents and descents on the first, or eastern division of the New York and Erie railway, a distance of seventy-one miles, is three thousand eight hundred and seventy-two feet, an average of fifty-four to the mile, or more than double the average grade of the proposed road. Heavy grades are, of course, objectionable, but the improvements which have been made in locomotive engines enable the engineer to overcome altitudes which have hitherto been deemed impossible to pass.

Hitherto heavy grades have been avoided, at whatever sacrifice, in favor of moderate grades, even when the sum of ascents to be overcome has been the same. In other words, it has been thought that in a road one hundred miles long, leading to a summit of one thousand feet of altitude, an average and uniform grade of ten feet per mile for the entire distance was preferable to eighty miles of level and twenty of a fifty feet per mile grade. But practically, the latter arrangement is said to have been found the best; that is to say, the

* The statement of grades at Tehuantepec is irrespective of half a mile of tunneling.

† "On this grade an engine weighing twenty-four tons, with a traction power of fifteen thousand one hundred and sixty pounds, has ascended with a train of loaded cars, weighing, in the aggregate, exclusive of tender, two hundred and eight tons, at a speed of from six to eight miles the hour. The same engine ascended the same grade with a passenger train of one hundred and eighteen tons at the speed of seventeen miles the hour."

concentration of grades at one point, compensated by an auxiliary power, is generally believed to be most advantageous both as regards cost and time.

How far this principle can be applied advantageously in the line of the proposed road, must be left to the discretion of the engineers to whom its construction may be confided. Fortunately, the nature of the country admits of such discretion. There may be a considerable concentration of grades within ten miles on either side of the summit by approaching it directly; or the road may be located at the bases of the parallel ranges of hills, on lighter and more nearly uniform grades.

By reference to the sectional map (*facing* p. 69), which presents a profile of the line that the proposed road will follow, it will be seen that the disposition of grades is favorable to the general course of travel and traffic, the heaviest grades lying on the side of the Pacific, and the lightest on the side of the Atlantic, from which direction, it may be calculated, three fourths of the freight, and two thirds of the passengers going between the seas, will pass. This is a consideration of no little importance in calculating the economic working of the proposed road.

X. LABOR, MATERIALS, AND CLIMATE.

Nearly all the materials necessary for the construction of the road exist on the line. There are inexhaustible quantities of the finest white and blue marble and sandstone, as also of the best pine, oak, and other varieties of useful timber. The country, with the exception, perhaps, of a narrow belt on the northern coast, is cool and salubrious, and proper for the employment of extra-tropical labor. In this latter respect (that of labor), the proposed line is remarkably favored, for it is probable the amount that may be required for the northern division may be obtained from the mahogany cuttings on the coast. There is probably no equal number of men under the tropics so inured to hard labor and exposure, or so well instructed in precisely the kind of work which will be required, as the mahogany-cutters. They are, furthermore, thoroughly disciplined, and accustomed to that unity of action so necessary to the prosecution of an enterprise like this. They are unsurpassed axemen, and expert in the clearing and grading of roads and construction of bridges.

The truck-roads in the mahogany cutting of the Messrs. Follin, on the Ulua, are often several miles in length, thirty feet in width, carefully leveled, grubbed, and bridged for the passage of loaded trucks drawn by six yoke of oxen. These roads are constructed by *task-work*, at the average rate of about fifty yards per man per day; or say fifty dollars per mile. The pay of these men is fifteen dollars per month* and rations; the latter consisting of a certain amount of flour and a fixed number of pounds of pork per week. Plantains, which grow in the greatest plenty on the coast, are substituted, to a considerable extent, for flour. The huts which the men occupy are constructed on the spot, and are made of poles or canes, covered with palm-leaves, and seldom require more than half a day in building. A hammock swung from one corner to the other, a couple of stones to support the cooking utensils, and the habitation of the workman is complete. He has few artificial wants, and no winter to provide against or to interrupt his labors. All he requires is a covering to protect him from the sun and the rain.

* One half of this is now paid in goods at high rates. If the wages were paid wholly in cash, they would rule considerably lower—say at thirteen dollars.

There is no doubt that the labor requisite to carry the road from the coast to the plains of the interior can all be obtained from this source. In the interior, and on the Pacific section, northern laborers can work with equal facility and less danger from the necessary exposure than in the United States. The greater part of the population of Central America exists on the Pacific coast, and on that division, therefore, a large supply of labor could be relied upon from the States of San Salvador and Nicaragua, and from Honduras itself. Upon this point I am supported by the opinion of Lieutenant Jeffers, who says that on this portion of the line "native labor can be obtained from this (Honduras) and the adjoining states in sufficient quantity; and, at the rate of wages (twenty-five cents per day), it would be very useful. There can, however, be no difficulty in introducing foreign labor, and its employment will be more satisfactory."

After passing the plain of Sula, the country is very open, with frequent savannas. The pine and oak forests are seldom so dense as to prevent the explorer from riding freely in all directions. The location of the road, therefore, for two thirds of its length, will be comparatively easy; and for this distance, also, the cost of clearing and grubbing will be diminished.

Respecting the climate, I can only repeat what I have already written on the subject from the country itself. "I do not believe there is a more healthful, and there certainly is no more agreeable climate in the world than that of Honduras in general. In this respect, the country surpasses the best parts of Italy. The Pacific coast is superior to that of the Atlantic in respect of health, and settlers might establish themselves around the Bay of Fonseca with no more risk than would attend any change of climate. Among temperate, cleanly people, all other circumstances being equal, I have no doubt the average of life would be ten years longer on that coast and in the interior of the country than in New York. In the first place, pulmonary complaints, and that large and fatal class of diseases resulting from colds and sudden changes of temperature, are here nearly or quite unknown. Intermittent fevers are less common than in our Western States, and yield more readily to the usual medicines. They are, after all, pretty much confined to persons of irregular habits, who disregard the precautions necessary to health in any climate. I have, for two years, undergone almost every kind of exposure and fatigue here, yet I have enjoyed uninterrupted good health—far better than I could have hoped to have enjoyed at home under similar circumstances."

The temperature on the line of the road is, of course, highest at its extremities. But the high temperature of the coast does not hold far inland. The modifying influence of the neighboring mountains is felt even before the increased altitude begins to have its natural effect. The temperature of Comayagua may be taken as approximately that of the entire line between the town of San Pedro Sula on the north, and that of Goascoran on the south; that is to say, of about three fourths of the entire line.

During the months of April, May, and June, which are the hottest of the year, the mean temperature, from six o'clock in the morning until the same hour in the evening, was 79° 1′. The highest or maximum point touched by the thermometer during these months was 88°; the lowest, or minimum, 68°; an extreme range of 20°.

The data bearing upon the temperature of the country in general, but more particularly that of the northern and least salubrious portion, have been presented elsewhere. (See *ante*, p. 32.)

XI. RESOURCES ON THE LINE OF ROAD.

Apart from the rich agricultural resources of the country through which the proposed road will pass, embracing every variety of tropical staple—coffee, cochineal, cotton, cocoa, sugar, rice, tobacco, indigo, maize, etc., there are other vast and undeveloped sources of wealth. The valley of the Ulua abounds in valuable and precious woods, and the hills and mountains of the interior contain numberless mines of the precious metals. There is hardly a stream on the Atlantic slope of the Cordilleras which does not carry gold in greater or less quantity. Recent examinations have shown that the sands of particular streams fully equal the placers of California in the extent and value of their yield. The silver mines of the interior, however, are unsurpassed in the amount and richness of their ores; and there is reason to believe, with the intelligence, enterprise, industry, and capital which will inevitably flow into the country with the prosecution of the railway, that Honduras will become, in proportion to its territorial extent, the largest silver-producing country in the world.

In the enumeration of the products of the state hitherto neglected, I may mention sarsaparilla, gum copal, India-rubber, gum arabic, fustic, dragon's-blood, vanilla, Brazil wood, liquid amber, Peruvian bark, quinine, etc., etc. Cattle are numerous in the state, and constitute a considerable part of the wealth of the inhabitants. Hides, therefore, which hardly pay to be carried to the coast on mules, will become an important article of export when new and cheap means of transportation are established.

Altogether, the establishment of regular communication with Honduras, and between its ports and the interior, will open to the world a rich and virgin field for the industrious and enterprising, create new markets for our manufactures, afford additional supplies for our use, and give a corresponding impulse to commerce and trade.

XII. INTERIOR NAVIGATION.

The capacities of the rivers of Honduras, coinciding in their course with the line of the proposed road, for purposes of accessory and general navigation, have been incidentally alluded to in the foregoing paragraphs. As will be seen by the sketch map of the line of the road accompanying these notes, the large river Ulua and the smaller Rio Goascoran run parallel to the projected road. The first may now be navigated by steamers for a distance of upward of sixty miles from its mouth, and to a point within ninety-five miles of the Bay of Fonseca. The latter, with some improvements, may be made to serve a useful purpose in the rafting of timber and the transportation of materials of construction.

In respect to the Rio Ulua, Lieutenant Jeffers observes:

"The mouth of the River Ulua is obstructed by a bar, having at this time but nine feet of water upon it; it may be said to be impassable for sailing vessels, as the outset is so strong that a fresh breeze is required to enable them to stem the current, and with a fresh breeze the sea is very heavy. Steamers drawing seven feet may enter at all times, and, from June to January, ascend as far as the junction of the Humuya.

"At any time between March and December, ships may, and do, anchor off the mouth of the Ulua, loading mahogany. There is, however, a cove about one mile to the westward, where a landing may be better effected, and at all times except during the continuance of the northers. From this landing to the river the distance is but about two hundred and fifty yards, and a light-draught steamer can, from this point, always ascend to the mouth of the Humuya, or, by the Rio Blanco, to a point near Yojoa.

"The Ulua can be used as accessory, and in the construction of the road may be of essential service; it can be navigated by a light-draught steamer at all seasons as far as the junction of the rivers, and the Humuya, for several months, as far as the mouth of the Sulaco, but beyond that point the river can not be made of service except in rafting down timber. The numerous rapids, sudden rise and temporary duration of the floods, and the character of the bottom, composed entirely of sharp rocks, forbid all hopes of improvement in the upper part of the river."

The Venta or Santiago River, which is the largest tributary of the Ulua, and which reaches into the rich departments of Santa Barbara and Gracias, can be navigated to some extent, as it is also possible the Chamelicon may be, at certain stages of the water. At any rate, the valleys of these streams offer advantageous means of communication with the departments above named, by improved cart or plank roads, for the construction of which all requisite materials are abundant on the spot.

Lieutenant Jeffers says of the Rio Goascoran:

"The Goascoran may be made available as a means of transport in the winter, or, rather, rainy season, and with some improvements, at *all* seasons. The mouth of this stream is obstructed by a sand-bar, but may be entered on the tide at a quarter flood: this bar may be removed by dredging. Above these are obstructions, caused by natural dams of large boulders: by removing these boulders from the centre of the river, we can create a series of ponds and sluices, forming a slack-water navigation as far as Caridad, probably to San Juan. For the purpose of rafting timber from above, should it be required, and transporting materials in boats, the river will be very serviceable."

Notwithstanding the facilities which the Ulua and other rivers may offer for navigation, it is not the purpose of the company to use them except as accessories in the construction of the road, in which respect they will be of great value. Frequent transhipments are inadmissible in any route of inter-oceanic communication looking to permanence.

XIII. SUMMARY OF THE CHARTER.

A charter for the construction of the proposed road was signed by Señors Don Leon Alvarado and Don Justo S. Rodas as commissioners of Honduras, and Mr. E. G. Squier as commissioner of the "Honduras Inter-oceanic Railway Company," on the 23d of June, 1853, which was subsequently ratified by the Legislature of Honduras, and proclaimed by the president of that republic, April 28th, 1854. It is far more liberal in its provisions than any charter ever conceded for any similar purpose, and, moreover, places the relations between the company and the state on a basis so plain and simple, and, withal, so mutually advantageous, as almost to preclude the possibility of difficulty or misunderstanding arising between them. The following is a rapid summary of its provisions:

Section I. concedes to the company the exclusive right for an inter-oceanic communication, by water or railway, through the territories of Honduras, and gives to the company all the lands and natural materials necessary for the purpose. Eight years from the date of the ratification of the contract are conceded for the completion of the work, with privilege of extension in case of interruption from natural or unforeseen causes. The charter is for *seventy years* from the completion of the work proposed, at the end of which time the state may purchase the road at a fair valuation, or extend the charter, in its discretion.

Section II. provides that the company shall have free passage over all lands, public or private, and concedes to the company a space of two hundred yards on each side of the line of the road; free use of all timber, stone, or other natural materials; free use of all the rivers and harbors of the state; and free introduction of all machines, instruments, provisions, and other materials for the construction and use of the road. Native laborers employed on the road are exempt from civil or military service. The company has the right to constitute itself a stock company, etc., and all of its rights, interests, and property are permanently exempt from taxation and charge on the part of the state.

Section III. provides that the company shall pay to the state the sum of one dollar for each through passenger over ten years of age. The company will receive the labor of convicts from the state on equitable terms, and agrees to fix the rates for interior transit and trade on the lowest terms consistent with its interests.

Section IV. provides that the citizens of the United States, and of all nations at peace with Honduras, shall pass over the route free of all taxes and charges, and without the requisition of passports. All goods and merchandise, *in transitu*, shall also pass free of charges on the part of the state, with the exception of a nominal sum for registry, to be paid by the company. Baggage of passengers to pass without examination or charge of any kind.

Section V. makes a gift to the company of four thousand caballerias of land, which, as the caballeria is fixed by law at one hundred and sixty acres, equals six hundred and forty thousand acres, or one thousand square miles. The company has also the exclusive right to purchase and locate, on the line of the road or elsewhere, an additional five thousand caballerias (eight hundred thousand acres), at twelve and a half cents the acre, payable in the stock of the company at par. All persons settling on the lands of the company are entitled to all the rights and privileges of native-born citizens of the state, and are exempt for ten years from all kinds of taxes, and all civil or military service, except with their own consent.

Section VI. stipulates that the ports at the extremities of the road shall be *free ports*. A commission of five persons, two named by the company and two by the state, who shall jointly elect a fifth, to constitute a "Tribunal of Reference," to frame all the necessary rules and regulations for carrying out the charter in its letter and spirit, and to decide finally and without appeal all disputes which may arise between the state and company. The government of Honduras to open negotiations with the leading maritime nations for the guarantee of the perpetual neutrality of the proposed route, in accordance with the Convention of Washington, July 5, 1850.* The company to have the

* *Extract from a Convention between the United States and Great Britain, signed April* 19, 1850; *ratified and proclaimed July* 5, 1850.

ARTICLE VIII. The governments of the United States and Great Britain having not only desired, in entering into this convention, to accomplish a particular object, but also to establish a general principle, they hereby agree to extend their protection by treaty stipulation to any other practicable communications, whether by canal or railway, across the isthmus which connects North with South America, and especially to the inter-oceanic communications, should the same prove to be practicable, whether by canal or railway, which are now proposed to be established by the way of the Tehuantepec or Panama. In granting, however, their protection to any such canals or railways as are by this article specified, it is always understood by the United States and Great Britiain that the parties constructing or owning the same shall impose no other charges or conditions of traffic thereupon than the aforesaid governments shall approve of as just and equitable; and that the said canals or railways, being open to the citizens of the United States and Great Britain on equal terms, shall also be open on like terms to the citizens and subjects of right to construct magnetic telegraphs. The government gives a bounty of fifty acres of land to each unmarried, and of seventy-five acres to each married laborer, who shall come to Honduras to work on the road, and who shall declare his intention to become a citizen.

In addition to this, the railway company, under the supplementary title of "*Honduras Steam-ship and Navigation Company*," enjoys the privilege of "ingress, egress, and passage to, from, and through the harbors, rivers, and waters of the state, free of all duties and charges of every kind."

XIV. COMPARISON OF THE ISTHMUS ROUTES IN RESPECT OF DISTANCE.

Time, not *distance*, is the true measure of the relations between places.

The saving of time, of course, depends more or less on the distance to be traversed, and hence a shortening of distance must always be an important element in calculating the advantages of the respective routes which have been proposed between the Atlantic States and California. But this is only one element. Good ports, where vessels may embark and disembark their freight and passengers with rapidity, at proper wharves, instead of through the means of small boats and lighters, is another important element to be considered, not only in respect of economy of time, but in respect also of convenience, cost, and security. Another element is the possession of easily accessible ports, and a general sailing course free from opposing periodical winds, and other similar detaining and obstructing causes. And still another element, and one of primary import-

every other state which is willing to grant thereto such protection as the United States and Great Britain engage to afford.

ance, is the avoidance of harassing delays resulting from frequent transhipments. These not only consume time, but are fruitful in annoyance, a source of constant dread to the traveler, and, I repeat, wholly "inadmissible in any route of inter-oceanic communication looking to permanence."

The proposed route *via* Honduras may therefore claim, in respect not only of distance, but in freedom from detentions and delays resulting from bad ports, adverse winds, and frequent changes, a clear and emphatic superiority over all routes which have been proposed across the Central American Isthmus. In respect of sailing distances, the following letter from Lieutenant MAURY must be received as conclusive:

"NATIONAL OBSERVATORY, Washington, June 26, 1854.

"E. G. SQUIER, ESQ.:

"SIR,—In reply to your note requesting to know the sailing distance from New York to San Francisco, *via* the various isthmus routes:

"You are aware that these distances can not be accurately stated, unless from more accurate charts than we now have. I suppose you do not want the distances stated except from port to port, exclusive of the distance to be run after the vessel crosses the bar or enters the harbor. I therefore send you the shortest steaming distance from port to port in round numbers.

From New York to San Francisco, *via* Panama,	5200 miles.
" " " " " Nicaragua,	4700 "
" " " " " Honduras,	4200 "
" " " Vera Cruz and Tehuantepec,	4200 "

"No allowance is made in the above for the distance across the continent. Respectfully yours,

"M. F. MAURY."

The distance across the continent at Panama is fifty-four statute miles, at Nicaragua one hundred and eighty-four, at Honduras one hundred and sixty, at Tehuantepec one hundred and eighty-six. Accordingly, the total distances are, from New York to San Francisco, *via* Panama, five thousand two hundred and fifty-four miles; Nicaragua, four thousand eight hundred and eighty-four miles; Honduras, four thousand three hundred and sixty miles; Tehuantepec, four thousand three hundred and eighty-six miles.

But it is also to be considered that the *shortest steaming course* is not always a practicable one. Thus, after passing the Capes of Florida, steamers can not safely steer direct for Vera Cruz. They must keep well to the northward, to avoid the dangerous reefs, shoals, and low islands which embarrass the great Campeachy Bank to the north of Yucatan. This *detour* augments the sailing distance between New York and Tehuantepec several hundred miles, and thus increases the relative superiority, in respect of distance, of the proposed Honduras route.

XV. COMPARISON OF ROUTES IN RESPECT OF PORTS.*

In order to institute a fair and impartial comparison between the various inter-oceanic routes proposed or in actual operation, we must first inquire what are the purposes of each. Taking them in their order, Tehuantepec, Honduras, and Panama are claimed to be proper and feasible points for railways; Nicaragua and Atrato for canal communications. We here leave out

* "It is necessary to remark farther, that, irrespective of climate and political considerations, there is one chief requisite, one main point to be insisted on, in connection with any route or line intended to be available for general utility, without which permanent success will be impossible. This indispensable adjunct is a *good port.* Without such a place of resort at *each end* of any canal or railway, easy of access, and sheltered at all times, shipping could not effect objects securely, and in definite times. Delay, expense, and risk must be the consequence of using a route unprovided with adequate harborage."—Capt. FITZROY, R. N., *Journal Royal Geographical Soc.*, vol. xx., p. 165.

the Chiriqui and Darien lines as exploded and impracticable. Nicaragua is simply impracticable for a railway; that is to say, for a continuous road leading from one ocean to the other. A road built up the valley of the San Juan River would require to be constructed through an unbroken wilderness, and, moreover, to be one hundred and nineteen miles in length. And even then a change to boats would become requisite to pass the lake (which can not be turned), with a resumption of land travel on the other side. The geographical position of the Atrato line, to say nothing of its proximity to the railway at Panama, renders a railway there unnecessary and valueless. The question of ports, then, as regards Atrato and Nicaragua, is of no consequence. It may nevertheless be observed that both are exceedingly defective in this respect. The present line of transit at Nicaragua has absolutely no port on the Pacific; and an adequate terminus on that sea can not be found short of the port of Realejo, a distance of upward of three hundred miles from San Juan de Nicaragua. The Atrato route labors under the same disadvantage on the Pacific, Cupica being small and exposed to the southwest; while on the Atlantic, the Atrato River has a bad bar, with only five feet of water.

Nor is it necessary, in this connection, to give much consideration to Panama. Its Atlantic terminus is not less than seven degrees of latitude to the southward of the corresponding terminus of the Honduras line, while its Pacific terminus is not less than four days' sailing distance below the latitude of the corresponding terminus of the Honduras line. Supposing all other circumstances to be equal, the saving in distance of the Honduras over the Panama line excludes the latter from any claim to a comparison. But Panama has bad ports on both sides; bad in respect to climate, and, if not absolutely unsafe on the Atlantic, certainly inadequate; while on the Pacific, the Bay of Panama, where vessels are compelled to lie several miles from the shore, can hardly be called a port. The time lost in effecting embarkation and disembarkation there, by means of small boats, to say nothing of the expense, annoyance, and danger, must always be a serious drawback.

It follows, then, that the routes which, in respect of latitude and consequent saving of distance, can bear a comparison with each other, are those of Honduras and Tehuantepec. In this respect, these are the only ones which meet the obvious requirements of commerce and travel. And here the general reader must bear in mind, that above lat. 14° N., the continent does not run north and south, but nearly east and west. The proposed northern terminus at Tehuantepec is in lat. 18° 8′ N.; that of Honduras in lat. 15° 49′ N.; the southern termini in lat. 16° 12′ and 13° 21′ N. respectively. The absolute difference in latitude is therefore but 2° 19′; and although Tehuantepec is in long. 94° 30′ W., and Honduras in long. 87° 57′ W., it is immaterial, in the voyage from New York to San Francisco, for instance, whether the *westing* is made in the Gulf of Mexico or the Pacific, except, perhaps, that the Pacific is a smoother sea than the Gulf, and that it could be made in the first quicker and more easily than in the second.

It would appear, then, that Tehuantepec has an absolute advantage over Honduras of 2° 19′ of latitude, equal to 4° 38′, or two hundred and seventy nautical miles in the whole voyage, as between New York and San Francisco. But this *apparent advantage* is lost in consequence of certain difficulties in the navigation of the Gulf of Mexico, and of certain requirements in the only charter for a railway at Tehuantepec which may be regarded as having any vitality for the present, viz., that of "la Compaña Mista." This charter provides that the steamers running in connection with the proposed Tehuantepec road must sail to Vera Cruz, and that there all passengers and freight must be transhipped in Mexican bottoms before going to the Isthmus.*

Vera Cruz is established as the only port of entry on the Gulf. Apart from all the detention which this transhipment involves—the fatality of the climate of Vera Cruz, and the insecurity of its harbor,† all steamers from the Atlantic states must give the great bank of Campeachy, with its thousand reefs and low islands, a wide berth, by keeping far to the northward. They can not, as I have already said, safely steer in a right line from the Straits of Florida for Vera Cruz, but must make a circuit to avoid the Alacranes and other dangerous impediments to navigation to the north of Yucatan, upon which the British West India Steamship Company lost a number of their best vessels, until strict orders were given to have them keep well to the northward of the Campeachy bank.

Calculating the deflection from this cause, and the increase of distance involved in going to Vera Cruz, not only is the apparent advantage in favor of Tehuantepec over Honduras lost, but the aggregate distance

* "ART. III. The company is obliged to establish a line of steamers, sufficient for the service of the route of communication, under the Mexican flag, in accordance with the laws of the country, to run between Vera Cruz and the point in the Rio Coatzacoalcos where the rail-road shall commence."

† "Vera Cruz does not even deserve the name of *roadstead;* it is a disagreeable anchorage among shallows."—HUMBOLDT, *New Spain*, vol. i., p. 2.

is so much increased as to give *an absolute advantage to Honduras of more than two hundred miles.*

I now come to the question of ports, upon which Captain Fitzroy, in the quotation at the head of this section, has laid a stress which all who have investigated the subject are aware is not too emphatic. To avoid any imputation of unfairness in this matter, which is necessarily one of testimony, I shall content myself with quoting from authorities not open to suspicion, whose impartiality can not be called in question, and who establish the fact that Tehuantepec has no ports worthy of the name on either sea. In respect to the Pacific terminus:

"The port of Tehuantepec is not more favored by nature [than the coast of Nicaragua]. It gives its name to the hurricanes which blow from the N.W., and which prevent vessels from landing at the small ports of Sabinas and *Ventosa*" [*Anglice*, "the windy"].*

Referring to Tehuantepec, M. Michel Chevalier observes, in his work on Inter-oceanic Communications, that

"It would be necessary to remedy, if possible, the *want of a moderately convenient port* on the Pacific. Tehuantepec scarcely deserves the name of roadstead. The sea recedes day by day from its shores; the anchorage yearly becomes worse; the sand deposited by the Chimalapa increases the height and extent of the bars of sand at the entrance of the first lake, in the second, and thence into the sea, and already is Tehuantepec accessible to small vessels only."

In fact, the plan of employing what is called the port of Tehuantepec was formally abandoned by the engineers of the Tehuantepec survey. They propose to create an artificial port at Ventosa by the construction of a "breakwater two thousand feet long." The

* Humboldt, "New Spain," vol. i., p. 20.

difficulty, not to say impossibility, of constructing artificial harbors to meet any important purpose, is too obvious and well understood to require remark.

In one word, Tehuantepec has absolutely no port on the Pacific. It is even less favored on the Atlantic; nor is it claimed that there is here the *remotest resemblance* of what is understood by a port.

This deficiency is proposed to be supplied by entering the Coatzacoalcos River, which is without shelter at its mouth, and which flows directly into the open sea. It has, moreover, a bar, which in bad weather would be impassable for vessels of a hundred tons. "*At high water, on the full and change, the depth of water on the bar is about thirteen feet, and falls as low as eleven feet,*" is the confession of those who have identified themselves with the Tehuantepec project.* Upon this point the authority of General Orbegoso, who was first employed by Señor Garay to examine the Isthmus of Tehuantepec, can not be accepted. He reported twenty-one to twenty-three feet on the bar, while the engineers of the Tehuantepec Company found but from eleven to thirteen, and Commodore Perry but twelve feet. Señor Moro seems to have been of the same school. He reported twenty-three feet on the bar at Boca Barra, at Tehuantepec, where the authority of the Tehuantepec report found but eight feet! Nevertheless, proceeding upon the erroneous assumption that the Coatzacoalcos carries eighteen feet at its bar instead of ten to thirteen, Captain Liot, Superintendent of the British West India steamers, observes:

"The soundings given in the preceding remarks (even those most favorable to the Tehuantepec project) are evidently insufficient for large vessels with full cargoes; for, although the prin-

* *The Isthmus of Tehuantepec, being the Results of a Survey, etc.*, p. 115.

cipal channel of the bar were always to maintain a depth of eighteen feet (as Señor Orbegoso asserts it does, but afterward admits that, 'under extraordinary circumstances, perhaps it does not'), how is a ship of six hundred tons burden, for instance (drawing eighteen feet of water, at least), to pass it? If there were much swell on the bar, it would be perilous for vessels of even fifteen feet draught to attempt it. Thus, then, this projected ship-canal would avail only for vessels of and under three hundred tons burden, and, in the seasons of 'norths,' great risk would attend their approach to that part of the coast where there is neither port nor shelter nearer than Vera Cruz (one hundred and twenty miles upon a northwest bearing from the bar of the Coatzacoalcos); and, during 'norths,' the land thereabout is not only a 'dead lee shore,' but it forms a perfect '*cul de sac*,' out of which sailing vessels could not escape under canvas except by risking the passage of the bar (which shifts), and that they would scarcely dare without a pilot; during a hard north, moreover, the surf on the coast is so heavy that pilots are unable to 'board' vessels, whatever their danger and distress may be."*

Evidence to this effect, but even more emphatic in language, might be accumulated to an indefinite extent.†

* "Considerations upon the question of communication between the Atlantic and Pacific Oceans, by W. B. Liot," etc., p. 8.

† Colonel ABERT, chief of the topographical bureau of the United States, in a review of the transits published by Congress, observes:

"The gulf-bar can not be considered as affording more than twelve feet of water. *Upon the Pacific side there is no harbor*. . . . Tehuantepec Bay is represented as shoal and much exposed, dangerous, and subject to frequent tempests."

Commodore SHUBRICK, commanding the Pacific squadron, in a letter to the Secretary of the Navy, dated October 7, 1847, says:

"There is, I understand, anchorage in the Bay of Tehuantepec, but all accounts agree with the letters of Mr. Forbes in describing it as exceedingly boisterous. Captain Hall says the hardest gales he ever experienced were in that bay, and the Spanish call it Ventosa."

Again, Mr. J. H. ALEXANDER, in a communication on the subject to the special Congress committee:

"What was said just now as to the defects of the harbor of San Juan del Sur, in connection with the Nicaragua route, applies also to the consideration of another, which has attracted much attention—I mean that over the Isthmus of Tehuantepec. . . In regard to the approaches on either side, Nature has been unkind;

As has already been observed, it has been proposed to remedy the deficiency of a port on the Pacific by the construction of an artificial harbor. To this end, it is designed to carry out a breakwater two thousand

and Ventosa Bay, on the Pacific, is, in its very name ('the windy'), an apt expression of the character of the roadstead; while, on the Coatzacoalcos side, there is nothing to protect the entrance of the river from the northers of the Gulf of Mexico."—J. H. ALEXANDER, *Congressional Report, No.* 145, 1849, p. 44.

Lieutenant-colonel GEORGE W. HUGHES, of the United States Topographical Engineers, in a letter to the Secretary of State on the subject of "Inter-marine Communications," sums up his account of Tehuantepec in the following words:

"One most serious objection to any communication across this isthmus for great commercial purposes is to be found in the want of safe and capacious harbors at either terminus. At the mouth of the Coatzacoalcos there is but twelve and a halt feet of water at low tide, and it is exposed to the full force of the northers which prevail from November till April. *I have seen thirty ships stranded in a single norther in the month of March.* It may be said that the bar may be removed, and an artificial harbor constructed at the mouth of the river. There is probably no more difficult problem in the system of engineering than the execution of such works under the best of circumstances; but I am far from asserting that skill and *money* may not accomplish them. The mouth of the Coatzacoalcos is peculiarly ill adapted to such improvements, which would scarcely be inferior in magnitude to the harbor of Cherbourg, and would assuredly require the munificence and resources of a Louis XIV. for their execution. The bar, created by the action of a certain natural law, would, if removed, be immediately re-formed by the same cause to which it owes its origin, unless that cause should be so modified as to direct elsewhere the deposition of earthy matter; and, in the present case, the question would be farther complicated by the silting up of the artificial harbor, if one should be built. Supposing that such a harbor should be constructed, it would still be liable to the objection of the difficulty and danger of access, especially for sail vessels, in the season of the northers. . . . The whole shore of Tehuantepec is subject to the visitation of terrific hurricanes (which take their name from the isthmus), sweeping with resistless fury along this inhospitable coast, where the tempest-tossed mariner seeks in vain for a harbor of refuge, even for the smallest class of sea-going vessels. For this there seems to be no remedy; the genius of man can not control the storms, and nature is constantly interposing new physical difficulties in the way of navigation."

Mr. PITMAN, in his work on the Practicability of an Inter-oceanic Communication (p. 204), arrives at a precisely similar conclusion:

"The prevailing weight of all extant authority shows that the mouth of the River Coatzacoalcos is not a sufficiently good port; that there is not a port at the mouth of the River Tehuantepec capable of receiving ships of considerable tonnage, and that there is no means of making the present port better. . . . From all these considerations, in addition to the before-mentioned reasons, it seems to be an unavoidable conclusion that the proposed route is *unsafe*, if not impracticable, for a ship navigation that would be adequate to extensive commerce."

feet long, to a depth of thirty-six feet. It is only necessary to look at the annual Congressional appropriations for breakwaters on our own coast, apart from their original cost, and to consider their comparative inadequacy, in order to estimate the practical value of this proposition.

The official survey of the entrance of the Rio Coatzacoalcos by Commodore Perry, published by the government, shows but twelve feet of water on the bar in a channel but one hundred and fifty feet wide. Outside of the channel the water shoals to eleven, ten, and nine feet.

The vessels which have been most largely employed in the California transit are the Ohio, Georgia, Illinois, etc., each having a capacity of upward of three thousand tons. The Falcon, one of the smallest of the ocean-going steamers, carries seven hundred and fifty tons, and draws fifteen feet of water, *or three feet more than the total depth of water on the Coatzacoalcos bar!* Tehuantepec, therefore, lacks the essential requisite of good ports: it has none worthy of the name, or capable of meeting the ordinary conditions of an interoceanic transit, on either sea. It would be difficult, if not impossible, to find in the Gulf of Mexico, or any where else on the whole Atlantic coast of America, a more dangerous point, or one less suited for a terminus of a route of communication across the continent than Tehuantepec. The northers, sweeping down the great valley of the Mississippi, have here their greatest force and influence; and, as observed by Captain Liot, no steamer or other vessel of ordinary sea-draught could cross the Coatzacoalcos bar during their prevalence, which is for six months in the year, from September to March. Ordinary waves are five or six feet from trough to crest, and with a moderate wind on shore, in conflict with the current of the river, the sea would break on the bar. Deducted from the total depth, no sufficient depth of water remains to float a vessel of a size and draught proper to venture into the open sea.

In respect to the climate of Tehuantepec, Señor Moro mentions that he had frequently seen the thermometer at Tehuantepec stand at 92° Fahr. at seven o'clock in the morning. The vomito (yellow fever), it is notorious, prevails along the whole coast of Mexico from Vera Cruz to Campeachy.

XVI. COMPARISON OF ROUTES IN RESPECT OF SAFETY.

In fixing upon a permanent route of inter-oceanic communication in this age of scientific research and discovery, we are called upon to take into consideration not only the more obvious and palpable conditions requisite to the success of such an enterprise, but the incidental circumstances which may affect it. Within a few years attention has been directed to winds and currents in their influences on navigation and commerce, and their careful investigation has already led to important results, which are practically exemplified in enabling vessels to make their voyages with increased rapidity and safety. The aggregate of saving in time, property, and life, more valuable than all, is but inadequately comprehended by the public.

Now, in making the voyage to the Central American Isthmus, vessels are not only obliged to traverse more than one thousand miles of the waters of the Atlantic, the most turbulent of oceans, but, in order to avoid the currents of the Gulf Stream, to pass to the windward, or eastward, of Cuba. The outward, and often the return track of the Panama and Nicaragua steamers is between Cuba and San Domingo, and of course to the eastward or outside of Jamaica.

As a consequence, no sooner do they pass from the stormy Atlantic than they enter precisely that part of the Caribbean Sea most frequently swept by hurricanes. The two great centres of these terrible elemental visitations are the West Indies and the China Sea. Beyond these limits they are of comparatively rare occurrence.

The accompanying chart, copied from the Standard Physical Atlas of Professor Johnston, shows the gen-

eral course of the West India hurricanes, and the subjoined table exhibits the date, and, so far as known, the range of the principal hurricanes which have occurred in the West Indies during the past one hundred and fifty years. From these it will be seen that the West India hurricanes commence near the Leeward Islands, sweep toward the northwest, taking Jamaica and Santo Domingo in their course, and after reaching the Gulf Stream, are deflected in the direction

CHRONOLOGICAL TABLE OF THE PRINCIPAL HURRICANES WHICH HAVE OCCURRED IN THE WEST INDIES WITHIN 150 YEARS.

Date of Occurrence.	Localities visited.	Date of Occurrence.	Localities visited.
1675, Aug. 31.	Barbadoes.	1807, October 14.	Between Jamaica and Santa Marta.
1681.	Antigua.	1809, August 3.	Porto Rico and St. Domingo.
1707.	Antigua.	1812, August 14.	Porto Rico and St. Domingo.
1712, Aug. 28.	Jamaica.	1812, October 12.	Jamaica.
1722, Aug. 28.	Jamaica.	1813, August 1.	Jamaica.
1726, Oct. 22.	Jamaica.	1815, Oct. 18 and 19.	Jamaica.
1740.	Antigua.	1818, Sept. 10 to 12.	Cayman Island and Campeche.
1744, Oct. 20.	Jamaica.	1818, Sept. 19.	Altevala, St. Domingo.
1751, Sept. 2.	Jamaica.	1818, Sept. 21.	Barbadoes and Dominica.
1766, Aug. 13.	St. Domingo.	1818, Sept. 22 to 25.	Windward of Antigua.
1772.	Antigua.	1818, October 7.	Port Royal, Jamaica.
1780, Oct. 3.	Savanna-la-Mar (Jamaica), (XI.).*	1819.	Barbadoes.
1780, Oct. 10.	Barbadoes, Martinique, Porto Rico,	1821, Sept. 1.	Bahamas, Carolina, Massachusetts, etc. (VIII.).
	Hayti, Bermuda (XII.).	1827, August 17.	St. Martin and St. Thomas (III.).
1781, Aug. 1.	Jamaica.	1830, August 12.	St. Thomas (VI.).
1784, July 30.	Jamaica.	1830, August 22.	On the north of the Bahamas (IX.).
1785, Aug. 27.	Jamaica.	1830, Sept. 29.	On the north side of the Caribbee Isl'ds (VII.).
1786, Oct. 20.	Jamaica.	1831, June 23.	Trinidad, Tobago, and Granada (I.).
1791, Oct. 20.	Jamaica.	1831, August 10.	Barbadoes (II.).
1792.	Antigua.	1835, August 12.	Antigua, Nevis, St. Kitts, St. Thomas (V.).
1795, Aug. 1.		1835, Sept. 3.	Barbadoes.
1804, Sept. 3.	Antigua, etc. (IV.).	1835, July 10.	Barbadoes, St. Vincent, St. Lucia.
1804, Sept. 19.	Bahamas.	1837, July 26.	Barbadoes, etc. (XIII.).
1805, July 25.	On the north side of the Bahamas.	1837, August 2.	Antigua, St. Thomas, etc. (XIV.).
1806, Sept.	In the neighb'd of the Bahamas.	1837, Aug. 16 to 25.	North side of Little Antilles (XV.).

* The Roman numerals refer to the hurricanes, the courses of which are delineated on the map.

of its current to the northeast. They all, therefore, as well as the few which reach the Gulf of Mexico, cross the track of the Panama and Nicaragua steamers and vessels.

It will be observed that of the fifty hurricanes, the ranges of which are above given, but *two* crossed the route which it is proposed to be followed by the Honduras line, namely, by land to Florida, and thence by steamers to Puerto Caballos.

Again: it is precisely in the line of all communication with Nicaragua and Panama that we find the region of rotatory or Caribbean hurricanes, as laid down by Professor Johnston. These would be wholly avoided by taking the direction of Honduras.

Hence it appears that the proposed route of interoceanic communication by way of Honduras would be almost entirely free from the dangers resulting from hurricanes. When we consider that not far from seventy-five thousand persons now pass annually, by way of the Isthmus, from the Atlantic to the Pacific coasts of the continent, security from dangers of this kind becomes an important consideration. The destruction of a merchant vessel, at the worst, involves but the loss of ten or twelve lives and a few thousand dollars of property, and, however deplorable the catastrophe may be regarded, it sinks into insignificance when compared with the loss of a California packet, with its five or six hundred passengers and millions of treasure. An important result, therefore, is gained if danger from this source be obviated or diminished, for any diminution of the contingencies of travel must be regarded as a public good.

There is still another point in the chart of Professor Johnston which deserves notice in this connection. It is the course of the "Nortes," or dreaded north winds of the Gulf of Mexico, which have been so often productive of the greatest disasters to shipping. These winds sweep down the valley of the Mississippi, and across the Gulf of Mexico, into the bight of the gulf lying between the peninsula of Yucatan and the lower states of Mexico. They blow with more or less constancy, and often with terrible force, for six months of the year, from September to March, on nearly a direct line from the mouth of the Mississippi to the Isthmus of Tehuantepec. As they advance across the gulf their force is augmented, and the contraction of the land contributes to give them a power, at times, almost equaling the hurricanes of the Antilles. This fact, in conjunction with the circumstance that Tehuantepec has absolutely no port at its northern or gulf terminus, in which steamers or sailing vessels could find refuge, demonstrates its utter inadequacy for the great purpose of inter-oceanic communication. The impossibility of any vessel entering the River Coatzacoalcos, which opens due north, over a bar on which the maximum of water never exceeds fourteen feet, during the prevalence of the northers, when the waves run to half that depth, and leave scarcely more than a fathom of water on the bar, is obvious to the dullest apprehension and the most prejudiced mind.

XVII. COST OF CONSTRUCTION AND PROBABLE REVENUES.

I am well aware of the difficulties in the way of calculating the cost of a great work like that proposed across the Isthmus of Honduras, not less before than after an accurate and minute survey has been made; and I am equally well aware that, in presenting any calculations of this kind, the cost of the Panama Railway will be adduced as a conclusive disproval of their accuracy, without a due consideration of the *entirely different natural conditions* of the two isthmuses of Panama and Honduras, and with a neglect of other circumstances of scarcely less importance.

The Panama Railway has a total length of forty-nine miles, and has cost, according to the report of the company presented to the Legislature of New York in January last (1855), in round numbers, $5,000,000. An additional sum of $1,000,000 or $2,000,000 will be required for the construction of an artificial port in the Bay of Panama; but this will be irrespective of the cost of the road proper, from which should be deducted the cost already incurred in creating the "City of Aspinwall" in Navy Bay, and which has certainly not been less than $500,000.

The actual cost of the Panama Railway has therefore been not far from $4,500,000, which, for forty-nine miles, gives an average cost, for building and equipment, of about $91,000 per mile. Assuming one hundred and sixty miles as the total length of the proposed road in Honduras, the same rate per mile would give a total cost of $14,560,000.

But I have no hesitation in claiming, in view of the different and more favorable conditions and circumstances of the case, that the road through Honduras will not cost half as much per mile as has been expended at Panama.

I. The first twenty-three miles of the Panama Railway are through what may be almost called a continuous swamp, which, under the tropics, and within the zone of constant rains, is equivalent to saying that it is through a section of country of the worst possible character for the construction of a railway. For this distance, the greater part of the road had to be built upon piles and crib-work, and subsequently filled in with earth. And it is but just to say, that the difficulties encountered and overcome by the engineers of that road upon this section are such as have never been surmounted elsewhere, in any country, since the introduction of railways. That section of road must stand as a marvel of engineering daring, skill, and perseverance. But its construction has only been effected at a startling cost both of money and of life. It is precisely upon this section that by far the largest amount of the capital of the Panama company has been expended.

No swamps of any kind exist upon the line of the proposed road in Honduras, nor is it believed that one hundred yards of piling will be requisite throughout its extent.

II. According to the Report of the Panama Railway above quoted, "A cutting is encountered at the summit thirteen hundred feet in length and twenty-four feet in greatest depth, containing thirty thousand cubic yards of excavation, which was supposed to be of an easy description, but which was found to be entirely different from any other part of the isthmus, occupying a large force more than two months in overcoming obstacles which were expected to be disposed of in as many weeks."

No cuttings of this kind are necessary upon the line of the proposed road in Honduras.

III. The Isthmus of Panama, narrow, sparsely populated, and "without supplies either of food or materials," rendered it "necessary for the company to send almost every thing from the United States. Even the timber for the cross-ties had to be obtained," continues the report, "from the United States, or from distant parts of New Granada."

By reference to a preceding paragraph (p. 256), it will be seen that every description of wood necessary for constructions on the proposed road in Honduras is found on the spot, or nearly on the spot where it will be needed. Mahogany, lignum-vitæ, cedar, oak, and pine are abundant, and the company of Americans who have established mills on the island of Tigre stand ready to contract for delivering the cross-ties for the entire road at prices below the ruling rates for which they are furnished in the United States.

IV. In respect of labor, the Panama company has encountered many and almost insuperable obstacles. "The workmen," continues the above report, "whether native or foreign, were conveyed to the Isthmus at a cost of from $15 to $50 each. They have been paid at rates far exceeding those given for similar services in the United States, and found in all their provisions, which were mostly sent out, as were also the cooks, from the United States. Sickness," says the engineer-in-chief, "although bearing no proportion to the exaggerated reports which have been circulated, is nevertheless a serious item of expenditure."

Upon the question of labor, so far as it relates to the proposed road through Honduras, nothing need be said in addition to what has been presented in the preceding pages. It can scarcely be doubted that a sufficient supply of the most efficient laborers can be procured for the construction of the northern sections of the road from the mahogany-works of the coast. It is believed, also, that many of the proprietors of these works will be glad to become contractors on the road, as affording them an opportunity of transferring their material, cattle, trucks, etc., etc., from a business which is no longer profitable, to one which holds out the promise of adequate returns. Upon the remaining sections of the road, a large supply of labor can be relied upon from the populous state of San Salvador and from the native population of Honduras. Furthermore, the climate is such as will admit of the comparatively easy and profitable introduction of foreign labor to any extent that may be desirable.

V. It appears from the Panama report that one of the principal causes which delayed the opening of that railway for a period of eighteen months longer than was anticipated "were the unprecedented rains" of 1853–4. Being under the zone of constant precipitation, with a merely nominal dry season, there can be no doubt that much of the heavy expenditure on the road, delay in its execution, and destruction of life with which its prosecution was attended, resulted from this cause. In this respect, Honduras offers a most decided and favorable contrast.

Again, Honduras affords an abundant supply of cattle broken to the yoke for trucking, and any desirable quantity of fine beef for food, at rates probably lower than any country in the world, excepting, perhaps, some of the states of Buenos Ayres. Nor can there be any doubt, with a population of nearly one hundred thousand existing on the line of the proposed road, or in its neighborhood, in a country of illimitable productiveness, that maize, plantains, yucas, and, in short, every variety of tropical vegetables, will be supplied to meet every demand.

In view of all these considerations, not less than of the fact that, even in what is called the rainy season, there need be no suspension of labor on the works, I am warranted in saying that the cost of constructing the Honduras railway will be, per mile, materially less than half what it has been on the Panama railway; that is to say, not exceeding $7,000,000 as the entire cost of construction and equipment.

In reference to the economic working of the proposed road, no comparison need be instituted in view of the obvious great cost of keeping in repair and working a railway in such a climate, and in a country so destitute of resources as that of the Isthmus of Panama.

The probable cost of the Tehuantepec road, as estimated by its engineers, exclusive of the indefinite cost of building a breakwater and constructing a port in the Bay of Ventosa, as also exclusive of the proposed excavation of the bar of the Coatzacoalcos, is as follows:

Exclusive of equipment . . .	$6,729,000
Equipment, etc.	1,118,000
Total cost . .	$7,847,000

Ordinary wharves of sixty feet in length, both at Puerto Caballos and in the Bay of Fonseca, would enable the largest ocean-going steamers to tie up by the side of the dépôts of the Honduras road with the greatest ease and in perfect security. The cost, therefore, of deepening the mouth of the Rio Coatzacoalcos, and of building an artificial port at Ventosa Bay, even if these operations were possible in the case of Tehuantepec, and of building up a terminus on a swampy island in an inadequate port, and constructing an artificial port in the Bay of Panama, as in the case of the Panama railway—the entire cost of these heavy undertakings is obviated, in the case of the Honduras road, by the great and controlling fact of the existence of unexceptionable ports at both of its extremities.

In respect of the probable revenues of the Honduras

road, from what has been said it will be seen that its construction will effect a positive saving of from five to eight days of time over any route of transit now in existence or likely to be constructed. All other circumstances being equal, this fact alone would give it the entire travel as between the Atlantic States and California. But when we add to this the ease with which the transit would be effected as compared with the frequent changes and transhipments on the Nicaragua line, and the embarkation and disembarkation at Panama (where steamers on the Pacific side have to lie several miles from shore, and where passengers and freight have to be taken on and off in small boats and lighters), then this advantage becomes greatly enhanced. Add to this the great fact of a salubrious climate, free from the "Chagres fevers" and "San Juan *calenturas*," and the great superiority of the Honduras line above all others becomes more manifest, and warrants the assertion that it would attract the *entire travel* between the two seas. The mails would, of course, take the speediest route; and a large amount of freight, which, in consequence of the difficulties that I have enumerated, can not now be carried over either the Panama or Nicaragua line, would also take this direction. Fifteen cents per pound, or three hundred dollars per ton, is the present cost of transporting freight across the Nicaraguan isthmus!

The immediate sources of revenue, therefore, upon which the proposed road could rely, are mails, passengers, express and other freight, including the transportation of bullion.

There is another consideration connected with the project of opening a railway through Honduras, viz., the fact that the country itself has vast resources, mineral and agricultural, which the construction of the road would rapidly develop, and which, in turn, would create a profitable and constantly increasing traffic for the road. It is not too much to anticipate that a country so favored in respect of soil and climate would attract to its shores a large emigration just as soon as the establishment of lines of steamers and the opening of interior means of communication would enable men to direct their enterprise thither with prospect of profit or of acquiring a competence. But, leaving out of view these prospective considerations, as well as the constant increase in travel and trade as between the two seas, still the positive *existing sources of revenue* are sufficient to make the proposed road one of the most profitable in the world.

The authors of the Report on the Isthmus of Tehuantepec (a work of value, to which I cheerfully yield my highest commendations for its large and well-digested collection of facts) have calculated that, for the four years preceding 1852, the number of passengers between the Atlantic States of the United States and California was 412,942, of which 241,522 went by way of Panama and Nicaragua (the route last named having then just been opened). They calculated the amount of freight which had been carried across the isthmus during the same period at 47,000 tons, the amount of gold at $138,620,000, and the average weight of mails per each steamer, 9000 lbs. In addition to the passengers above enumerated, 11,021 went to California by way of Cape Horn.

Leaving out the year 1848, it appears that, for the three remaining years, the annual emigration between the Atlantic States and California, including that overland, amounted to 141,350. Of these, 80,190 went annually by sea.

It may be alleged that these figures relate to years when the California emigration was at its height, and that the average returns will now fall below these numbers. But such is not the fact. The number of passengers between the Atlantic States and California for 1854, it is well known, was materially diminished by the general financial depression during the last six months of that year. Nevertheless, the arrivals and departures by sea from San Francisco amounted to 59,000.* The number of arrivals and departures for the last six months of the year was 9000 *less* than during the first six months. In other words, had the current of travel been sustained at the rate with which the year opened, the emigration would have come up to 70,000 persons, irrespective of the arrivals and departures by land.

This statement respecting the number of arrivals and departures from California is from a table published in a recent California newspaper. I find, on application at the New York Custom-house, the following statement of departures and arrivals for this city:

Departures from New York for California, and Arrivals at New York from California, by steamers, for the year ending March 16th, 1855.

DEPARTURES per Nicaraguan steamers . .	13,373
" " Panama " . .	11,746
" " Independent " . .	4,172
ARRIVALS per Nicaraguan steamers . . .	11,195
" " Panama " . . .	8,025
" " Independent, " . . .	3,340
Total . . .	51,851

* This is irrespective of 16,084 Chinese who arrived in San Francisco during the same period. But 2330 Chinese returned during this period, so that the net accession of Chinese to the population of California for the year amounted to 13,754!

This is irrespective of passengers for South America and the Pacific ports generally, apart from California. These figures are conclusive upon one point of much importance in calculating the revenues of the proposed Honduras road, viz., *that passengers will always take the shortest or speediest route between given points.* The Nicaragua route is about two days shorter than that by Panama, and this circumstance has given it a majority of the passengers between the seas, notwithstanding that its steamers are inferior in accommodations and management to those sailing to Panama, and notwithstanding that it has miserable boats on the River San Juan, and not less than from four to six transhipments, according to the season. In the dry season, when the water in the river is low, besides the transfers at San Juan del Norte and San Juan del Sur, there are changes at the Rapids of Machuca, the Rapids del Castillo, Rapids del Toro, and at Virgin Bay. There are transhipments in all seasons at the Castillo and at Virgin Bay. The revenues to be derived from freight could not fail to increase in amount with every year. Indeed, there is no parallel to the rapidity with which our trade with the Pacific has been developed. The amount of tonnage which cleared from the ports of the United States for the Sandwich Islands, China, East Indies, and the Pacific Ocean generally, *exclusive of California and Oregon*, for three years, from 1850 to 1852 inclusive, was as follows:

Years.	American.	Foreign.	Total.
1850,	93,588 tons.	11,640 tons.	115,228
1851,	114,330 "	20,880 "	135,210
1852,	198,210 "	91,640 "	289,850

Increase in two years, 173,522 tons, or about 140 per cent.

Apart, however, from all speculations of this kind, there exist positive data for estimating the prospective revenues of the proposed road, derived from the experience of a single section of the Panama railway. I copy from the report of the directors of the company to the Legislature of New York:

"*Receipts.*—The gross receipts to February, 1854, being for most of the time from 23 miles of road, were $771,526 41

And from February, 1854, to October 31, 1854, during which period 31 miles were open .		416,000 00
Gross receipts		$1,187,526 41
The running expenses were	$324,720 95	
Credit to New Granadian gov't.	13,090 28	
Transportation of mails .	217,632 63	
New Granada's proportion for mails	3,470 68	
		558,914 54
Net receipts		$628,611 87

Out of which and the estimated receipts for November and December there have been paid dividends as follows:

July, 1853, 5 per cent. on	$2,194,062 10	$109,703 10
January, 1854, 3½ per cent. on	2,716,372 00	95,080 02
July, 1854, 3½ per cent. on	2,832,000 00	99,120 00
January, 1855, 3½ per cent. on	2,875,000 00	100,625 00
Total		$404,928 12

besides paying the interest on bonds."

That is to say, with but thirty-one miles of road open, and carrying less than one half of the passengers between the seas, still the road has paid, for eight months, at the rate of $52,000 per month, equal to $624,000 per annum. Had the road possessed a monopoly of the transit, as the proposed road in Honduras would be certain to secure for itself, its revenues would have been not less than at the rate of $1,250,000 per annum on thirty-one miles of road, equal to a gross receipt of twenty-five per cent. per annum upon the cost of the entire road. The cost of working the road, it will be seen, has been less than one half the gross receipts, and, at the same rate for the future, would leave the net profit of the road not less than fifteen per cent. on its capital!

Now the diminished cost of working the Honduras road, resulting from the greater cheapness and abundance of supplies of all kinds, joined to the diminished cost of keeping it in repair as compared with Panama, would unquestionably, on the same basis of gross receipts, enable it to pay an annual interest on its estimated total cost of $7,000,000 of not less than eighteen per cent.

In other words, I estimate that the revenues which would accrue to the Honduras road, were it now in operation, at not less than $1,750,000 per annum. By the natural increase of travel and trade, it may safely be assumed that this amount would be swelled to $2,000,000 per annum by the time the road could be completed, were it to be commenced immediately.

There are other considerations which, although not directly connected with the profits of the road in itself, should not be overlooked. I mean the great public advantages which would result from the opening of the proposed communication. It is demonstrable that, if the road were built, there would be an absolute average saving of time in the voyage between the Atlantic States and California of not less than seven days. It would therefore result:

I. That, on the basis of 70,000 passengers per annum, there would be an aggregate saving of 490,000 days to the public. At two dollars per day, a low valuation of time in the United States, this would equal in round numbers $1,000,000.

II. The saving in the form of interest, insurance, etc., etc., on the precious metals in transit.

III. The saving of seven days in the transmission of the mails, and the consequent increased facilities in the transaction of business as between the Atlantic and Pacific coasts of the continent.

I am perfectly aware that there are many whose interests and prejudices will lead them to denounce all these estimates as bold and unfounded assertions. But sooner or later the road through Honduras will be built, and I am willing to risk my judgment on the practical issue, viz.:

That its construction will be effected at a cost not exceeding $7,000,000; that its average revenues for the first four years of its working will not be less than $2,000,000 per annum; and, finally, that it will effect an average saving of time over existing routes of not less than seven days in the voyage between New York and California.

SAN SALVADOR.

CHAPTER XV.

REPUBLIC OF SAN SALVADOR—GEOGRAPHICAL AND TOPOGRAPHICAL FEATURES—PRODUCTIONS, REVENUES, ETC.

THE State of San Salvador lies upon the Pacific Ocean, between the parallels of 13° and 14° 10′ N. latitude, and the meridians of 87° and 90° W. longitude. It has a coast-line of about one hundred and sixty miles, extending from the Bay of Fonseca to the River Paza, which divides it from Guatemala. Although the smallest of the Central American states, it has relatively the largest population, most industry, and the largest commerce.

SAN SALVADOR—CAPITAL, SAN SALVADOR.

Departments.	Capitals.	Population.
San Miguel	San Miguel	80,000
San Vicente	San Vicente	56,000
La Paz	Sacatecoluca	28,000
Cuscatlan	Suchitoto	75,000
San Salvador	San Salvador	80,000
Sonsonate	Santa Anna	75,000
Total		394,000

The area of the state is, approximately, nine thousand six hundred square miles, or one thousand and sixty-six square leagues,* nearly equal to that of Ver-

* Mr. Baily estimates the area of this state at five hundred and seventy-seven square leagues, which is manifestly erroneous. He puts Chiquirin Point, the southeastern extremity of the state, in long. 87° 42′ W., and the Rio Paza in long. 89° 50′ W., while it is in long. 90° 15′ W., a difference of about twenty-five miles

mont, and somewhat greater than that of New Hampshire.

The topographical features of San Salvador are remarkable. The coast presents, for the most part, a belt of low, rich alluvial land, varying in width from ten to twenty miles. Back of this, and presenting an abrupt face seaward, rises what may be called a coast-range of mountains, or, rather, a broad plateau, which has an average elevation of about two thousand feet, and is relieved by numerous high volcanic peaks.

Between this range and the great primitive chain of the Cordilleras lies a broad valley, varying in width from twenty to thirty miles, and having a length of upward of one hundred miles. The coast plateau subsides generally toward this magnificent valley, which is drained by the great River Lempa, and is unsurpassed for beauty and fertility by any equal extent of country under the tropics. Its northern border rests upon the flank of the mountains of Honduras, which tower above it to the height of six or eight thousand feet, and is comparatively broken and rugged. To the south of the Lempa, however, the country rises from the immediate and proper valley of the river, first by a terrace with a very abrupt face, and afterward by a gradual slope to the summit of the plateau. This feature is illustrated in the physical section already presented facing p. 69. Another considerable basin, of great beauty and fertility, is formed by the system of small rivers which rise in the western parts of the state, around the feet of the volcano of Santa Anna, and fall into the sea near Son-

in the total length of the state. This is not the sole error. He calculates the coast-line of the state at forty-five to fifty leagues, which, on the assumption that the state has an area of five hundred and seventy-seven square leagues, would give but about eleven leagues of average width, which is palpably wrong. Its average width is upward of twenty leagues.

sonate. It forms a triangle, the base resting on the sea, and the apex defined by the volcano. Another and still larger basin is that of the Rio San Miguel, lying transversely to the valley of the Rio Lempa, in the eastern division of the state, and separated only by detached mountains from the Bay of Fonseca.

The mountain system of San Salvador, if its isolated volcanoes and volcanic groups can be called a system, is peculiar and interesting. Not less than eleven great volcanoes bristle along the crest of the plateau which I have described as intervening between the valley of the Lempa and the sea. They form nearly a right line from northwest to southeast, accurately coinciding with the great line of volcanic action, which is clearly defined from Mexico to Peru. Commencing on the side of Guatemala, they occur in the following order, viz., Apeneca, Santa Anna, Izalco, San Salvador, San Vicente, Usulutan, Tecapa, Sacatecoluca, Chinemeca, San Miguel, and Conchagua. There are also some others of less note, besides numerous extinct craters, sometimes filled with water, and various volcanic vents or orifices called "Infernillos." In the Bay of Fonseca the series is represented by the volcanic island peak of Tigre, and is resumed on the opposite shore by the memorable Coseguina, succeeded by El Viejo, Telica, Momotombo, and the other volcanoes of Nicaragua.

The Rio Lempa, considered under every point of view, is unquestionably the most important natural feature of San Salvador. In respect of size it ranks with the Motagua in Guatemala, and the Ulua and Segovia in Honduras. For a considerable part of its course it is a navigable stream, and therefore destined to become of great value in the development of the resources of the state. It rises on the confines of Guatemala, at the foot of the high peak (sometimes called volcano) of Chingo, and flows in a southeast direction, through the great basin which I have described, for a distance of more than one hundred miles, when it turns abruptly to the south, and, breaking through the coast-range, finds its way, a distance of fifty miles farther, to the sea. Its mouth, according to the Conde de Güeydon (who visited this coast in command of the French brig-of-war "Genio" in 1847), is in lat. 13° 12′ 30″ N., and long. 91° 1′ W. from Paris, equivalent to 88° 41′ W. from Greenwich.

The Lempa receives several considerable tributaries from the north, the principal of which are the Sumpul, Guarajambala, and Torola. The Sumpul rises on the confines of Guatemala, near Esquipulas, and flows on a course nearly parallel with the Lempa for upward of ninety miles before joining the latter. Throughout its length it constitutes the boundary between the states of Honduras and San Salvador.* It flows, for the most part, among high mountains, in a narrow valley, affording but little room for cultivation. The Torola is a much smaller stream, rising in the Mountains of San Juan, in Honduras, and flowing southwest into the Lempa. For the greater part of its course, in common with the Sumpul, it divides the two states above named. It collects its waters in a section of country remarkable for its mineral wealth. The tributaries of the Lempa from the south are, the outlet of Lake Guija, Rio Quesalapa, rising near the city of San

* Mr. Baily, in his Map of Central America, makes the Lempa proper the boundary between Honduras and San Salvador, whereas, for nearly the whole of its course, it flows through the very centre of the latter state. It forms the boundary between these states for only a very few miles, from the mouth of the Sumpul to that of the Torola.

Salvador, the Titiguapa, and Acajuapa, rising near San Vicente, all comparatively small streams.

I crossed the Lempa at two points; the first more than a hundred miles above its mouth, near the city of Suchitoto, and the second about thirty miles above its mouth, on the *camino réal* between the cities of San Vicente and San Miguel. The time of my crossing at Suchitoto was the latter part of July, 1853, or about the middle of the rainy season. The river at that point was then not less than one hundred and thirty yards broad, deep, and so rapid that the mules swam across with difficulty. The banks, although only of moderate height, are here seldom if ever overflowed, and, from the various indications on the shore, I should estimate the greatest rise of water during the floods at not more than from fifteen to eighteen feet.

At the second point, where I crossed it (called "La Barca") on the first of September, 1853, it is a magnificent stream, upward of two hundred yards in width, and flowing with a strong, deep current. The country on both sides is flat, but elevated from fifteen to twenty-five feet above the water at its average stage. The houses at the crossing I computed to be twenty-one feet above the water in the river, which was then high, and probably not less than five feet above its average stage. Yet, during the great rain or *Temporal* of October, 1852, the water rose two and an eighth Spanish varas in the houses, equal to *twenty-eight feet* above the stage marked at the time of my visit, or not far from *thirty-five feet* above ordinary or average stage! The whole surrounding country was overflowed, and the people at the ferry carried the large barges in which they escaped upward of six miles inland. This rise, however, was unprecedented, and the result of heavy rains such as had never before been known in the country.*

The river was examined about three miles above "La Barca," by order of the government of San Salvador, in 1852, with a view to the erection of a suspension bridge. The point selected was one where the stream is compressed by high banks. The width here was found to be one hundred and fifty-two *varas*, and the depths, measured at intervals of ten yards, were as follows, in feet, commencing at the left shore, viz., 6, 10, 12, 15, 14, 12, 11, 10, 9, 7, 6, 5, 4, 4, 3½, 3, which gives an average depth of nine feet at ordinary stages of the water. Assuming a current of three and a half miles per hour—and it is probably greater—we find the river at this point, and at low stage, discharging 1,227,150 cubic feet of water per minute.

From these data it results that, unless obstructed by shallows and falls, the Lempa must be navigable for steamers of light draught for nearly one hundred miles above its mouth. I did not learn of the existence of any such obstacles, and, although the current is strong, I think the river is available for steamers such as are in constant use on our Western waters. At present it is little used, owing to the difficulty, if not impossibility, of ascending the river in boats proper for commercial purposes without the aid of steam.

The mouth of the Lempa is obstructed by a bad bar, carrying but six feet of water, but the estero of Jaltepeque approaches to within a league of the river, which, in fact, is connected with it by a natural canal,

* An account of this sudden rise of the river at this point was written at the time of its occurrence by Señor Don José Maria Cacho, and published in "*El Siglo de San Salvador*," Nov. 5, 1852. Señor Cacho was detained at the huts of La Barca during the flood. From his account, the river must have risen not less than fifteen feet in a single night.

through which the water flows at high stage in the river. The land between the river and estero is low, and the two might be permanently connected by means of a new canal, or by deepening the channel which now exists. The Bay of Jiquilisco (Espiritu Santo) sends some considerable estuaries to within a short distance of the Lempa, if, indeed, they do not connect with it. Both Espiritu Santo, the port of which was named, in 1846, Puerto del Triunfo, and the port of La Concordia, have every necessary capacity for commercial purposes. The Count de Güeydon reported, in reference to the first named, that it is always easy for merchant vessels to pass the bar, since at low tide there is never less than twelve feet of water on it, and at high tide twenty-two feet.

The Rio Paza (or Pazaca), separating San Salvador from Guatemala, and the Rio San Miguel, are the only remaining rivers of considerable size in San Salvador. The latter drains a considerable geographical basin, of great fertility, but for the most part low and unhealthy. In common with the Jiboa, Comolapa, and numerous other small streams flowing into the Pacific from the volcanic coast-range or plateau, these rivers take the form of estuaries in passing through the low country bordering the sea, and become navigable for small boats.

San Salvador has two considerable lakes, one in the northwestern part of the state, called Guija or Guijar, and another, very nearly in the centre of the state, named Ilopango or Cojutepeque. The former is said to be about fifteen miles in length by six in width. It receives several considerable streams, and discharges itself into the Rio Lempa, of which it may be regarded as one of the principal sources. It abounds with fish of good quality. There is a large island in this lake, on which, according to Juarros, are some ancient ruins, called by the natives Zacualpa, *i. e.*, Old Town. Lake Ilopango is about twelve miles long by perhaps five in greatest width, and is clearly of volcanic origin. It seems to have been an ancient crater, and is surrounded on every side by high, abrupt hills, composed of scoria and volcanic stones. It receives no tributary streams, although it has a small outlet, flowing through a deep ravine into the Rio Jiboa, near the base of the volcano of San Vicente. The surface of the water is not less than twelve hundred feet below the general level of the surrounding country, which, as will be seen farther on, is wholly volcanic.*

In addition to these principal lakes, there are others of comparatively small size, which are simple extinct craters, or were caused by the subsidence of the earth during volcanic convulsions. They rarely have outlets, and the water which they contain is generally im-

* "Toward the southern shore, but at a considerable distance, there are three or four small islets, or rather rocks, a little above the surface of the water. In the lake there is very rarely a perceptible increase, but the depth is very great; and as there is no remembrance of its having been sounded at any period, the popular opinion of its being unfathomable has obtained implicit credence with the illiterate inhabitants of the adjacent towns. The water, when taken up, is beautifully pellucid, but it is not considered wholesome either for drinking or bathing, nor suitable for domestic purposes. When at rest, it reflects, in the same manner as the deep sea, the azure of a generally bright sky; but when the surface is ruffled by a breeze, it has the peculiarity of assuming a green color, of that tint which the common people designate, very appropriately, as verde de perico (parrot green), and exhaling a sulphurous odor, not slight, but powerful and sufficiently disagreeable, becoming more intense as the wind increases in strength. When the upper stratum of the water is thus moved, fish, pepescos, and moharras are taken in great quantities; at other times, when the lake is still, scarcely any can be caught. This fishery is a source of profit to the people of the neighboring towns, who are proprietors of different portions of the shores, the exclusive possession of which is secured to them by immemorial custom. The fish is of indifferent quality, yet much esteemed and praised by the inhabitants of San Salvador, because it is almost the only aliment of the kind they are acquainted with; for, although the city is no more than seven leagues from the ocean, sea-fish is very rarely brought to it."—*Baily*.

From Nature and on Stone by D. C. Hitchcock

Printed by Sarony & C? New York

PORT OF LA. UNION.

pregnated with saline substances to a degree to be unfit for use.

The principal ports of San Salvador are La Union, on the Bay of Fonseca, La Libertad, and Acajutla. The last two, however, are unprotected, and can only be regarded as roadsteads. They derive their importance from their proximity to the respective cities of San Salvador and Sonsonate. It sometimes happens that vessels are obliged to lie off the port of Acajutla for many days without being able to communicate with the shore; indeed, landing is at all times difficult, and frequently dangerous. It is, nevertheless, the port which was designated as the stopping-place of the galleons under the crown, and has still the extensive *bodegas* or warehouses which were then erected. Efforts are now making to direct trade to the newly-established port of Concordia, by opening roads to connect it with the considerable town of San Vicente.* La Union, however, although situated at one extremity of the state, must continue to be its principal port, and must increase in importance with the development of the resources of the Bay of Fonseca. Although constituted a port at a comparatively recent period, it now receives the principal part of the imports of the state. Its situation, under the lee of the volcano of Conchagua, which shuts it off from the benefit of the sea-breezes, is unfa-

* This port is situated on the Pacific, about midway between the well-known ports of La Union and La Libertad, seven leagues from Sacatecoluca, ten from San Vicente, and fifteen from the city of San Salvador. Bodegas, or store-houses, have been erected, a commandant appointed, and pilots qualified for the port. As an inducement to the opening of commerce at this point, the government has issued a decree to the effect that the first vessel which enters the port will be required to pay but one third of the regular duties and charges on vessel and cargo; the second but one half; the third but two thirds; the fourth but three fourths. The port may be entered without difficulty by vessels drawing twelve or thirteen feet. The date of the decree creating the port is August, 1853.

vorable to general health, and gives it a temperature higher than that of any other point on the entire bay. This circumstance has led to the discussion of the question of its removal to a point nearer to the entrance of the bay called Chiquirin, where the sea-breezes reach, and where the depth of water is such as to enable the largest vessels to lie close in shore. Until this change shall be effected, the tendency of things will be to concentrate commerce at the free port of Amapala, on the island of Tigre. The population of La Union may be estimated at about two thousand, irrespective of the inhabitants of the dependent Indian pueblo of Conchagua, situated about a league distant, on the flank of the volcano of the same name.

San Salvador, from its conformation of surface and the nature of its soil, is essentially an agricultural state. The basin of the River San Miguel, that of Sonsonate, and the valley proper of the Lempa, not less than the alluvions bordering on the Pacific, are of extraordinary fertility, and eminently adapted for the production of tropical staples. Around the Bay of Jiquilisco and the port of La Libertad, cotton has been cultivated with success; but up to this time, the principal products of the state have been, in the order of their importance, indigo, sugar, and maize. Indigo constitutes the chief article in the exports of the state, and enters most largely into its resources as an article of trade. The production, however, in consequence of the falling off in price since 1830, has materially diminished. At one time it amounted in quantity to not less than twelve thousand *ceroons* of one hundred and fifty pounds net each, and in value to not far from $3,000,000. As has been observed by Mr. Baily, some idea of the extent of ground which must have been covered with the plant may be formed from the fact that it takes, on the average, three hundred pounds of the plant to produce one pound of indigo. It is produced from an indigenous triennial plant, known by the Indian name of *Jiquilite* (*Indigofera Disperma*). This plant flourishes luxuriantly on nearly all kinds of soil. The land requires comparatively little preparation, being merely burned over and slightly plowed. The seed is then scattered broadcast. This is done in the months of February and April; and the growth of the plant is so rapid, that by the first of August it has attained a height of from five to six feet, and is fit for cutting. "On land freshly sown," says Baily, "the product of the first year is but moderate; the quality, however, is good. The strength of the crop is in the second year. The product of the first year is called *tinta nueva;* that of the second, *tinta retoño*. Experienced cultivators manage to have a portion of each description in each season. After the cutting, the stems and roots remain without signs of vegetation until the early part of the following year, when they shoot out again. The *retoño*, as being the most advanced, is first ready for cutting, as the *tinta nueva* seldom reaches the proper state before September. The manufacture of the indigo is then carried on daily until the whole crop is got in, and by the end of October or the beginning of November the produce is fit for market."

The manufacture of the indigo requires no very difficult nor expensive processes; but it must be cut promptly at the proper period, or else it becomes worthless. It is then necessary for the proprietors of estates to have a large and reliable supply of labor. The difficulty of obtaining this at such times, during political disturbances, when laborers seclude themselves as much as possible to escape conscription, has been one of the principal causes of the falling off of the production of this commodity. It is not easy to calculate the present product of indigo in the state; but as it constitutes about the only reliance of the merchants in paying for their imports, it can not fall much short of $1,000,000 in value.

Sugar is widely produced in San Salvador, from petty *trapeches* or mills which are scattered all over the state. The largest quantities are manufactured in the vicinity of the town of Santa Anna. It is of excellent quality, the crystals being remarkably large and hard.*

Cacao was anciently produced in the neighborhood of Sonsonate and San Vicente in great abundance, but its cultivation is now insignificant. "Coffee," observes Mr. Baily, "is another article which might become of great agricultural importance in San Salvador. There are many localities favorable to its growth about Ahuachapam, Santa Anna, San Salvador, Sonsonate, and San Vicente. In the first three places it grows kindly, and there are some thriving plantations that yield fruit of good quality; but the home consumption being small as yet, though gradually increasing, they are not looked to as a source of much profit.

Tobacco of good quality, but only in amounts necessary for home consumption, is produced in various parts of the state. That grown in the neighborhood of the towns of Tepetitan and Istepec is most valued.

The geological conditions of San Salvador, as may

* "Sugar and raspadura (candy) have much increased in production, and the distilling of rum to an extraordinary extent, in the neighborhood of Sonsonate, by the opening of the California market. Vessels now find at Acajutla an ample supply of these articles, ready packed for mule carriage: the rum in small fourteen and fifteen gallon casks, and gray-beards of from three to six gallons, suitable for easy transport at the diggings or to places in the gold regions."—*Baily's Central America*, p. 89.

be inferred from the physical facts already presented, preclude the existence of the precious metals, except in those portions of the state directly dependent on the primitive range of the Cordilleras, or, rather, on the mountain system of Honduras. The silver mines of Tabanco, Sociedad, and others, in their immediate vicinity, lying in the northeastern part of the state, in the Department of San Miguel, on the confines of Honduras, have nevertheless a wide celebrity. They have been extensively worked, with very profitable results. Two leagues from Tabanco are the gold mines of Capetillas, of great richness. The group of silver mines known under the general name of "Minas de Tabanco," hold the silver in combination with galena and sulphuret of zinc. They are easily worked, and yield from forty-seven to two thousand five hundred and thirty-seven ounces to the ton. The particular mine called Santa Rosalia is richest, and gives the maximum yield here stated. A considerable part of its ores are shipped direct to England. An attempt was made about the year 1830 to work these mines on a large scale by an English company, which sent out a large corps of Cornish miners for the purpose. The machinery sent out at the same time was nevertheless so heavy that it was found impossible to transport it from the coast, which difficulty, in conjunction with others, entirely broke up the enterprise. Nevertheless, with the construction of proper roads, whereby modern improvements in mining with the requisite machinery could be introduced, there is no doubt that these mines could be made of great value, both to their owners and to the state. Their proximity to the Bay of Fonseca is favorable to their complete development.*

* "Five leagues north of San Miguel are a number of mines of silver. Among

"Near the village of Petapa," says Dunlop, "nine leagues from Santa Anna, are some rich mines of iron, which produce a purer and more malleable metal than any imported from Europe. The ore is found near the surface, and is very abundant; and there are extensive forests in the immediate vicinity, which serve for making charcoal." But the amount of iron manufactured is not equal to the consumption of the state, not exceeding seven hundred tons per annum. It is worth about $10 the 100 lbs., or $200 per ton! Were these mines worked properly, the enterprise could not fail to be a profitable one to all employed. Mr. Baily assures us that some of this iron, sent to England a few years ago for the purpose of examination, proved to be a "very valuable variety for conversion into fine steel, approaching in this respect very nearly to the celebrated *wootz* of India."

Among the many undeveloped resources of San Salvador, and one which may perhaps come to have a first value in the state, is its coal, of which there is reason for believing vast beds exist throughout the valley of the Rio Lempa, and in the valleys of some of its principal tributaries, over a region of country one hundred miles long by not far from twenty miles broad. Coal had long been reported to exist in the state, previously to my visit in 1853. The investigations which were

them is one called La Carolina, which was worked by a Spanish *empresario* about thirty years ago. He invested his own property, borrowed $100,000, and, after getting his mine in order, in less than six months was able to pay his obligations, and, although he died before the end of the year, he left $70,000 in gold and silver, the produce of the mine. After his death the ownership was disputed, the works fell into ruins, and the mine became filled with water, in which condition it remains. The mines of Tabanco were more celebrated than those in this vicinity, and when worked, yielded upward of $1,000,000 annually (?), although worked in a rude manner without machinery. The principal one once yielded $200,000 annually to the proprietors."—*Dunlop's Travels in Central America*, p. 277.

From Nature and on Stone by D. C. Hitchcock. Printed by Sarony & C° New York.

VALLEY OF THE RIVER LEMPA.

then made, under my directions, may, however, be regarded as having put the question at rest. Coal was found at a number of places in the valley of the Rio Titiguapa, flowing into the Lempa from the west, of good quality, proper geological conditions, and with every indication of abundance. This river, it may be observed, is navigable for seven months in the year. The coal occurs about two leagues above its junction with the Lempa; also in the valley of the Rio Torola, about three leagues from its junction with the Lempa, of good quality, apparently abundant, and having all the geological conditions perfect. Near the town of Ilobasco, close to the Rio Lempa, it is reported to exist in large beds, and to have been used for many years by the village smiths.

The coal of San Salvador is all of the variety called *brown coal*, and is a later formation than what is known as *pit* coal. In Germany it is found in vast deposits in Croatia, Moravia, Bohemia, Tyrol, Saxony, Silesia, etc., and it is worthy of remark, that all the coal which has been found south of the Mississippi Valley, in Mexico, Central America, New Granada, Chili, etc., appears to be of this variety. In the county of Mansfeldt, in Germany, the brown coal is used for toughening copper, and for melting the white metal for the blue metal in reverberating furnaces. All the steam-engines in the above-named German coal districts are fed with this coal. It can be used for refining lead and silver, for the calcination of ores, and generally for all the operations performed in reverberatory furnaces. Trials which have hitherto been made to coke it, for use in blast furnaces, have not been successful. I am not aware that its use has ever been attempted for locomotives and steam-ships. This is not remarkable, as it has hitherto been found where no opportunity has existed of submitting it to this kind of trial. That found in the valley of the Rio Titiguapa, already alluded to, has a specific gravity of 1.57; ashes 10.5 per cent.* It is of that peculiar kind of brown coal called *pitch coal*, and is rich in bitumen.

That part of the coast of San Salvador extending from Acajutla to La Libertad is termed "Costa del Balsimo," from the circumstance of producing what is known in the materia medica as "balsam of Peru." Lying to the seaward of the volcanic coast-range of mountains which I have described, the whole tract is much broken by the spurs and ranges of hills which the latter sends down toward the sea, and so thickly covered with forests that it is difficult, if not impossible, to penetrate it on horseback. It is exclusively occupied by Indians, who, as it will appear farther on, are little altered from their primitive condition. They support themselves by the produce of the balsam-trees, and by hewing out cedar planks and scantling, which they carry on their shoulders to Sonsonate and San Salvador. Their chief wealth, however, is the balsam, of which they collect annually about twenty thousand pounds, which is sold to dealers in the cities at an average price of half a dollar per pound. "The trees yielding this commodity," according to Baily, "are very numerous on the privileged spot, and apparently limited to it; for on other parts of the coast, seemingly identical in climate, rarely an individual of the species is to be met with. The balsam is obtained by making an incision in the tree, whence it gradually exudes,

* This result compares favorably with that of the analysis of the best varieties of American bituminous coals. The Virginia bituminous coal leaves 10.7 per cent. of ashes; the Pennsylvania free-burning coal 13.3 per cent.; the Maryland bituminous (Cumberland), 10 per cent.

and is absorbed by pieces of cotton rag inserted for the purpose. These, when thoroughly saturated, are replaced by others, which, as they are removed, are thrown into boiling water. The heat detaches the balsam from the cotton, and, being of less specific gravity than the water, it floats on the top, is skimmed off, and put in calabashes for sale. The wood of the tree is of close grain, handsomely veined, nearly of a mahogany color, but redder. It retains for a long time an agreeable, fragrant odor, and takes a fine polish. It would be excellent for cabinet-work, but can seldom be obtained, as the trees are never felled until by age or accidental decay their precious sap becomes exhausted. This balsam was long erroneously supposed to be a production of South America; for in the early periods of the Spanish dominion, and by the commercial regulations then existing relative to the fruits of this coast, it was usually sent by the merchants here to Callao, and, being thence transmitted to Spain, it there received the name of 'balsam of Peru,' being deemed indigenous to that country. The real place of its origin was known only to a few mercantile men."

As I have said, the volcanic features of San Salvador are both numerous and striking. Only two of the eleven great volcanoes of the state are what are called "vivo," alive or active, viz., San Miguel and Izalco. The first-named rises sheer from the plain to the height of six thousand feet, in the form of a regular truncated cone. It emits constantly great volumes of smoke from its summit, but its eruptions have been confined, since the historical period, to the opening of great fissures in its sides, from which have flowed currents of lava, reaching, in some instances, for a number of miles. The last eruption of this kind occurred in 1848, but it resulted in no serious damage.

It is difficult to conceive a grander natural object than this volcano. Its base is shrouded in densest green, blending with the lighter hues of the grasses which succeed the forest. Above these the various colors melt imperceptibly into each other. First comes the rich umber of the scoriæ, and then the silver tint of the newly-fallen ashes at the summit; and still above all, floating in heavy opalescent volumes, or rising like a plume to heaven, is the smoke, which rolls up eternally from its incandescent depths.

The volcano of Izalco may, however, be regarded as the most interesting volcanic feature of the state. This volcano and that of Jorullo, in Mexico, described by Humboldt, are, I believe, the only ones which have originated on this continent since the discovery. It arose from the plain, near the great mass of the extinct volcano of Santa Anna, in 1770, and covers what was then a fine cattle hacienda or estate. About the close of 1769 the dwellers on this estate were alarmed by subterranean noises and shocks of earthquakes, which continued to increase in loudness and strength until the twenty-third of February following, when the earth opened about half a mile from the dwellings on the estate, sending out lava, accompanied by fire and smoke. The inhabitants fled, but the *vaqueros* or herdsmen, who visited the estate daily, reported a constant increase in the smoke and flame, and that the ejection of lava was at times suspended, and vast quantities of ashes, cinders, and stones sent out instead, forming an increasing cone around the vent or crater. This process was repeated for a long period, but for many years the volcano has thrown out no lava. It has, however, remained in a state of constant eruption, and received, in consequence, the designation of "El

From Nature and on Stone by D. C. Hitchcock.

Printed by Sarony & Co N.Y.

VALLEY OF JIBOA.

Faro del Salvador," the Light-house of Salvador. Its explosions occur with great regularity, at intervals of from ten to twenty minutes, with a noise like the discharge of a park of artillery, accompanied with a dense smoke, and a cloud of ashes and stones, which fall upon every side, and add to the height of the cone, which is now about twenty-five hundred feet in altitude.

The volcanoes of San Vicente and Tecapa have several orifices or vents, emitting smoke, steam, and sulphurous vapors, which are called "*Infernillos*," literally, "Little Hells." In a word, it may be said, with truth, that San Salvador comprehends more volcanoes, and has within its limits more marked results of volcanic action, than probably any other equal extent of the earth. For days the traveler within its borders journeys over unbroken beds of lava, scoriæ, and volcanic sand, constituting, contrary to what most people would suppose, a soil of unbounded fertility, and densely covered with vegetation.

There are also many extinct craters, which are now generally filled with water, constituting lakes without outlets, and of which the water is brackish. One of these, called "Joya," occurs about four miles to the southwest of the city of San Salvador.

Near the town of Ahuachapan, in the extreme western part of the state, are some remarkable thermal or hot springs, called *ausoles*, "emitting a dense white steam from a semi-fluid mass of mud and water in a state of ebullition, continually throwing large, heavy bubbles to the surface." These ausoles are described by Montgomery in his Narrative as follows:

"Of these lakes or ponds there are several, and they occupy a considerable tract of land. The largest is about a hundred yards in circumference. In this, as in all the others, the water, which was extremely turbid, and of a light brown color, was boiling furiously, and rising in bubbles three or four feet high. The steam ascended in a dense white cloud, and spread for a considerable distance round, as I stood for some time on the bank of this natural caldron, gazing with awe upon its tremendous vortex. The heat was so great on the surface of the ground near the borders of the lakes that, had our feet not been protected with thick shoes, it could not have been endured. On thrusting a knife into the ground, the blade, when drawn out after a few seconds, was so hot as to burn the fingers. Our horses, which, according to the custom of the country, were not shod, exhibited such symptoms of uneasiness, owing to the state of the ground beneath them, or in consequence of the strong smell of the steam, that it was found necessary to leave them tied some distance from the scene. In some places a little column of smoke issued fiercely from a hole in the ground, while in others, the water, in a boiling state, gushed out like a fountain. The ebullitions of these lakes or springs have formed on the borders of them a deposit of the finest clay, and of every variety of colors; but it does not appear that the natives have profited by the facility thus afforded them for the manufacture of pottery; and although nothing would be more easy than to establish there the finest mineral baths in the world, this object has never occupied their attention."

But, notwithstanding its numerous volcanic features, San Salvador has suffered less from earthquakes than either Costa Rica or Guatemala. The greatest catastrophe that has befallen the state from this cause occurred last year (April, 1854), when the capital of the state was utterly destroyed by a violent earthquake. Previous to this event, the city of San Salvador, in point of size and importance, ranked third in Central America; Guatemala, in the state of the same name, being first, and Leon, in Nicaragua, second. It was founded in 1528 by George Alvarado, brother of the renowned Pedro Alvarado, the next in command to Cortez in his conquest of Mexico, and afterward the conqueror and governor of Guatemala. Its foundations were first laid at a place now called Bermuda, about six leagues to the northward of the present site. In 1539 it was removed to the place which it occupied until the period of the recent catastrophe. Its name was given to it by Alvarado in commemoration of his final decisive victory over the Indians of Cuscatlan, which was gained on the eve of the festival of San Salvador.

During the dominion of Spain in America the city was the seat of the governor intendente of the province of San Salvador, dependent on the captain-generalcy of Guatemala. After the independence it became the capital of the state, and was early distinguished for its thorough devotion to the principles of the liberal party in Central America.

After the confederation of the states it was selected as the capital of the new republic, and a district was laid off around it, called the Federal District, after the example of the United States in erecting the District of Columbia. It continued to be the seat of the federal government until the dissolution of the republic in 1839.

I spent the month of August, 1853, in the city of San Salvador, and was much impressed with the great beauty of the town, and the general intelligence, industry, and enterprise of its inhabitants, who surpass, in these respects, the people of any of the other large towns of Central America. The position of the town was remarkably beautiful; in the midst of a broad, elevated plain, on the summit of the high table-land or coast-range of mountains which intervenes between the valley of the River Lempa and the Pacific. Its elevation, by barometrical admeasurement, is two thousand one hundred and fifteen feet above the sea. As a consequence, its climate is cool as compared with that of the coast alluvions, although unfavorably modified in this respect by a low range of hills on the southern border of the plain, which shuts off the sea-breeze. Were it not for this obstacle, the breezes of the ocean, which is only twenty miles distant, would reach the city. During the month of August, 1853, the maximum of temperature was 81° of Fahr., the minimum 70°, and the mean average 76° 3′, which constitutes a delicious climate.

The hills around the plain of San Salvador are covered with verdure, which, as the dews are considerable, keeps green throughout the dry as well as the rainy season. About three miles to the westward of the city is the great volcano of San Salvador. The cone, which rises on the northern border or edge of the crater, is (approximately) eight thousand feet in height. The volcano proper, however, is a vast mass, with a broad base of irregular outline, its summit serrated by the jagged edges of the crater, and is much less in altitude than the cone. This cone seems to have been formed by ashes and scoriæ thrown out of the crater, which is represented as a league and a half in circumference, and a thousand *varas*, or nearly three thousand feet, deep. At the bottom of this crater is a considerable lake of water. Very few persons have had the temerity to venture into the chasm of the volcano, and none of these are likely, judging from the accounts which they give of their efforts, to repeat the undertaking. Two Frenchmen, who ventured down a year or two since, became exhausted and incapable of returning.

They were rescued with great difficulty by a detachment of soldiers from the garrison.

San Salvador stands, or rather stood — for its destruction has been so complete as to justify the use of the past tense—upon a table-land wholly made up of scoriæ, volcanic ashes, sand, and fragments of pumice, overlying, to the depth of hundreds of feet, the beds of lava which had flowed from the volcano before their ejection. Those who have seen the scoriaceous beds which cover Pompeii can form an accurate idea of the soil on which San Salvador was built.

The channels of the streams are worn down to a great depth through this light and yielding material, and constitute immense ravines, which render the approaches to the town almost impassable, except at the places where graded passages are cut down on either side, paved with stone, and sometimes walled, to keep them from washing out and becoming useless. Some of these approaches are so narrow that it is customary, when mounted, to shout loudly on entering, so as to avoid encountering horsemen in the passages, which are frequently so restricted as to preclude either passing or turning back. San Salvador has more than once owed its safety, in time of war, to these natural fortifications, which confounded the enemy with their intricacies and difficulties, while affording means of defense to the inhabitants.

The facility with which the soil above described washes away has been the cause of several disasters to San Salvador. During a heavy rain of several days' duration, called a "*Temporal*," which occurred in 1852, not only were all the bridges which crossed a small stream flowing through one of the suburbs of the town undermined and ruined, but many houses destroyed in the same manner. One of the principal streets, extending into the suburbs, began to wash at its lower extremity, and the excavation went on so rapidly that no effort could arrest it. A considerable part of the street became converted into a huge ravine, into which the houses and gardens on either side were precipitated. The extension of the damage was guarded against, when the rains ceased, by the construction of heavy walls of masonry, like the faces of a fortification. How serious an undertaking this was regarded may be inferred from the fact that its completion was deemed of sufficient importance to be announced in the annual message of the President.

San Salvador, like all other Spanish towns, covered a large area in proportion to its population. The houses were built low, none being of more than one story, with very thick walls, designed to resist the shocks of earthquakes. Each was built around an inner court, planted with trees and flowers, and frequently containing a fountain. To the circumstance of the existence of these courts the people of San Salvador owe their general preservation in the late catastrophe, as will be seen from the accounts below given. They afforded ready and secure places of refuge from the falling dwellings.

The population of San Salvador was estimated in 1852 at twenty-five thousand. Including the little towns in its environs, and which were practically a part of it, such as Soyopango, San Marcos, Mexicanos, etc., its inhabitants might have been estimated at thirty thousand. It was the seat of a bishopric, with a large and beautiful cathedral church, and of a large and flourishing university, the buildings for which were only finished about a year ago. It had also a female seminary, several hospitals, and numbered some eight or ten churches. In 1852, a very large and beautiful cemetery, with a fine façade and dependent chapels, was constructed. Two aqueducts, one of which is five miles in length, supplied the city with water. It was also a place of considerable and improving trade. Under the auspices of the late president, Dueñas, a cart-road was surveyed, and carried nearly, if not quite, to a successful conclusion, from the city to its port on the Pacific, called La Libertad, a distance of about twenty-two miles. This, in a country where the best roads are hardly equal to what we would here call cattle-paths, was certainly no inconsiderable advance.

The market of San Salvador was well supplied from the numerous Indian villages around it. On feast-days, and on the occasions of the fairs, such as that falling on the anniversary of the victory of Alvarado, the town overflowed, not only with people gathered from within a radius of fifty leagues, but with foreigners and merchants from every part of Central America. At these fairs the accounts between dealers were adjusted, and contracts, sales, and purchases made for the ensuing year; the whole concurrence and bustle contrasting strangely with the usual monotony and quiet.

With the exception of the central and paved part of the city, San Salvador was eminently sylvan, being literally embowered in tropical fruit-trees. The red-roofed dwellings, closely shut in with evergreen hedges of cactus, shadowed over by palm and orange-trees, with a dense background of broad-leaved plantains, almost sinking beneath their heavy clusters of golden fruit, were singularly picturesque and beautiful. In recalling the picture, it is sad to think that all is now abandoned and desolate; that the great square is deserted, and that a silence, unbroken even by the fall of water from the lately glittering fountains, reigns over the ruined and deserted, but once busy and beautiful city of "Our Saviour!"

It will be seen from the following account of the catastrophe of April 16th, that the work of devastation was accomplished in the brief space of ten seconds. Fortunately, a premonitory shock had induced the wary inhabitants to abandon their houses, and seek safety in the public squares and in the court-yards of their dwellings. Had it not been for this, the loss of life would, of necessity, have been very great.

San Salvador has suffered greatly in past times from earthquakes. Severe ones are recorded as having occurred in the years 1575, 1593, 1625, 1656, and 1798. Another, which occurred in 1839, shattered the city, and led the people to think of abandoning it. The volcano has also several times thrown out sand, and threatened general devastation.

But none of the earthquakes alluded to were comparable in violence with that now recorded. It will be seen that the event has inspired so profound a terror, that the people do not propose to return again to the same site, but to select a new locality for their capital. In this they follow the example of the people of Guatemala, which city was originally built at a place now called the Antigua, or Old City. In 1773 an earthquake occurred of such power as nearly to ruin the town, which was removed in consequence. It may be doubted if the earthquake of that year was as violent as that which ruined San Salvador, and which in that respect may be compared with that which destroyed Caraccas in 1812, and in which ten thousand lives were lost. The earthquake of Caraccas consisted of three terrific shocks, each one lasting but two or three seconds. The shocks which destroyed San Salvador did not collectively extend over ten seconds.

The subjoined account of the destruction of the city is from the "*Boletin Extraordinario del Gobierno del Salvador*" of May 2d, 1854, and may be recorded as authentic:

"The night of the 16th of April, 1854, will ever be one of sad and bitter memory for the people of Salvador. On that unfortunate night, our happy and beautiful capital was made a heap of ruins. Movements of the earth were felt on the morning of Holy Thursday, preceded by sounds like the rolling of heavy artillery over pavements, and like distant thunder. The people were a little alarmed in consequence of this phenomenon, but it did not prevent them from meeting in the churches to celebrate the solemnities of the day. On Saturday all was quiet, and confidence was restored. The people of the neighborhood assembled as usual to celebrate the Passover. The night of Saturday was tranquil, as was also the whole of Sunday. The heat, it is true, was considerable, but the atmosphere was calm and serene. For the first three hours of the evening nothing unusual occurred, but at half past nine a severe shock of an earthquake, occurring without the usual preliminary noises, alarmed the whole city. Many families left their houses and made encampments in the public squares, while others prepared to pass the night in their respective court-yards.

"Finally, at ten minutes to eleven, without premonition of any kind, the earth began to heave and tremble with such fearful force that in ten seconds the entire city was prostrated. The crashing of houses and churches stunned the ears of the terrified inhabitants, while a cloud of dust from the falling ruins enveloped them in a pall of impenetrable darkness. Not a drop of water could be got to relieve the half-choked and suffocating, for the wells and fountains were filled up or made dry. The clock tower of the cathedral carried a great part of that edifice with it in its fall. The towers of the church of San Francisco crushed the episcopal oratory and part of the palace. The church of

Santo Domingo was buried beneath its towers, and the college of the Assumption was entirely ruined. The new and beautiful edifice of the University was demolished. The church of the Merced separated in the centre, and its walls fell outward to the ground. Of the private houses a few were left standing, but all were rendered uninhabitable. It is worthy of remark that the walls left standing are old ones; all those of modern construction have fallen. The public edifices of the government and city shared the common destruction.

"The devastation was effected, as we have said, in the first ten seconds; for, although the succeeding shocks were tremendous, and accompanied by fearful rumblings beneath our feet, they had comparatively trifling results, for the reason that the first had left but little for their ravages.

"Solemn and terrible was the picture presented on the dark, funereal night, of a whole people clustering in the plazas, and on their knees crying with loud voices to Heaven for mercy, or in agonizing accents calling for their children and friends, which they believed to be buried beneath the ruins! A heaven opaque and ominous; a movement of the earth rapid and unequal, causing a terror indescribable; an intense sulphurous odor filling the atmosphere, and indicating an approaching eruption of the volcano; streets filled with ruins, or overhung by threatening walls; a suffocating cloud of dust, almost rendering respiration impossible—such was the spectacle presented by the unhappy city on that memorable and awful night!

"A hundred boys were shut up in the college, many invalids crowded the hospitals, and the barracks were full of soldiers. The sense of the catastrophe which must have befallen them gave poignancy to the first moments of reflection after the earthquake was over. It was believed that at least a fourth part of the inhabitants had been buried beneath the ruins. The members of the government, however, hastened to ascertain, as far as practicable, the extent of the catastrophe, and to quiet the public mind. It was found that the loss of life had been much less than was supposed, and it now appears probable that the number of the killed will not exceed one hundred, and of wounded fifty. Among the latter is the bishop, who received a severe blow on the head; the late president, Señor Dueñas; a daughter of the president, and the wife of the secretary of the Legislative Chambers, the latter severely.

"Fortunately, the earthquake has not been followed by rains, which gives an opportunity to disinter the public archives, as also many of the valuables contained in the dwellings of the citizens.

"The movements of the earth still continue, with strong shocks, and the people, fearing a general swallowing up of the site of the city, or that it may be buried under some sudden eruption of the volcano, are hastening away, taking with them their household gods, the sweet memories of their infancy, and their domestic animals, perhaps the only property left for the support of their families, exclaiming with Virgil, '*Nos patriæ fines et dulcia linquimus arva.*'"

The revenues of San Salvador are derived from duties on imports, and the proceeds of the government monopolies of tobacco and *aguardiente* (rum). The receipts of the state from all sources, and its expenditures, for five years, are reported by the treasury as follows, the fiscal year commencing October 1st, and terminating September 30th:

Years.	Receipts.	Expenditures.
1848–49	$397,405	$384,227
1849–50	353,127	342,453
1850–51	402,619	385,836
1851–52	454,113	415,207
1853–54	600,188	579,460

For the fiscal year 1851–52, $205,191 were derived from duties on importations, $110,592 from the monopoly of *aguardiente*, and $10,290 from that of tobacco. The expenditures on account of the army for the same year were $69,000; public debt, $185,747; and civil and general list, $160,360. For the fiscal year 1853–54, the payments on account of the domestic debt were $312,901.

The interior debt of the state on the first day of January, 1853, including bonds in circulation, was about $350,000. On the first of October, 1852, according to the statement of the treasurer, the amount of "*bonos y vales*," bonds and treasury notes in circulation, was $213,938. During the fiscal year $141,243 had been issued, and $185,747 redeemed.

The "bonos" are classified, and received at fixed valuations, and in certain proportions, in payment of duties and other obligations to the state. Their valuation is wholly arbitrary, and is determined by legislative enactment, ranging from ten to eighty per cent. on their face. They have mostly, if not entirely, originated in the political disturbances of the country, having been issued on account of the forced loans from proprietors, or in the way of compensation for property taken for public purposes, and probably do not represent more than one third of the original value on account of which they were issued.

The foreign debt of the state on the first day of January, 1853, amounted to not far from $325,000, of which the greater part was the proportion of the debt of the old federation assumed by San Salvador. This has been augmented by various claims, made mostly, if not exclusively, by British subjects, and which, in the aggregate, have amounted to about $100,000. The interest on the old debt has not, I believe, been paid, and its accumulation since 1848 is probably chargeable upon the state. The report of the treasurer for 1852 puts down $18,205 as paid on account of debts due to individual foreigners. For 1851 the amount of this item was $5800; for 1850, $20,200.

The exports of San Salvador for the year 1851 were 7000 bales of indigo, valued at $700,000. The exports of ores, balsam, skins, rice, sugar, etc., for the same year, were estimated at $500,000. Total exports, $1,200,000. The imports for the same year were valued at $1,500,000.

The political organization of San Salvador corresponds generally with that of Honduras, with which it has always closely sympathized. In 1853, under the temporary ascendency of a reactionary government, it withdrew its delegates from the Constituent Assembly, then in session in the city of Tegucigalpa, for the purpose of framing a Constitution for the organization of a Federal Republic, which should comprehend the three states of San Salvador, Honduras, and Nicaragua. At the same time, it declared itself a distinct and sovereign state, under the title of the "Republic of San Salvador."

In 1850 I had the honor, on behalf of the United States, of negotiating a treaty with Don Agustin Morales, plenipotentiary of San Salvador, which subsequently received the requisite ratifications upon both sides, and is now in full force and effect. It secures to the citizens of the United States all the rights, privileges, and immunities of citizens of San Salvador in commerce, navigation, mining, and in respect of holding and transferring property in that state. It guarantees to American citizens resident in the country the fullest protection in the enjoyment of religious and civil freedom, and, in short, every other right and privilege which has been conceded in any treaty negotiated between the United States and any other nation on the globe. And here it may be mentioned, as an illustration of the sympathy and good feeling which has always existed among the people of San Salvador in respect to this country, that in 1823, when doubts existed as to the possible organization of the Federal Republic of Central America, the State of San Salvador formally and solemnly decreed its aggregation to the United States.

San Salvador, as I have said, is relatively the most populous of the Central American states. It has, indeed, a relatively larger population than most of the states of the United States—nearly four times as many to the square mile as Maine, and more than Vermont or New Hampshire. Considering that it has no large capitals, like Mexico or Lima, within its borders, it is unquestionably more populous than any other equal portion of Spanish America. The traveler, however, would not be apt to receive this impression in traveling through the country, since comparatively few of the people live outside of the numerous villages which dot over the state in every direction. The inhabitants of these towns have their little patches of ground at distances varying from one to five miles from their residences, and think little of traveling that distance in the morning to work them, returning at night. It is this circumstance which lends much of picturesqueness and life to the journeys of the traveler, who, as he approaches the villages in the evening, or departs from them in the early morning, finds the paths thronged with people bearing their implements of cultivation, or loaded with the produce of their little *huertas* or *chacras*.

There is little public or unclaimed land in the state, and few large tracts held by single individuals. This is a circumstance favorable to the general industry, which contrasts creditably with that of the other states; and, upon a second and more extended acquaintanceship with the state and its people, I can only repeat what I have before had occasion to say of San Salvador, that in respect of industry, general intelligence, and all the requisites of good order, its people are entitled to rank first in Central America. There is no part of Spanish America where individual rights are better respected, or the duties of republicanism better understood; and, whatever may be the future history of Central America, its most important part, in all that requires intelligence, activity, concentration, and force, will be performed by San Salvador.

CHAPTER XVI.

ABORIGINAL POPULATION OF SAN SALVADOR.

THE inquirer into the history and relations of the aborigines of America is often surprised to find enigmatical fragments of the great primitive families of the continent widely separated from their parent stocks, and intruded among nations differing from them in manners, language, government, and religion. These *erratic* fragments—to adopt a geological term—in some instances present the clearest and most indubitable evidences of their origin and relationship, in an almost unchanged language, and in a civil and social organization, manners, and customs, little, if at all, modified from those of their distant progenitors. The inference from this would naturally be that their separation had been comparatively recent; yet these identities have been found to exist in cases where tradition fails to assign a cause or period for the disruption, or even to indicate the manner in which it took place.

At the period of the discovery of America, a colony or fragment of that primitive stock, which, under the name of Quichés, Kachiquels, Tzendales, Mayas, etc., occupied nearly the whole of what is now Guatemala, Chiapa, and Yucatan, was found established on the River Panuco. They bore the name of Huastecas, and from them had proceeded those beneficent men who carried the arts of civilization and the elements of a mild religion into those regions, where the Acolhuas and Aztecas, or Nahuales, afterward built up the so-called Mexican empire. It was one of their leaders, bearing the hereditary name Quetzalcoatl in the Nahual dialect, and Cuculcan in the Tzendal, who taught the higher arts to the inhabitants of Cholula, and who afterward returned to the primitive seats of his fathers in the valley of the Usumasinta by way of the isthmus of Coatzacoalcos. The period of this migration to the Panuco dates back beyond the foundation of the principalities of Anahuac, and is anterior to the Tezcucan and Aztec dynasties.

In Central America, on the other hand, two considerable fragments of the true Nahual or Aztec stock were found intruded among the native or original families of that portion of the continent. One of these, as I have shown in my work on Nicaragua, occupied the principal islands in the Lake of Nicaragua, the narrow isthmus which intervenes between that lake and the Pacific, and probably a portion of the country to the southward as far as the Gulf of Nicoya. Their country was less than a hundred miles long by scarcely twenty-five broad; yet here they preserved the same language and institutions, and practiced the same religious rites with the people of the same stock who dwelt more than two thousand miles distant, on the plateaus of Anahuac, from whom they were separated by numerous powerful nations, speaking a different language, and having a distinct organization.

I have elsewhere indicated the character, habits, and religion of the Nahuals of Nicaragua, and shown in what respect their language was modified, or differed from that spoken by the Nahuals of Mexico.* I do not propose to go over that ground again, but to con-

* See article on the "Archæology and Ethnology of Nicaragua," part i., vol. iii. of Transactions of the American Ethnological Society.

fine myself to some account of another and larger colony or fragment of the Nahual stock, which was situated between Nicaragua and Guatemala, principally in what is now the State of San Salvador, where their descendants still remain, retaining to this day their original language, and many of their primitive manners and customs.

Their existence here was affirmed by the earliest chronicles, but, as I have had occasion to say in treating of the Nahuals of Nicaragua, the fact does not seem to have been generally accepted by modern ethnographers. In the absence of direct proofs, such as might be derived from a comparison of their language with that of the Nahuals of Mexico, this is not surprising. The science of ethnology is now happily so far advanced as to require a closer authentication of the facts upon which it proceeds than can always be derived from the vague and frequently obscure allusions and statements of the ancient chroniclers.

The data necessary to establish the statements of the conquerors in the respect above indicated I was fortunate enough to obtain in my recent visit to Central America in the year 1853. During that visit I not only traveled extensively through Nicaragua and Honduras, which bound San Salvador on the south and north, but also traversed that state throughout its entire length and breadth, visiting in succession each of its departments.

As a general rule, the aboriginal population has been much modified by three centuries of contact with the whites, and an equally long subjugation to the Spanish rule; yet there are towns, even in the immediate vicinity of the capital, which have retained to a surprising degree their primitive customs, and in which the aboriginal blood has suffered scarcely any, if indeed the slightest intermixture. In most places, however, the native language has fallen into disuse, or only a few words, which have also been accepted by the whites, are retained. The original names of places, however, have been preserved here with the greatest tenacity, and afford a very sure guide in defining the extent of territory over which the various aboriginal nations were spread.

In the neighborhood of Sonsonate there are several large towns, inhabited almost exclusively by Indians, who also use the national language in ordinary intercourse among themselves. The same is true of some of the towns on the southern flank of the volcano of San Vicente, whose inhabitants, no later than 1832, attempted to reassert their ancient dominion, and exterminate not only the whites, but all who had a trace of European blood in their veins.

There is, nevertheless, one portion of the State of San Salvador where the aborigines have always maintained an almost complete isolation, and where they still retain their original language, and, to a great extent, their ancient rites and customs. This district is known as the "*Costa del Balsimo*," or Balsam Coast. It is about fifty miles in length by twenty to twenty-five in breadth, lying between La Libertad, the port of the city of San Salvador, and the roadstead of Acajutla, near Sonsonate. This district is entirely occupied by Indians, retaining habits but little changed from what they were at the period of the conquest. It is only traversed by foot-paths so intricate and difficult as to baffle the efforts of the stranger to penetrate its recesses. The difficulty of intercourse is enhanced, if not by the absolute hostility of the Indians themselves, from their dislike to any intrusion on the part of the whites, be they Spaniards or foreigners. I was, however, fortunate in numbering among my warmest friends in Central America two gentlemen, who are the principal purchasers of the celebrated "Balsam of Peru," which is obtained exclusively by these Indians, and constitutes their only article of sale and sole source of wealth. They not only have an extensive acquaintance with the Indians, but also great influence over them, which was exercised in putting me in relation with some of the more intelligent ones in their visits to the city of San Salvador. I was thus enabled to obtain a vocabulary of their language, which is nearly identical with the ancient Nahual or Mexican. The differences which exist are indicated in the comparison which is elsewhere made.

The towns of the Indians of the Balsam Coast occupy generally the level summits of the low range of mountains which extend parallel to the coast at the distance of about three leagues inland. Their houses are all thatched with grass or palm leaves, the churches only being covered with tiles. The largest town has no more than two thousand inhabitants. Very few among these Indians know how to read or write, but in this respect considerable advance has been made since the independence.

The mechanical arts are little understood, and, of course, the fine arts still less practiced. Music is cultivated to some extent, but only as an accessory to public worship. They profess the Catholic religion, but with no very clear idea of its more exalted tenets; and its ceremonies are interpolated with many peculiar aboriginal rites.

Their necessities are very limited. The women dress

in a blue skirt of cotton cloth woven in San Salvador, but go naked above the waist. They make two braids of their hair, trimming it with pearl-colored ribbon, and when they go out, cover their heads with a *tiara* of *mappoyan*. The men dress in a trowsers of cloth, made of the native cotton, woven by themselves in a species of hand-loom. This, with a palm-leaf hat, such as are manufactured for sale in other parts of the state, completes their dress.

Matrimony is celebrated both as a civil rite and religious sacrament, as in other parts of the state; but the ceremonies which precede it are different and peculiar. As soon as the boy attains the age of fourteen years, and the girl twelve, the parents agree upon the match, perhaps without consulting the inclinations of the principals, and sometimes in contravention of them. When the betrothal is effected, the father of the son takes the girl to his house, and is obliged to educate and maintain her as if she were his own child. The labor of both boy and girl is at his service, but when it is supposed the new couple are able to sustain themselves, the parents jointly build a house, and give them means to start in life.

It is, nevertheless, not uncommon to see among these Indians a family of three generations, all married, living in the same house, and dependent upon the oldest pair.

These Indians respect not only the parental and public authority, but also the authority of age, in their public and especially in their private gatherings. They style the old persons "*Ahuales*." This title and authority is only conceded to persons over forty years of age, who have had charge of the treasure-boxes of their various saints, or who have served in some public capacity. But among these "officers" there is a rigorous scale of rank.

Their laws are ostensibly those of the state, but, in point of fact, these are not consulted in their civil and criminal decisions. Custom and common sense constitute their code of procedure. The meetings of their *cabildos*, or municipal courts, are always held at night, commencing at seven in the evening, and lasting until ten, or even later, if the matter in hand require it. The cabildo is lighted by a fire of dry wood, built in one of its angles. Here the people assemble, with their hats in their hands, exhibiting the greatest submission and deference to the authorities.

Their votes for president, deputies, etc., are always given in consonance with the indications which they receive from the seat of government, and which they regard in the light of orders.

Agriculture among them is carried on only to the extent of producing the maize requisite for the year, and nothing more. Their sole wealth consists of their balsam, calculated approximately to amount to twenty thousand pounds annually, and which they sell at four rials, or half a dollar the pound. This, it might be supposed, would gradually place in their hands some property, but it is quite spent in the festivals of the saints, which are rather eating and drinking bouts than sacred feasts.

Physically, these Indians have more angular and severer features than those of the other families of Guatemala and Nicaragua. They are not so symmetrical in form, and are darker in color, more taciturn, and apparently less intelligent. Their women are much smaller than those of the other Indian nations, are generally ugly, and, when old, little short of hideous. Throughout the state they are industrious, and San Salvador, favored generally with a fertile and arable soil, is undoubtedly the best cultivated, as it is the best populated state of Central America.

Having thus indicated the present condition of the Nahuals of San Salvador, and the district within which the ancient race has preserved its blood unmixed and its peculiarities almost unchanged, I now propose to define the extent of its occupation of the country at the period of the conquest. Upon this point the testimony of the early chroniclers is unusually direct, and, even if it were less so, the easily recognizable peculiarities of the Nahual names of places, of rivers, and other natural objects, would afford us a very sure guide in our researches.

When, in 1524, Pedro de Alvarado had subdued the kingdom of the Quichés, and received the submission of the Kachiquels, another powerful nation of the same stock, whose capital was not far from where the old city of Guatemala now stands, he obtained information of a great people situated farther to the southwest, on the coast of the South Sea, who were called *Pipiles*, and with whom the Kachiquels had little or no intercourse, and were in a state of almost constant warfare. Incited by his Kachiquel allies, and still more by his own ambition, he determined to undertake their reduction, and for that purpose set out from the Kachiquel capital with a large force of Spaniards and Indian auxiliaries.

Of this expedition Alvarado has himself given us a summary in his second letter to Cortez, and it is still easy to trace the route of his army, from the names of the places which successively fell under his arms, and which, with scarcely an exception, are still retained.

Between the territories of tribes or nations in a state of constant hostility or warfare against each other, there must necessarily be a "disputed ground," depopulated and desolate. Such a belt of country was traversed by Alvarado after leaving the Kachiquel capital which it took him three days to pass. "His advance," says Juarros, "was slow, for the reason that there was no intercourse between the people of Guatemala and the *Pipiles*, and roads were unknown."

On the third night, however, which was dark and rainy, he reached the town of Escuintepeque, and, although most of the inhabitants, seized with terror, fled without striking a blow, yet those who remained opposed an obstinate resistance. After five hours' hard fighting, he was obliged to fire the town, which was done at several points. But even these desperate measures failed, and it was not until he found means to threaten the principal cazique with the destruction of the neighboring plantations of cacao and maize that he was induced to surrender. Alvarado spent eight days here in reducing the neighboring towns and collecting the inhabitants from the forests, where they had fled in their alarm. He then advanced with his force, which now numbered three hundred Spanish infantry, one hundred horse, and six thousand Guatemalan and Tlascalan auxiliaries, the latter being a portion of those who had accompanied him from Mexico.

The next obstacle which opposed his course was the River *Michatoyat*, which reaches the sea at the roadstead of Istapan, where Alvarado afterward built the vessels used in his expedition to Peru, and which is now the Pacific port of Guatemala. He crossed this river with difficulty, and, after much hard fighting, reduced the towns of Atiquipaque (called Atipar by Alvarado), Taxisco (Tassisco), and finally reached Guazacapan, which, supported by Nextiquipaque, Chiquimulla, Guaimaiga, and Guanagazapan, made a vigorous resistance. The Spaniards finally carried the place, but only to find it deserted by its inhabitants. Alvarado, after spending several days in vain attempts to induce them to return to their homes and submit to the Spanish authority, was obliged to leave them unsubdued. They, however, ultimately submitted, of their own accord, to the authorities of Guatemala. Juarros mentions, as a singular circumstance, that the Indians of Guazacapan fought with little bells fastened to their wrists.

Proceeding onward beyond the Rio de los Esclavos, Alvarado encountered the strong town of Pazaca, supported by the neighboring towns of Sinacantan, Naucinta, Tecuaco, and others more distant. The Indians here strewed the ground with poisoned prickles, which wounded many of the horses and men, and caused them to die, in the course of two or three days, in great agony. The battle before Pazaca was long and bloody, and finally resulted in favor of the Spaniards; "but the victory," says Juarros, "did not entirely decide the conquest of the district; for, although some of the towns (among them Texutla) submitted, others, in strong force, still retained their liberty and native governments."

Alvarado continued his advance past the Rio Paza (or Pazaca) into the district of Izalco, which then, as now, was densely populated. Here he encountered a stout resistance, and was himself severely wounded. He nevertheless captured Moquisalco (the present Mohuisalco), Acatepeque, Acasual (Caxocal), Tlacusqualco, and other towns, and finally reached the principal or capital town of the Nahuals, called Cuscatlan, a name which was also applied by them to their country at large.

After remaining here seventeen days, the rainy season coming on, Alvarado returned to the capital of the Kachiquels, near which he founded the ancient city of Guatemala. The details of the subsequent gradual reduction of Cuscatlan to the Spanish authority have not reached us in a connected form. We only know that the people resisted the Spaniards with great intrepidity, and that the latter only succeeded here, as elsewhere, through the agency of their horses and fire-arms. Without these the conquest of America could never have been effected.

The name of the first town reduced by Alvarado in this expedition, namely, Escuintepeque, written also Iscuintepec, is undoubtedly Nahual, and probably derived from *itzcuintli*, the name of a species of indigenous dog, and *tepec*, mountain, or *altepetl*, place, *i. e.*, Place or Mountain of the Dog. This town, which still exists, gave its name to the district which lies to the westward of the Rio Michatoyat, and within which, according to Juarros, the Sinca dialect was generally spoken. This may have been true, for the Nahuals often translated into their own language the names given to places in the territories of their neighbors, or, from inability to pronounce them, gave them names of their own. Thus Atziquinixai (the Home of the Eagle), which was the name of the capital of the Zutugil kingdom, was called *Atitlan* by the Pipiles or Nahuals, which means, literally, place by the water, it being situated on the banks of a lake. *Quesaltenango* was thus substituted for the Quiché Xelahuh, *Zapohitlan* for Xetuhul; and in Nicaragua, *Xolotlan* for Nagrando.

It is not improbable, therefore, that Escuintepeque was a name given by the Nahuals to a town of the Sincas, and preserved by the Spaniards in consequence of their previous greater familiarity with the Mexican language.

Nor is it impossible, on the other hand, that the Nahuals were spread along the coast, not only as far as Escuintepeque, but even to the River Nagualate.* Be this as it may, Alvarado expressly informs us that, after crossing the River Michatoyat, he came to Atiepas (Atiquipaque), *where the people spoke a different language from those of Escuintepeque.*† If the people of the latter town spoke the Nahual or Mexican, then it follows that the inhabitants of the district or province of Guazacapan, which extended from the Rio Michatoyat to the Rio Paza (or Aguachapa), had a different language. This conclusion would derive some support from the apparent total absence of Nahual names in that district. Herrera, however, gives us the probable key to the entire difficulty. He says, "*The natives of this province are humble, and speak the Mexican tongue, although they have another peculiar to themselves. When heathens, they observed the rites of the Chontals of Honduras.*" We may fairly infer from this testimony that the district of Guazacapan was occupied by a people probably of the same family with the Chontals of Honduras, who had either been subjected by their Nahual neighbors and compelled to adopt their language, or who had gradually gained a

* The name of this river seems to be compounded of *Nahual*, or, as it was universally written by the old chroniclers, *Nagual*, and *atl*, contracted into *at*, water, *i. e.*, River of the Nahuals.

† Fuentes states that the Nahual language was confined to "certain parts on the sea-coast, commencing at the town of Escuintepeque." Elsewhere, referring to the march of Alvarado, he says he advanced on Escuintepeque, "que es la tierra de los Pipiles."

knowledge of it, and assimilated in other respects with them from long contact and association. Their assimilation probably had become sufficiently complete to justify us in classing them under the same general designation.

After passing the Rio Paza (Pazaca, or Aguachapa) into the district of Izalco, all doubts as to the relationship of the inhabitants disappear. They were, at the period of the conquest, as they now are, undoubted Nahuals; and from that river to the banks of the River Lempa, the people were entirely homogeneous. That the Lempa constituted their boundary on the southwest appears not only from the total absence of Nahual or Mexican names to the eastward of that river, in the ancient province of *Chaparristique*, now San Miguel, but also from the direct testimony of Herrera, who informs us that the town of Iztepeque, situated at the foot of the volcano of San Vicente, in the immediate vicinity of the city of the same name, was the last town of the Nahuals in that direction. I quote his own language: "At this town of Iztepeque begins the country of the Chontals, speaking another language, and a brutish people."*

The Lempa seems also to have bounded the territory of the Nahuals upon the north; at any rate, there are but one or two towns bearing names in their dialect on the left bank of that river; and even if they did pass it at any point, their farther spread in that direction must have been speedily arrested by the high, desert ranges of the Cordilleras, which lie parallel to the valley of the Lempa in that direction, and which constituted the southern limits of the district of Corquin, whose inhabitants were allied politically, if not by

* Herrera, vol. iv., p. 154.

blood, to the people of Copan, who were themselves of the Kachiquel family. Lempira, the last of the chiefs of Corquin, made his final stand against the Spaniards on the mountain of Piriera, which overlooks the valley of the River Lempa, in the name of which beautiful stream his own is commemorated.

It follows, then, that the Nahuals of San Salvador, at the period of the conquest, were spread over the entire country embraced between the River Michatoyat (possibly the River Nagualate) on the northwest, the River Lempa on the southeast, and between the Pacific Ocean on one side, and the abrupt ranges of the Cordilleras, overlooking the valley of the Lempa, on the other; that is to say, over a territory from one hundred and eighty to two hundred miles in length, by an average of sixty miles in width, and embracing an area of not far from eleven thousand square miles.

The chroniclers are unanimous in representing this district of country as "one of the best peopled in all America." It had many large towns, well built, and in all respects equal to those of Mexico. In his letter to Cortez, Alvarado tells us that, beyond the city of Cuscatlan, the farthest point which he reached in his first expedition, "there were great cities and villages, built of lime and stone." He adds also, by way of apology for not continuing his enterprise, that the country was too extensive and densely populated to admit of his subjugating it before the setting in of the rainy season.

The name given to the country of the Nahuals of San Salvador was Cuscatlan, which, according to the chronicler Vasquez, signified "*tierra de prefeas ó freseas*," or, freely translated, "land of riches," a name which, considering the great beauty of the country, its fertility of soil, and variety and luxuriance of vegetation, was equally appropriate and beautiful.* It was also called, according to the same authority, *Zalcoatitlan.*

According to Juarros, the name *Pipil* was given to the people of Cuscatlan from the circumstance that "they spoke a corrupt dialect of the Mexican language, with a childish pronunciation: the word *pipil* signifying children." This name is certainly no longer known, and it may be doubted if it was ever accepted or applied as a general designation. It may, indeed, have been used contemptuously by the Mexicans who accompanied Alvarado, and who, no doubt, affected a superiority over their kindred in Cuscatlan. *Pipilpipil* is rendered by Molina, in his Dictionary, by the Spanish term *muchachuelos*, small boys; and *pipillotl* by *niñirea*, childishness. The translator of the "Codex Chimalpopoca," quoted by Bourbourg, renders *pipilpipil* by *viejitos*, little old men.

The term *Nahual* or *Nagual*, and its ancient plural *Nanahuatl*, are the names under which all the tribes who spoke the Mexican idiom were known. It signified, in this application, an expert man, who spoke well his own language. In its primitive sense, the word *nahualli* meant secret, occult, mysterious, and in later periods came to designate a man versed in judicial astrology and the arts, a sorcerer or magician. The Spaniards gave the name of *nagualismo* to certain mysterious rites which are practiced to this day by the Indians, as also to their idolatrous practices generally. Nuñez de la Vega, in his "Constituciones Diocesanas," has given us an account of the *Nagualistas* of his day, at

* *Cuscatl*, in the Mexican language, signifies jewel or precious stone, and *lan* is a common terminal signifying place or locality.

which time the term *nagual* was used to express the idea of a demon or familiar spirit.

The form of government which existed in the ancient Cuscatlan seems not to have differed from that which prevailed among the people of the same stock in Mexico; that is to say, there were a large number of petty chiefs, who exercised authority over single towns or districts and their immediate dependencies, but all, from their affinity in blood, language, and religion, more or less allied politically, and generally acting in concert. Such was the case in Mexico; but the relationship was not so intimate as to prevent them from occasionally warring upon each other. A primitive state of society is inconsistent with extended dominion. Power, to be great, must be concentrated, and concentration without means of easy and rapid communication is impossible. The transmission and execution of orders, collection of men and supplies, and the movements of forces, all requisites to the establishment and support of an empire of any considerable extent, are impossible without the aids to be derived from navigation, the subordination of horses, or other beasts of burden, and the opening of roads; without these, conquests can not be retained, nor local ambitions or discontents held in check. The empire of the Incas, the only one worthy of the name which was established by the aborigines in America, owed its existence, in a great degree, to the naturally easy means of communication between its various parts, improved by the construction of a vast system of roads and bridges, traversed regularly by a well-organized corps of messengers for the transmission of intelligence.

Juarros, quoting at second-hand from Fuentes, speaks of a monarchy as having been established over the Pipiles a short time previous to the conquest, but, for reasons elsewhere given, the whole account may be regarded as apocryphal. Neither Alvarado, nor any of the chroniclers, with this exception, refer to any higher authority in Cuscatlan than the local chieftains. Had there existed a king, or a chief having a general supremacy like that exercised by Montezuma in Mexico, the fact would not have escaped a special mention, for the vainglory of the *conquistadors* was more apt to lead them to exaggerate than undervalue the importance of the chiefs whom they subjugated. No doubt there were individual chiefs who possessed a power superior to the others, exercising a great influence over them, and perhaps arrogating a qualified authority; but, as I have said, this is a point upon which we have no precise information.

Upon the general subject of the religion and the manners and customs of the people, our information is also exceedingly scanty, and what we know is chiefly derived from the imperfect summary given by Herrera. We may, however, safely assume that, in these respects, they corresponded very closely with the affiliated nations of Mexico. It appears certain that they had an organized priesthood, and a class of persons corresponding to the keepers of the records of the valley of Anahuac. Their high-priest, says Herrera, wore a long blue dress, had a species of mitre on his head, from which depended bunches of feathers of various colors, and carried in his hand a species of staff or crosier. Next to him in rank was "a notable doctor in their books and sorceries, who explained their omens." Besides these there was a kind of ecclesiastical council, composed of four persons, who were consulted on all matters pertaining to the rites of religion. In case of the death of the high-priest, a successor was selected from these four by the chief and council, by lot.

They paid adoration to the rising sun, and "had two idols, one in the shape of a man and the other of a woman," to whom they offered sacrifices. Their sacrifices were made at particular periods, which were fixed by their calendars. There were, however, two principal ones, viz., "at the beginning of winter and the commencement of summer," probably at the periods of the summer and winter solstices. On these occasions, according to Herrera, they sacrificed human beings, illegitimate children of their own nation, "from six to twelve years of age." The ceremony and accompanying rites were the same as those practiced in Mexico, and consisted in tearing out the heart of the victim, and scattering his blood to the four points of the compass. The priests were consulted on the subject of declaring war, and successful wars were celebrated by festivals, which lasted for fifteen days, each of which was distinguished by the sacrifice of a prisoner. If the sacrifices were made to the female divinity, the festival lasted for but five days.

Marriages seem to have been made under the direction of the chiefs, and consisted in first submitting the parties to lustrations, such as washing them in a river, and afterward tying them together in the bride's house, whither the relations brought presents to the new couple, the priest and cazique being present at the ceremonies. Children received their names from the priests, to whom presents were made on the occasion of naming the child. After childbirth the mother was obliged to submit to a lustration in a running stream, to the waters of which an offering of copal and cocoa was subsequently made, "that it might not hurt her."

Only the kindred lamented for the death of ordinary persons, but the death of a cazique or war-chief was signalized by a general mourning of four days, at the end of which time the priest announced that the soul of the deceased was with the gods. The son of the chief, or, in default of one, his nearest relative, succeeded to his authority. Rape was punished with death; adultery by making the offender the slave of the injured husband, "unless pardoned by the high-priest on account of past services in war." There were certain degrees of relationship, seven in number, within which it was unlawful to marry, and within which all sexual intercourse was punished with death. Upon matters of this kind there existed the greatest rigor; "for," says Herrera, "he who courted or made signs to a married woman was banished." Fornication was punished by whipping. Robbers, according to Juarros, were banished, and murderers put to death by being thrown from a high rock.

The assertion of Herrera as to the practice of human sacrifices is distinct and unqualified; but if we are to credit the Pipil MS. quoted by Fuentes, and after him by Juarros, these sacrifices were so repugnant to the people that the attempt of Cuaucmichin to introduce them led to the general insurrection of the people, and his own deposition and death; but, as I have already had occasion to observe, I attach but little value to this authority, and have no doubt of the existence of human sacrifices, as affirmed by Herrera.

Juarros gives us an account of the origin of the Pipil Indians, which appears to have been chiefly drawn from Fuentes, who, in turn, seems to have relied mainly upon a certain MS. history of that people, written by one of the Pipil chiefs. It represents that Autzol

(Ahuitzol), the eighth king of Mexico (who reigned from 1486 to 1502), failing in his attempts to reduce the Tzendals, Quichés, Kachiquels, and their affiliated nations to his authority by force, sought to effect the same object by fraud. To this end he directed a great number of his Indian subjects to introduce themselves by degrees into the country, under the disguise of merchants, so as to be ready to co-operate with him when he should next undertake its subjugation. This plan was defeated by his own sudden death in 1502. The Indians, however, who had thus obtained a footing in the country, "multiplied immensely," and spread over the provinces of Sonsonate and San Salvador. Being of the lowest class of the population, and speaking a corrupt dialect of the Mexican language with a childish accent, they were called Pipiles, "which signifies children."

Their rapid increase alarmed their Kachiquel and Quiché neighbors, who sought every opportunity to oppress them. They nevertheless made a firm resistance, and established a large army, under the direction of warlike chiefs, for their defense. These chiefs gradually came to exercise supreme authority over the people, and the principal cazique, named Cuaucmichin, finally undertook to introduce human sacrifices. This attempt aroused the people, who killed him in their rage. They then elected a chief of mild character named Tutecotzimit as their head, and reduced all the other chiefs to the class of *alahuaes*, or heads of *calpuls*. Nevertheless, Tutecotzimit was not without ambition; and, desirous of perpetuating the sovereignty in his own family, he created a council of eight members, composed of his own relations and adherents, whom he constituted nobles. These officers were invested with high authority, and distinguished from all others by long robes of particular colors, the use of which was interdicted to every other rank. While doing this for his own benefit, he ameliorated the condition of the people at large, and made himself so popular that the supreme power was vested in him and his family without opposition. The descent was fixed in the eldest son, provided, in the opinion of the council above alluded to, he was competent to the administration of affairs; if not, the second son was made king, or else the nearest relative of the deceased sovereign. Females were excluded from the succession, but this limitation did not prevent them from inheriting property. All high employments, civil and military, were the prerogatives of the nobles, "who could only reach that dignity through the gradations of inferior offices."

This traditionary account, so far as it professes to relate the origin of the so-called Pipil population, is simply puerile and absurd. Both Fuentes and Juarros must have forgotten that Ahuitzol ascended the throne of Mexico no earlier than 1486, only thirty-six years before Alvarado invaded Guatemala. The latter found the country, from the River Michitoyat to the Lempa, a distance of more than one hundred and sixty miles, entirely and densely populated by these Indians of the Nahual stock, who were regularly organized, and possessed large and well-built towns. On the hypothesis of this tradition, "the merchants" sent by the cunning Ahuitzol must not only have dislodged the original occupants of the country and built many large towns, but also increased their numbers to this incredible extent, all in the short space of thirty years, for the tradition distinctly says that the Mexican monarch did not resort to this scheme until after his attempts to reduce the Guatemalan nations by force had failed.

The relations which existed between the Nahuals or Pipiles and their neighbors of Guatemala are represented by all the chroniclers as the reverse of cordial. "The people of Guatemala," says Fuentes, "held them in great contempt, and never mixed with them."

Without at present venturing into any speculations on the subject of the origin of the Nahuals of Nicaragua and San Salvador, it may nevertheless be observed that the hypothesis of a migration from Nicaragua and Cuscatlan to Anahuac is altogether more consonant with probabilities and with tradition than that which derives the Mexicans from the north. And it is a significant fact, that in the map of their migrations presented by Gemelli, the place of the origin of the Aztecs is designated by the sign of water (*atl* standing for *Aztlan*), a pyramidal temple with grades, and near these a *palm-tree.* This circumstance did not escape the attention of the observant Humboldt, who says, "I am astonished at finding a palm near this teocalli. This tree certainly does not indicate a northern region." We must look for the primitive country of the Nahuals to the south of Mexico. No history, chronicle, or known hieroglyphic of the Mexicans assigns a northern origin to the Nahual tribes, except the relation of Ixtlilxuchitl, who wrote at the expiration of a considerable period after the conquest, and who, in this, only followed Cortez and the Spanish authors who had preceded him. Even Montezuma, in his conversation with Cortez, affirmed that his ancestors came from a different direction; but the Spaniards, conceiving that they must have come from the north, pronounced the emperor in error, as if he were not better acquainted with the traditions of his own people than themselves!

Upon the subject of the language of the Nahuals of Cuscatlan there is very little to be presented. As I have already said, I obtained a short vocabulary of the dialect now spoken on the Balsam Coast from one of the principal men of the village of Chiltiapam, which falls within that district. I also obtained a few words from an Indian of the large town of Izalco, near Sonsonate. In both cases I adopted the Spanish orthography, and have not only given the sounds of the words as closely as it was possible for me to convey them, but also without any attempt to harmonize them with the Mexican. From the subjoined comparative table it will be seen that the variations from the Mexican of the dictionaries is very slight—hardly greater than would be made by different investigators in writing down the same words as they might be sounded to them by the same person. The principal variation is precisely that which I have elsewhere had occasion to remark in the pronunciation of the Nahuals of Nicaragua, viz., the general omission or contraction of the well-known Mexican terminal *tl* or *tli.* Some other peculiarities are indicated in a MS. note prefixed to a copy of Molina's Mexican Dictionary (1571), which I had the good fortune to obtain in the city of San Salvador, and which I have reason to believe belonged to the now extinct convent of the San Franciscan monks, who were the first to introduce Christianity in the ancient Cuscatlan. This note is partially obliterated, but the paragraphs which can be made out are are as follows:

"In this province the *l* is not pronounced; thus, in *tlativez*, to throw, the *l* is omitted, and the word becomes *tativez:* nor do they * * * * * * as, for example, *totox* becomes *toto*, or * * * The *c* is confounded with the *q*, and thus for *cue* they say *que.*

* * * Nor do we find *tla* in these parts, nor *ta*; thus, for *tlatemu*, to descend, they say simply *temu*."

English.	Nahual of Mexico.	Nahual of Balsam Coast.	Nahual of Izalco.
man,	tlacatl,	tacat.	
woman,	cihuatl,	ciguat.	
head,	tzontecon,	tzunteco.	
hair,	tzuntli,	tzunka.	
hand,	maitl,	mapipi.	
heart,	yullotli,	yul.	
bread (wheat),	tlaxcalli,	tashkat.	
heaven,	ylhuicatl,	ilhuicac.	
sun,	tonatiuh,	tona,	tonal.
moon,	metztli,	mezti,	metzti.
star,	citlali,	citatl,	cital.
night,	tlalli,	tailua.	
wind,	ehecatl,	ehecat.	
fire,	tletl,	titl,	tet.
water,	atl,	at,	at.
earth,	tlalli,	tal,	tal.
mountain,	tepetl,	tepetl.	
stone,	tetl,	tetl,	tet.
maize,	centli,	cinte,	cinte.
tree,	quauitl,	quahuit,	quahuit.
grass,	çacatl,	sacat.	
pine-tree,	oco-quauitl,	ocot.	
deer,	mazatl,	mazat.	
rabbit,	tochtli,	tutzti.	
snake,	coatl,	coatl,	cahuat.
bird,	tototl,	totot.	
fish,	michin,	mitzin.	
white,	yztac,	itztac.	
black,	tliltic,	tiltic.	
red,	chichiltic,	chiltic.	
great, big,	vey,	hue.	
many,	miec,	miak.	
church,	teupan,	teupan,	tupan.
house,	calli,	ka,	cal.

English.	Nahual of Mexico.	Nahual of Balsam Coast.	Nahual of Izalco.
1	ce,	ce,	ce.
2	one,	ome,	home.
3	yey,	yae,	yey.
4	naui,	nahue,	nahue.
5	maquilli,	maquil,	maquil.
6	chicace,	chicuasin.	
7	chicome,	chicome.	
8	chicuey,	chicuei.	
9	chicunaui,	chicunahue.	
10	matlactli,	mahtlati.	
11	matlactlionce,	mahtatice.	
12	matlactliomome,	mahtatiome.	
20	cempoualli,	cempual.	

MISCELLANEOUS NOTES.

A.

SEGOVIA, CHONTALES, AND THE MOSQUITO SHORE.

THE map accompanying this memoir presents some new information respecting the northern districts of Nicaragua, known respectively as Nueva Segovia and Chontales. This is one of the most interesting and valuable portions of Central America. It is, in fact, part of the great central plateau of Honduras, and, like all the other sections of that state, is comparatively cool and salubrious, well watered, abounding in minerals and the precious metals, and producing many of the fruits of the temperate zone. Segovia is very sparsely populated, and but an insignificant portion of its surface has been brought under cultivation. The principal occupation of its inhabitants is mining. Silver ores are most abundant; the ores of gold are common, and there are streams in which the Indians carry on gold-washing, but in a rude way and on a small scale. Copper and the inferior metals are also found in quantities which, in other countries and under different circumstances, would contribute greatly to the general wealth. Chontales is described by Chevalier Friedrichsthal as having, "in general, an alluvial soil, being an undulating country, without any very determinate character, furrowed by gullies and narrow runs of water, and dipping generally to the southwest. Porphyry appears but rarely on the surface."* It is chiefly a grazing region, but has lately obtained some notoriety from its mines of gold. Recently, it is alleged, coal has been discovered. The large river Escondido (called Bluefields on the English maps, and known as Lama by the people of Segovia, and as Siquia by the Indians) flows through this department.

In case emigration from the United States or Europe should

* Journal of the Royal Geographical Society of London, vol. iii., p. 78.

ever take the direction of Central America, there is no doubt but the elevated districts of Honduras and Segovia would become rapidly populated, and rise to be among the most important sections of the entire country; and had the several European attempts to plant settlements in Central America been made here, instead of on the low, hot alluvions of the coast, it is probable they would have escaped the complete and disastrous failures which have overtaken them all.

The principal towns in Nueva Segovia are Ocotal, Matagalpa, Jalapa, Acoyapa, and Depilto. The latter is a mining town in the centre of a rich mineral district. Six leagues distant are the mines of Marquilisa, lately worked by citizens of the United States. There is here a fine stream, with thirty feet fall, capable of carrying extensive machinery. The other mines best known are those named Mina Grande, de St. Albino, Santa Maria, Santa Rosa, Esquipulas, Limon, and Agua Podrida. In respect to the general mineral wealth of this department, I am, fortunately, able to present the following letters, the first of which was addressed to me in 1850, while residing in Leon de Nicaragua,

MINING TOWN OF DEPILTO, NUEVA SEGOVIA.

by Don F. D. Zapata, then prefect of the department. The second was written, in reply to some inquiries of my own, by a gentleman recently engaged in mining in that district.

"Prefect's Office and Military Commandancy of Nueva Segovia, Ocotal, Oct. 4, 1850.

"DEAR SIR,—Appended hereto is a list of various mines of the precious metals and gold-washings known to exist to the east and northwest of this city, which I have obtained from responsible persons for transmission to you. They are worthy of attracting the attention of all Nicaraguans, and especially of the industrious and enterprising people of the United States. I am indebted to Don Gregorio Herrera, an inhabitant of the valley of Arrayan, for much of my information. He has been occupied for many years in the gold-washings of that district, and has sent to me here a load of the auriferous sand from the ravine (*gulch*) of Salamaji. It is proper to add that, in the vicinity of these gold-washings, the land is of the richest quality, and that the hills are covered with valuable woods and medicinal herbs. The district is well watered, maintaining the grass always green, and is therefore well adapted for cattle.

"In conclusion, I can only say that I shall avail myself of all the leisure which I may have to inform you of the character and resources of this interesting region. As ever, truly your obedient servant, F. D. ZAPATA."

Report on the Gold-washings, and the Mines of Gold and Silver, which exist to the east of this City (Ocotal), on the Main Road to Jalapa.

"1. At the distance of two leagues and a half from this city are the ravines (*quebradas*) of Chachaguas, with gold dust mingled with the sand.

"2. On the same road to Jalapa, at the distance of four leagues from this city, are the ravines of Salamaji, containing several gold-washings, yielding gold in considerable quantities, and of superior quality.

"3. In the same direction, six leagues from this city, is the ravine of Alali, gold-washings worked by the Güirises, and whence the neighbors of the valley of Arrayan have constantly obtained large quantities.

"4. Eleven leagues from this city is the ravine of Leones, where there is a gold mine; gold-washings also exist here.

"5. Sixteen leagues from this city is the rich silver mine of Limon, from which has been taken much native silver. It is now filled with water.

"6. Returning from Limon, and taking the road to the left toward Jicaro, before arriving at Muyuca, at the distance of seventeen leagues from this city, is to be found a vein rich in shining metal, but which has not yet been assayed. It is called Higuera.

"7. Following the road to Jicaro, in the vicinity of Sabana-grande, twelve leagues from this city, is the mine of Macuelisito, rich in silver ore.

"8. Taking a course to the right from here, and fourteen leagues from this city, are the mines of Santa Albino, and in their vicinity those of Tirado, both of gold.

"9. From this place to the left, on the road to Ciudad Vieja (old Segovia), twenty-seven leagues from this city, is the ravine of Quilali, whence the Güirises have taken considerable quantities of gold dust of superor quality.

"Submitted to the Prefect of the Department Ocotal, October 1, 1850.

"MIGUEL ARTOLA.
"BENITO PENA.
"FRANCISCO IRIAS."

Addition to the above, by Don Gregorio Herrera, living in the Valley of Arrayan.

NAMES OF RAVINES AND STREAMS.

"1. *Chaguite*—Gives large grains of gold in abundance, and of good quality.

"2. *Perillos*—Abundant in the same class of metal.

"3. *Quebrachos*—Good gold, but in smaller grains, and less abundant.

"4. *Javonera*—Gold abundant and good.

"5. *Rio de Alali*—Carries gold, and on the banks are five mantos (banks or placers) of the same metal.

"6. *Ravine San Lorenzo*—Gold in large grains abundant.

"7. *Ravine Zapote*—Like the above, with two placers.

"8. *Rio Apali*—Carries gold, and has a placer.

"9. *Ravine Santa Albino*—Like the above, and near it many abandoned works.

"10. *Ravine Almorzadero*—Rich in good gold.

"11. *Ala de Quilali*—Here are three small ravines, carrying much gold, and two placers.

"12. *Rio Jicaro*—From the direction of Quilali, three ravines, with gold.

"13. *Rio Santa Pablo*—Has much gold and abundant supplies of food.

"14. *Ravine Las Cucharas*—Here runs the Yauli into the Rio Jicaro, with gold of good quality in abundance.

"15. *San Francisco*—Three ravines, with abundance of gold.

"From Ocotal to the most distant ravines, the distance, more or less, is twenty-five leagues. From the above it appears that there are twenty-one gold-bearing streams and ten placers. F. D. ZAPATA."

"New York, April 12, 1854.

"DEAR SIR,—In answer to your letter regarding the Department of Segovia, in the State of Nicaragua, I would say that I have resided there for nearly three years, and that its mineral wealth is very great.

"On leaving the city of Granada for that department, the road lies through a low plain, covered with the mahogany and other valuable trees, for the distance of twelve leagues, until you arrive at the town of Tipitapa.

"This town is on the river of the same name, which is the outlet of the Lake of Managua. It is a small place, inhabited by a dark population. There is a boiling spring here, near the falls of the river.

"After crossing the river, the road runs along its borders through a dense forest, with a very rich soil. Here is found the logwood (Nicaragua-wood) in great abundance.

" Two leagues from Tipitapa is the hacienda of San Ildefonso, a large cattle estate. The land from this point begins to rise. After passing three other large haciendas, the first difficult ascent is found. It is an abrupt hill, very toilsome for mules, covered with small stones made round by their passage. On reaching the top of the hill, the country opens into a large plain, covered with '*guacal*' trees. The soil of this plain is a black clay, very difficult to pass in the rainy season. In the summer it is dry and destitute of vegetation.

" The hacienda of La Concepcion completes the second day's journey, being fourteen leagues from the town of Tipitapa.

" From La Concepcion to the town of Chocoyas is eight leagues, over the same plain, covered with broken lava. One league from Chocoyas the road crosses, by a ford, the large river of Matagalpa.

" Chocoyas is a large old Spanish town. In the plaza are the ruins of a large church, commenced many years since, but never completed.

" In the hills which surround the town many veins of gold and silver ore have been found, and in the gulches near are very beautiful white carnelians.

" Magnetic iron ore is also found near this place. The road, after leaving the town, crosses the same river. The character of the country is the same, being a perfectly level plain for about six leagues, when the land rapidly rises, till the town of La Trinidad is reached. This is a beautifully-situated place, lying in a lovely valley, surrounded by the most fertile land in the world. To the right are the gold mines of Jicora. From La Trinidad the ascent is very abrupt for about four leagues, when the table-land is again reached. The distance to the town of Esteli is seven leagues.

" Esteli is a little town in a small plain, through which winds a river of the same name, which empties into the Lake of Managua. There is a grist-mill here, and the country produces considerable wheat, of medium quality. There are large quantities of wild silk in the forests, and many veins of silver ore have been found in the hills. From here to the hacienda of Ablandon the land rises in abrupt ascents, alternating with table lands, producing the best grass in the state. From this hacienda the land again rises, and, on attaining the summit, a lovely plain of about three leagues in length is crossed. The descent from the plain is equally abrupt with the ascent. From the summit the volcano of Momotombo is plainly seen. The road then follows the river of Condega for about six leagues, crossing it thirteen times, until the pretty town of the same name is reached. This is one of the finest towns in the state, having a church and many good dwellings. From this place to the Indian town of Palacaguina is two leagues, through a highly fertile country. From Palacaguina to Totogalpa is four leagues; from Totogalpa to Marquilisa is seven leagues. This town is the centre of the mining district in this state. In every direction about it the hills are filled with silver and gold ore. Within a circuit of three leagues there are over fifty veins of silver ore known. These have not been explored, as there is no capital here to carry on any works of the kind. Copper mines have also been found near.

"There is a fine vein of iron ore, and also a tin mine, in the vicinity. Seven leagues from Marquilisa is the town of Depilto. Here are the works of Don F. Paguaga and Don Felix Cerra. They have several very valuable mines, and in the town and in its vicinity are over a hundred of the best veins known. Copper ore is also found, though not to the same extent.

"Respectfully yours, J. S. BRADBURY."

Several large streams flowing into the Atlantic take their rise in Segovia. The largest of these are the Rio Escondido, running along the base of the range of mountains which shuts in the basin of Nicaragua on the north, and the Rio Coco, Wanks or Segovia, which, for the greater part of its course, constitutes the boundary between Nicaragua and Honduras. It flows into the Atlantic at Cape Gracias á Dios, in latitude 15° N. Neither of these streams is well known. From all accounts, with the exception of the parts flowing through the alluvions and level lands of the coast, they are rapid, and the navigation is impeded by rocks and falls. Canoes and piraguas, nevertheless, do ascend both, almost to their sources, but always with difficulty.

I have in my possession an original letter from Don Francisco Irias, who descended this river in 1842. He observes that it has several large tributaries, the Coa and Poteca from the north, and the Bocay and Pantasma from the south, and proceeds:

"I pass now to describe the rapids, which commence at the place called Pailla. They are, *Gualiquitan*, which has a strong current, and a broken, narrow channel between the rocks, but which may be passed without the least danger. *Ulacuz*, which is similar, but also without danger, abounding in water derived from the great river Ulacuz, which falls from the right, from fearful (*espantosa*) mountains, in my opinion extending to the southeast. *Guascuru* has its rapids, which, though somewhat abrupt, are without risk in the passage. *Quiroz* is similar, although there is a fall before arriving to it, around which, however, nature has formed a canal, so that the navigation of the river is uninterrupted. *Turuquitan* is a rapid or narrows, which is only dangerous for the transportation of cattle, on account of a great rock in the middle of a stream, upon which, if the rowers are not dexterous, the rafts are sure to run. But accidents are rare, inasmuch as the oarsmen are accustomed to this kind of navigation from their youth. *Suginquitan* is another unimportant rapid. At *Crantara* the current is strong, but the passage is entirely practicable, as is also the case at *Pistalquitan*. The rapid of *Cairas*, at first sight, terrifies the voyager with its rushing, foaming, and tumultuous waters, yet does not prevent his passage, for nature has also here provided marvelously for overcoming the difficulty, and made a side canal, before arriving at the dangerous point, by means of which the boats can be passed by the oarsmen in an hour with entire safety. *Tilras* and *Quipispe* are the final rapids, and are unimportant.

"These are the sole obstructions to the navigation of the river from the point of embarkation to the sea, at Cape Gracias á Dios. At present the descent occupies about ten days. Two days are taken up in descending the rapids here described, and four in ascending them. It will be observed that only about a fifth part of the river is in any way obstructed. The delay in the voyage is chiefly occasioned by unloading and reloading at some of the points above mentioned. From the last-named rapids to the cape there is scarcely any current, and it is necessary to use the oars. This part of the country through which the river passes is very beautiful, being composed of open plains covered with grass and scattered trees. It is a section well adapted to raising black cattle and horses, as also to the introduction of colonies, which, in a few years, could attain to prosperity and riches upon its virgin soil in cultivating its numerous valuable fruits, and in consequence of its proximity to the cape and the Great Antilles affording easy means of exportation and a market. Mules and horses may here be raised in the greatest abundance, and profitably shipped to Cuba, Jamaica, and other points where most valued.

"It is lamentable to find so beautiful a coast with no other population except a few worthless *Moscos* (Mosquitos), unable, from want of education, as unfitted by disposition, to attain to any improvement in the future. I will endeavor to give some idea of their savage situation and customs. Most of them subsist by hunting and fishing, and a very few by a rude and petty agriculture, planting, in little patches on the borders of the river, small quantities of plantains, yucas, sweet cane, and cotton, the last of which is rudely spun and woven by the women in the form of blankets, sails for their canoes, strings for their bows, and netting for feather-work. Some of their feather-work is quite beautiful. They make a kind of cloth of the bark of a tree, called *uni*, which serves for dress and for covering at night.

"They celebrate the anniversaries of the death of their parents or friends with most doleful and unharmonious songs and wailings, which are enough to put the timid traveler to flight. This mourning or lamentation is chiefly performed by the women, under a tent of *ule* bark. Some perform the ceremony walking backward and forward for the distance of about one hundred yards, in the following manner: they advance four or five steps, and then fall flat on their chest and face, with a force apparently great enough to kill themselves, repeating the same barbaric ceremony until the night closes. Some paint their faces with *achiote* or *tile*, and, though they exhibit some skill in this, most are rendered horrible from the operation. They are all very much addicted to strong drinks, and when a dram is given them they exhibit great satisfaction, and endeavor to return some article which their situation enables them to give; but this is done on the moment, and the favor is soon forgotten.

"They appear kind, and exert themselves to please strangers who may visit their huts; for, though there are among them some bad and disorderly Indians, yet there are very few who will offer any violence to the traveler, principally, however, on account of the fear in which they stand of their chiefs, to whom they pay great deference. For any fault of obedience or any crime they are severely punished, so that traders may carry on their traffic with little fear of insult or injury. They are fond of dances, for which they provide fermented liquors of cane-juice and yuca in great abundance, and when the day fixed upon arrives, a great number of families collect, all having their faces fantastically painted. When they are gathered, two designated dancers open the ceremony, appearing suddenly from the depths of the forest, where they are previously hidden, dressed in palm leaves, and painted of various colors. These extraordinary figures enter a square covered with *pacaya* leaves, where they dance a whole day, joined by many people. Meanwhile, most of the guests remain in or about the hut of their host, drinking eagerly the fermented liquors, which, being strong, soon upset them, producing violent vomiting. Upon recovering a little, and the sun somewhat declining, the males form their dance apart from the women, making use, as instruments of music, of a dull-sounding drum, and of some great, hoarse-sounding pipes of hollow reeds, the noise of which is frightful, accompanied by some small pipes, to the measure of which rude instruments the musicians as well as the people dance until nine or ten o'clock at night. The women, also apart, commence their dance at eight o'clock at night, and continue until five in the morning. They form a right line, each taking the hand of the other, occasionally separating and shaking a rattling gourd, to the sound of which, accompanied by a low chant, they dance. It can hardly be said that any of these dances are worth seeing; but it is certain that, in spite of their extravagance, they do not fail greatly to amuse the civilized spectator.

"Some of these Moscos (Mosquitos) raise a few mares, and some cows, besides which they have a little commerce with Belize, from which place are brought a little clothing, iron pots, guns, axes, and other articles, which are carried to different points in the valley of Pantasma, the old Look-out, and to the town of Talpeneca, where they are exchanged for calves of one or two years old, which are carried in *balsas* (rafts) down to the coast.

"The chief or 'king' who at this time governed these savages was a man of small stature, thin, with an aquiline nose, dark color, descended from *Xicaque* and *Mosco* ancestors, and had some education. His residence was generally upon the banks of the river. He was hospitable to the voyagers, inviting them to his hut, and feasting them to the best of his ability while they remained with him. He also insisted on all who were fond of *aguardiente* (rum) to drink until they could not move, on pain of being regarded as wanting in consideration to him.

"Cape Gracias á Dios unfortunately has no commerce, but it has a favorable and picturesque situation. It has in front a salt lake of large capacity, which is separated from the ocean by a strip of land covered with mangroves, opening from the sea upon the south, where vessels may enter to reach the town or settlement. The coast is here occupied by Moscos and Sambos.

among whom are one or two Englishmen. One of these is named Stanislaus Thomas Haly, who has about one hundred head of cattle, with some mares and saddle-horses. The climate at this point is healthy, as is also that of the valley of the river, for in all my journey I saw but one sick person.

"Of the islands on the coast I have no personal knowledge. In returning from the cape I was occupied twenty days. Mr. Haly assured me that a road might be opened by which the journey from the cape to this point might be made in six days. He also stated that, in his opinion, at a cost of ten thousand dollars, the few difficulties in the river, which obstruct the transportation of commodities, could be removed."

The coast of Central America bordering on the Caribbean Sea, from Bluefields Lagoon (seventy miles north of San Juan) to Cape Cameron, some distance to the north and westward of Cape Gracios á Dios, has long borne this somewhat vague geographical designation, "Costa del Mosquito," or Mosquito Shore. The name was always purely geographical, and never conveyed, or was intended to convey, any idea of political separation from the rest of Central America. Nor is the name derived, as has been supposed, from the abundance of the insects called mosquitoes, but from a horde of Sambos, or mixed Indians and negroes, which has sprung up there, called *Moscos* by the Spaniards, *Moustics* by the buccaneers, and *Mosquitos* by the English. These barbarians never occupied the whole of this coast, but were always confined to a narrow strip of the shore in the neighborhood of Sandy Bay.

This coast, as I have already had occasion to observe, is, for the most part, alluvial. The climate is moist, warmer than that of the interior, and not as salubrious, although, in the latter respect, it is entitled to rank as high or higher than any of the West India islands. Besides the rivers Wanks and Escondido, it is traversed by several other large streams, rising in the table-lands of Nicaragua and Honduras. Toward their sources these are rough and rapid, but as they approach the ocean they lose their turbulent character, and flow majestically into the sea. Some of these have formed large salt-water lakes or lagoons at their mouths, which constitute very good harbors for vessels of light draught. The greater part of the country is fertile, and capable of producing in the greatest abundance cotton, sugar, coffee, indigo, rice, and tobacco. It has also immense savannas or open fields covered with grass, which are well adapted to pasturage and the raising of cattle; and almost inexhaustible supplies of mahogany, cedar, rosewood, and other valuable timbers may be obtained on the coast and in the neighborhood of the streams.* Roberts assures us, also, that, back from the rivers, there are broad, sandy plains, covered with fine pines, some of them large enough for the masts of ships. These fine savannas, he adds, much resemble the pine lands of North Carolina. The cays, bays, and islands near the coast abound in turtle, and their shells have always been the chief article of export from the shore.

The geography of the Mosquito Shore is very imperfectly known. Upon the coast, however, there are several very good harbors, and positions capable of easy settlement. Bluefields Lagoon derives its name from a Dutch pirate named Blauvelt, who had his head-quarters there during the predominance of the buccaneers in these seas. It is a considerable body of water, some thirty or forty miles in length, and almost completely land-locked. There is a bar at its entrance, with but fourteen feet of water, but within the bar it has from four to six fathoms. The great river Escondido, and some smaller streams, flow into it. The lands bordering on these rivers are said to be extremely fertile, and capable of producing all the staples of the tropics.

* The following passage is from a Memorial on the Mosquito Shore, prepared by the Council of State of Jamaica, and transmitted to the Board of Trade and Plantations in 1773:

"The climate of the Mosquito Shore is milder than any in the West India islands, and the air is more salubrious; the lands are every where well watered, and every where fertile. The soil is rich in an uncommon degree. The necessaries, and even the luxuries of life, present themselves on all sides. The rivers, lagoons, and sea abound in excellent fish, and the coasts afford the greatest number of excellent turtle, both for food and the shell, of any country of equal extent in the world. The cotton-tree, cacao, and vanilla flourish spontaneously all over the country. Indigo, too, is a native, and seems to be the same with that of Guatemala, which is accounted the best of any. The sugar-cane here arrives at as great perfection as in any of the islands; and of mahogany and sarsaparilla the quantity exported annually is so great as to render the settlement already an object of no small importance to the commerce of Great Britain—no less than 800,000 feet of the former, and 200,000 pounds of the latter, exclusive of 10,000 pounds of tortoise shell, having been shipped to England in 1769. The banks of the rivers and lagoons are equally well adapted to the growth of logwood as any part of Honduras; and we have reason to think that there is here enough to supply all Europe."

Thirty miles to the north of Bluefields is Pearl Cay Lagoon. It affords a tolerable harbor for small vessels, but ships of large size can not pass the bar at its mouth. A considerable river, the Wawashaan, falls into this lagoon. The country around it corresponds generally with that in the neighborhood of Bluefields. Thirty miles farther to the northward, a large river, the Rio Grande, flows into the sea. It has a dangerous bar at its mouth, but when this is passed, it is said that it may be navigated by small boats for a distance of a hundred miles into the interior. Farther to the northward are the Prinzapulka, the Tongla, Brackma, Wava, Duckwara, and some other considerable streams. Next in order is the Rio Wanks at Cape Gracias á Dios. Above this cape, Carataska and Brus Lagoons, and the Patuca and Rio Tinto, or Black River, are the most striking geographical features of the coast.*

It has already been intimated that but a very small portion of the Mosquito Shore is inhabited or occupied by what are called the Mosquito Indians. These are few in number, and are composed chiefly of Sambos (*i. e.*, negroes crossed with Indians), and of the children of Jamaica traders, captains and crews of coasting vessels, by Indian, negro, or Sambo women. The negro element in this extraordinary mixture was introduced by the slaves from a vessel wrecked nearly two hundred years ago at Cape Gracias á Dios, by runaway slaves from the Spanish districts, and by the slaves which came with the settlers from Jamaica, at the time when England attempted to take possession of the coast, about the middle of the last century. At first these hybrids were confined to the vicinity of Sandy Bay and Cape Gracias,† but afterward, with the aid of the pirates and Jamaica traders, established themselves farther to the south-

* "A great part of this coast," says Roberts, "is overflowed during the rainy season, and it is possible for a canoe to pass at that period, by inland navigation, from Para Lagoon and Wava rivers. This is the case, generally speaking, with all the low savanna land from Pearl Cay Lagoon and the Cape, and thence to Plantain River."

† Robert Hodgson, who was sent out by Governor Trelawney, in 1740, to excite these Indians against the Spaniards, reports that the territory occupied by them was eighty leagues in length, from Cape Gracias southward. The extension to Pearl Cay and Bluefields Lagoon took place subsequently, and was effected through English aid.

ward, at Pearl Cay and Bluefields Lagoon. But they never occupied any portion of the coast below the point last named, although it is not to be doubted that they occasionally accompanied the English buccaneers in their descents upon other portions of the Spanish Main.

The entire number of these people does not probably exceed two thousand, certainly not three thousand. In the estimates heretofore made, the pure Indians (Woolwas, Tonglas, Cookras, etc.) have been included, with the view of giving the Mosquitos an importance which they do not possess. But these Indians do not recognize what is called "Mosquito authority," and have always been in a state of hostility with the Sambos.

The true Mosquitos are principally established at Bluefields, Pearl Cay, Prinzapulka, Rio Grande, Sandy Bay, and Cape Gracias. Their character and habits at Cape Gracias have been impartially described by Colonel Irias, whose account is equally applicable to the entire stock. From their indiscriminate intercourse with the traders and others, as from the total absence of marriage relations, they have contracted a leprous taint, similar to that which has diseased and is destroying the Sandwich Islanders. For this reason, as also from the detestation in which they are generally held, the Indian tribes of the interior permit no intermixture with them, visiting with death, it is said, individuals guilty of such intercourse. The nature of their social relations may be inferred from the account of Roberts, an English trader on that coast, whose prejudices naturally inclined him to favor these *protégés* of Great Britain. His work was written in 1827. He says:

"I have never known a marriage celebrated among them. These engagements are mere tacit agreements, sometimes broken by mutual consent. The children here and at Bluefields [which, it will soon be seen, is the royal capital] are, in general, baptized by the captains of trading vessels from Jamaica, who, on their annual visit to the coast, perform this ceremony, with any thing but reverence, on all who have been born during their absence; and many of them are indebted to these men for more than baptism. In proof of this, I could enumerate more than a dozen acknowledged children of two of these captains, who seem to have adopted, without scruple, the Indian idea of polygamy to its fullest extent. By this licentious and immoral conduct they have, however, so identified themselves with the natives as to obtain a sort of monopoly of the sale of goods. They have also insinuated themselves into the good graces of some of the leading men, so that their arrival is hailed with joy by all classes as the season of festivity, revelry, christening, and licentiousness."

This free and easy relationship is even now but little altered, for Macgregor, in his statement of the Mosquito question, prepared and published under order of Parliament in 1849, makes the following confession, which illustrates, incidentally, the origin and nature of British influence on the coast:

"In the Mosquito Shore a plurality of mistresses is considered no disgrace. It is no uncommon circumstance for a British subject to have one or more of these native women at different parts of the coast. They have acquired great influence through them," etc.

From the frequent mention, of late years, of a personage styled the "King of the Mosquitos," some portion of the public may have fallen into the error of supposing that what are called the Mosquito Indians do really recognize and obey some such potentate. Nothing could be farther from the truth. No form of government ever existed among these people except such as was vested in their local head men or chiefs, who have often been at variance and in open hostility among themselves. Some of these have assumed the title of governor, others of general, admiral, etc., without, however, having the slightest comprehension of the meaning of the terms. Thus, at the time of Roberts's visit, a chief called Governor Clemente was recognized as head man over the coast from Pearl Cay Lagoon to Sandy Bay; and another, styled General Robinson, held authority in the vicinity of Cape Gracias. When the English superintendent at Belize found it convenient to manufacture a king on the Mosquito Shore, a number of these head men were got together, and, by liberal appliances of rum, induced to affix their marks to a paper, which was afterward produced as an "act of allegiance" to a Sambo selected for the purpose by the English agents. But the chiefs neither understood what they did nor regarded it afterward. The fiction, however, answered its purpose, as will be seen in another place, when we come to speak of the British pretensions on the Mosquito Shore.

Since the English agents have come to reside here permanently, Bluefields has been selected as their place of abode. Roberts says of this place that, when he was there, it was "under the influence of two young men, who claimed affinity to the late British superintendent," and that, "although it was not acknowledged as such by the British government, it might truly be considered a British settlement." What has become of "the two young men" is not known; but Bluefields is now the residence of the supposititious "King of the Mosquitos." It is described as follows in the English paper published at Belize, which, of course, makes the most of it:

"Bluefields is the capital of Mosquitia. It is situated on the river and lagoon of the same name. In the midst of the palms bordering the river is the residence of the king, and his English tutor or guardian, over which floats the British flag At some distance from this is the House of Justice, which is under the Mosquitia flag. Says Macgregor, 'An ensign and standard for the Mosquito nation was sent to the country from England.' In October, 1847, Bluefields and its dependencies contained 599 inhabitants, of all ages, of which 111 were whites, and 488 blacks. These occupied two villages, the largest of which is Bluefields proper, containing 78 houses; the lesser, 'Carlsruhe,' the Prussian colony, consisting of 92 souls, occupying 16 houses. Very few of these houses are built of boards; but one of this kind is the residence of Mr. Walker, diplomatic agent and consul general of England, with whom his Mosquito majesty resides. There is neither church nor priest in the place; but Mr. Green, an English doctor, reads some passages from the Bible on Sundays, in the House of Justice."

The Mosquitos have no settlements except immediately upon the coast. The interior country is occupied by a number of tribes, generally, if not universally, recognizing the Spanish authorities, and, to a greater or lesser extent, using the Spanish language. Between Bluefields and San Juan are the Ramas, who are said to be a mild, inoffensive people, having little communication with the other tribes. Upon the Escondido, or Bluefields River, are situated the Cookra and Woolwa Indians, of whom, however, little is known except that they entertain a hostility toward the Mosquitos, originating at the time when the latter, in concert with the people of Jamaica, made forays into their territories for the purpose of capturing prisoners for slaves. Between the Ramas and Woolwas and the San Juan River is a tribe, or fragment of a tribe, called the Melchoras. Byam, an English traveler, asserts that they are Caribs, who were driven by the English pirates from the islands on the coast, and who retreated thence to this secluded portion of the main land. He adds that they have a great dread of the English, and will hold no communication with the whites unless previously assured that there are no English among them. Upon the Rio Grande and the Prinzapulka, and to the northward of the Woolwas and Cookras, are the Toacas and Payas Indians. Above these, and occupying the country in the direction of Carataska and Brewer's Lagoons and the Patuca River, are Caribs, or, as the name is here pronounced, Kharibees, from the Leeward Islands. They extend to Truxillo, and constitute part of the inhabitants of that port. They are held in dread by the Mosquitos, and have made a greater advance in civilization than any of the other tribes on the coast. There are some other tribes, including those anciently called the Xicaques, Pantasmas, Tahuas, Gaulas, Iziles, Motucas, &c., who are scattered over the territory intervening between the coast and the mountainous regions of the centre of the continent. None of these hold intercourse with the Mosquitos, or recognize their authority; nor can they be included in any estimate of the population of what is facetiously called the "Mosquito kingdom."

B.

(*Note to Chapter VII.*)

THE BAY ISLANDS,

The islands in the Bay of Honduras, as I have already had occasion to say, are of great beauty, salubrity, and fertility, as well as important from their geographical position, and the possession of large and secure ports. These circumstances give peculiar significance to the fact that, on the 17th of July, 1852, a proclamation was issued by the superintendent of the British establishment of Belize, declaring that "*her most gracious majesty the Queen has been pleased to constitute and make the islands of Roatan, Bonacca, Utilla, Barbaretta, Helena, and Morat to be a colony, to be known and designated as 'the Colony of the Bay Islands.'*" This proclamation was issued, as will be seen from its date, nearly two years after the formal promulgation of the convention of Washington of July 4, 1850 (known as the "Clayton and Bulwer Treaty"), which provides, among other things, that "*the governments of the United States and Great Britain, neither the one nor the other, shall ever occupy, or fortify, or colonize, or assume or exercise any dominion over Costa Rica, Nicaragua, the Mosquito Shore, or any part of Central America.*" It may be added here that the organization of these islands as a British colony attracted the attention of the Congress of the United States. The committee of Foreign Relations of the Senate, after a full consideration of the subject, reported "*that the islands of Roatan, Bonacca, Utilla, etc., in and near the Bay of Honduras, constitute part of the territory of the republic of Honduras, and therefore form a part of 'Central America;' and, in consequence, that any occupation of these islands by Great Britain would be a violation of the treaty of July* 5, 1850."

The disregard of solemn treaty obligations, not less than the invasion of the territorial rights of Honduras, involved in the seizure and occupation of these islands by Great Britain, justify me in departing from the general design of this memoir so far as to give an outline of the events which led to this extraordinary result.

Bonacca, then called Guanaja, was discovered by Columbus on his fourth voyage, in 1502. He took possession of it on behalf of Spain, and subsequently discovered, and in like manner took possession of, Roatan.

Among all maritime nations, and at all periods, discovery has been understood to convey the title of sovereignty; and, therefore, these islands, and these coasts of the continent, were universally recognized as pertaining to the dominions of Spain. She remained in undisputed possession of them until the swarming of the buccaneers, when the Gulf of Mexico and the Caribbean Sea became infested with piratical hordes. A great majority of these freebooters were Englishmen—not Malays nor Bornese; their vessels were of British build—not awkward junks and open prahus. Nor was there any fleet, or self-constituted neighboring rajah ready, with British officers and seamen, to inflict a terrible chastisement upon them by wholesale butcheries, as in the case of the Saribas Dyaks. On the contrary, they were openly aided by the English of Jamaica, who, with scarce an exception, were either pirates or the accessories of pirates. Jamaica at this time was supported by the buccaneers, and it is notorious that its governors themselves became associated with their leaders, and shared their plunder. So scandalous became the conduct of some of them, that the crown, although little disposed to disturb a system which contributed so largely to its wealth and revenues, was compelled to remove them. "The King of England," says the pirate Esquemeling, writing in 1670, "to satisfy the King of Spain, recalled some governors of Jamaica; but this did not prevent the pirates from doing as before."

Not satisfied with their depredations on the sea, the pirates, emboldened by success, made descents upon the land, and captured, pillaged, and burned almost every accessible city or town on the Spanish Main. They organized a system of land piracy, in many respects more terrible than that which they had practiced on the ocean. They made excursions into Costa Rica, Nicaragua, Honduras, and Guatemala, as well as in the frontier provinces of New Granada and Mexico. They even made permanent stations at various secluded places on the main land and on the adjacent islands, where they rendezvoused after their various expeditions, to divide their spoils, refit, and organize for new adventures. Bluefields and Cape Gracias á Dios on the Mosquito Shore, and that part of Guatemala now called Belize, were favorite localities with these outlaws. Bluefields and Belize both derive their very names from pirate chieftains.

It can readily be supposed that the island of Roatan, with its safe and excellent harbors, fine climate, and abundant supplies, could not long escape the attention of the cut-throat rovers. An English detachment of that honorable fraternity made a descent upon it as early as 1642, and at the same time captured Guanaja and the neighboring islands. "These positions," says the historian Juarros, "were exceedingly advantageous to them, and proportionately injurious to the Spaniards, because, being near the main land, the English (pirates) were enabled to make their descents whenever they pleased, and with equal facility intercept the commerce between the kingdom of Guatemala and Spain." The annoyance from this source finally became so serious, that the Viceroy of Guatemala, the Governor of Havana, and the President of the Audiencia Real of San Domingo, united in fitting out an expedition to expel the English from this stronghold. The expedition consisted of four ships of war, under the command of Francisco Villalva y Toledo, who endeavored to surprise the pirates, but failed in the attempt. He found the harbors fortified, and was obliged to bear away to the main land for re-enforcements. He subsequently returned, and in the month of March, 1650, after some hard fighting, succeeded in driving the freebooters from the island.

The Spanish regained possession only to find it a waste. The few natives which the pirates had spared and reduced to slavery were too much afraid of their return to remain on the island, and emigrated to the main land, where the government allotted them lands. The island, thus abandoned, seems to have remained deserted until 1742, when the English entertained and attempted the project of obtaining possession of the whole of the Atlantic coast of Central America. In furtherance of this plan, they forcibly seized upon several important points of the main land, captured Truxillo, and made establishments and erected forts at the mouth of Black River. They also occupied Roatan, and fortified it with materials carried off from Honduras. These events, in conjunction with others, led to a war with Spain, which lasted until 1763, when a treaty was concluded, the seventeenth article of which provided that "*his Britannic majesty shall cause to be demolished all the fortifications which his subjects have erected in the Bay of Honduras, and other places of the territory of Spain in that part of the world, within four months*," etc., etc. The forts at Black River and at other places were accordingly evacuated early in 1764. But, in violation of the treaty, the English seem to have continued their occupation of Roatan. They also kept up relations of an improper nature with the Indians on the coast, and engaged largely in smuggling, and in other employments closely allied to piracy, which so exasperated Spain, that in 1780 she once more declared war. In this year the authorities of Guatemala again expelled the English from Roatan. The treaty of peace of 1783, with, it would seem, a special reference to these islands, provided not only that the English should abandon the continent (except a certain well-defined territory, in which they might cut logwood, and nothing more), but "*all islands whatever dependent upon it.*" The English evading the stipulations of the treaty, Spain insisted on more stringent terms, which were incorporated in the treaty of 1786, by which it was provided that the English should "*evacuate the country of the Mosquitos, as well as the continent in general, and the islands adjacent, without exception.*" Nothing could be clearer or more explicit than this; and it seems that, failing to find any means of evading the provision, England did really abandon not only these islands, but the whole coast.

The provisions of this treaty were suspended by the war of 1796, when England, still covetous of these valuable islands, again occupied them, and constituted them the penal settlements of the much-injured natives whom their cruel rapacity had spared in St. Vincent and the other Leeward Islands. Two thousand of these, it seems, were located upon Roatan; but, as soon as the invasion became known in the capital of Guatemala, the captain general directed the Intendant of Honduras to effect its resubjugation. Accordingly, Don José Rossi y Rubia, well supported by officers and men, was sent to the island, which, on the 17th of May, 1797, quietly surrendered. This seems to have been the final attempt of the English during that century forcibly to seize upon these islands, which thenceforward remained in undisputed possession of the Spanish crown.

The stringent provisions of the treaty of 1786 were revived and incorporated in a new treaty between England and Spain, which was concluded August 28th, 1814. The treaty, in its terms, was word for word the same with that which we have quoted, and excluded England "*from the country of the Mosquitos, the continent in general, and the islands adjacent, without exception.*" This treaty was therefore in full force and effect, and the Spaniards in undisputed possession of the island, when, in 1821, the Central American provinces threw off their allegiance to the Spanish crown. Up to that time England had acquired no shadow of a title, by conquest or otherwise, to the island. Four times she had attempted to seize it by force, and had been as often expelled. She had finally, and as late as 1814, by solemn treaty bound herself utterly to abstain from any farther attempts at occupation. At this time we have the testimony of a British officer, Captain Henderson, in command of the forces at the establishment of Belize, that the island was in the occupation of Spain. "*The island of Roatan, as has been previously remarked, belongs to Spain, and a military station is retained on it.*"*

At the time of Central American independence, Roatan and the neighboring islands were dependent upon and under the jurisdiction of the province of Honduras. When that province assumed the rank of a state, the republican authorities, as a matter of course, took possession of these islands. They passed within her jurisdiction, and were occupied by her without dispute or hinderance from any quarter. Her title to them was clear and unquestioned, and she exercised over them freely all the rights of sovereignty.

This state of things continued after Honduras entered the

* Henderson's Account, etc., p. 204.

Federal Republic of Central America, until May, 1830, at which time the British superintendent of Belize, who had become embittered against the republic in consequence of its refusal to surrender certain runaway slaves, in a fit of anger and revenge made a descent upon Roatan, and seized it in behalf of the British crown. At this time the states of Central America were united, and not to be outraged, as now, with entire impunity. The federal government made an immediate and energetic remonstrance to the British government, by whom the act was formally disavowed, and the islands abandoned by the invaders.

From this time until 1841, the island appears to have remained in the peaceful occupation of the people and government of Honduras, although it is not to be doubted that the superintendents of Belize, who seem generally to have had a proclivity to piracy, in virtue of their office, were constantly on the watch for pretexts to add Roatan to their usurpations on the coast; but the rights of Honduras had been too distinctly and too often recognized to admit of being set aside. It was not until 1838 that any pretext was afforded them for putting their designs in effect.

In that year, a party of liberated slaves from the Grand Cayman Islands came to Roatan to settle. The commandant, Don Juan Bta. Loustrelet, who was stationed at Port Royal with a sergeant's guard and a number of convicts, informed them that foreigners desiring to settle on the islands were required by the laws of Honduras to apply to the state government for permission. A portion of emigrants made the requisite application, but another portion refused to do so, and at once applied to the Superintendent of Belize, Colonel Alexander Macdonald, for his support. This officer shortly after made his appearance in the British sloop-of-war "Rover," landed forcibly at Port Royal, ran down the Central American flag, and hoisted that of Great Britain. No sooner had he re-embarked than the commandant again put up the flag of Central America, whereupon Macdonald again went on shore, seized the commandant and his soldiers, and carried them over to the main land, threatening them with death if they ventured to return.*

* The particulars of this outrage are thus gleefully related by Young:

"A British sloop-of-war appeared off the port; a boat full of men was dispatched

Thus, in time of peace with Honduras, whose authority over Roatan the British government had distinctly recognized, that island was again forcibly seized by the officers of Great Britain. The Republic of Central America had in the mean time been dissolved, and the State of Honduras was too feeble and too much distracted by internal factions to make any resistance to this most flagrant aggression. It nevertheless protested energetically against the invasion, but its communications do not appear to have been answered. Macdonald, in the interim, had made himself so obnoxious to all the Central American states that the British government found it politic to remove him. This was done in 1843, when Colonel Fancourt was appointed in his place. This gentleman, it is presumed, was instructed to preserve greater moderation than his predecessor; at any rate, the government of Honduras thought the occasion favorable to renew its representations concerning the unjust and piratical seizure of Roatan. It therefore addressed a letter to Colonel Fancourt, complaining of Macdonald's conduct, and requesting the immediate surrender of the island; to which that officer replied in polite but general terms, evading all responsibility by referring the latter to the British government. The result was an instruction forwarded to Mr. Chatfield to acquaint the government of Honduras that when Colonel Macdonald hauled down the flag of that state in Roatan, it was *by order* of the British government.

Of course this was untrue, for the seizure was Macdonald's own affair; but the British government, by this declaration, assumed the responsibility of the act. This step seems to have been taken for the purpose of screening an over-zealous officer; for it seems incredible that Great Britain cherished the cold-

to the shore, the Central American flag hauled down, and that of Old England planted in its place. Shortly after the vessel set sail, the commandant pulled down the English colors and hoisted his own, which was no sooner observed than the vessel put back, and landed a party of seamen and marines. *The Central American flag was lowered, and two or three of the middies amused themselves by dancing on it.* The commandant and his soldiers, notwithstanding his vociferous protestations, were put on board the vessel, and had the mortification of seeing, on their departure, the meteor flag of Old England waving in the breeze. They were landed on the beach at Truxillo, with a few gentle hints as to their future behavior."—*Young's Narrative*, p. 147.

blooded design of robbing Honduras of these portions of her territory, in the face of her own treaties of 1786 and 1814, and her own disavowal of the seizure of the islands in 1830. The assumption of the responsibility of Macdonald's misdeeds did not necessarily imply that Great Britain pretended to territorial rights in the islands; but, kept in awe by threats, blockades, and other violent measures, on frivolous pretexts, Honduras hesitated to reassert her authority, and confined herself to the only resort of a weak power, remonstrance and protest.

In the mean time, attracted by the superior resources of Roatan, considerable numbers of the Cayman Islanders abandoned the impoverished soil of the Caymans, and established themselves here, so that in the course of a few years, the population, by increase and emigration, amounted to upward of a thousand. For some time they appear to have been without any form of government, living in very primitive style; but with the increase of inhabitants they organized a kind of council, and elected its members from among themselves. This condition of things did not escape the watchful eye of the Belize superintendent, who, as the Cayman Islanders were British subjects, failed not to discover here some kind of pretext for assuming the control and sovereignty of the islands. He seems to have informed the inhabitants at various times that, as English subjects, he should be glad, if they desired it, to nominate magistrates in the island to keep the peace between them; that he did not claim the authority to interfere in their local affairs, but that he was willing to do so on their application to that effect. It would appear, however, that the islanders preferred to elect their own magistrates, the principal of whom was a Mr. Fitzgibbon, a citizen of the United States. It was not until the commencement of the year 1849 that, having been properly instructed in their *rôle*, they "applied" to Colonel Fancourt "to establish a regular form of government in the island!" How far this "application" was brought about by the English agents it is not necessary to inquire; it was certainly a very adroit and plausible way of consummating the violence of Macdonald.

Colonel Fancourt thereupon recommended to the inhabitants to choose twelve representatives to form a Legislative Assembly for the enactment of laws, etc., subject to his veto. He nominated five magistrates, but in a short time the people grew dissatisfied with their conduct, and elected others. The superintendent declared that this was an encroachment on the prerogative of the crown, and, unless they submitted to his nominees, he should withdraw her majesty's protection. They respectfully informed him that, he being a non-resident and unacquainted with the qualifications of individuals, he ought to allow them the privilege of electing municipal authorities. The inhabitants were then divided into two parties, one of which was desirous of being taken under her majesty's protection. They drew up a petition, soliciting the appointment of a stipendiary magistrate, pledging their honor to raise a sufficient revenue to pay his salary and contingent expenses.

The state of affairs existing at this time, *i. e.*, 1850, is thus described by Captain Mitchell, R.N., from which it appears that neither the people themselves nor the British government regarded Roatan as under British authority.

"The people aver that they are quite ignorant under what government they are placed, and whether her majesty's Superintendent at Belize has any authority over them; they are desirous of knowing in what position they are regarded. Some discontented people, such as are found in all communities, have poisoned the minds of others, inducing them to collect together and appoint magistrates in opposition to those recommended by his excellency the superintendent of Belize.

"At times the island has been (from their not knowing their exact position, and from the influence of the discontented) without any sort of government, every man fearing for himself and what he possessed. Such was the state of things when I arrived; they have now elected magistrates, from universal suffrage, to act until the pleasure of the Governor of Jamaica shall be known, to whom they have sent a petition."

The history of this petition is somewhat remarkable. There being two parties, one favorable, and the other opposed to British protection, it became necessary for the former to make their petition as imposing as possible. To this end, the names of the children at the school of the Wesleyan Mission were all added to the list. This precious document was sent to the Superintendent of Belize for transmission to the British Secretary of State for the Colonies. In consequence, Captain Jolly, of the British navy, was sent to Roatan by Sir Charles Grey, Colonial

Secretary, to ascertain of the inhabitants (the 1500 or 2000 negroes aforesaid) whether, if the government appointed a paid magistrate in the island, they would consent to pay a land-tax of a shilling an acre to the British crown. To this proposition, commended by the guns of a vessel of war, and a variety of other arguments equally potent, it is not at all surprising that the negroes gave their consent.

A new superintendent of Belize, Colonel P. E. Wodehouse, who qualified himself for his position as the accomplice of Torrington in Ceylon, had in the mean time been appointed. One of his earliest acts was to visit Roatan in person. He proceeded there in her majesty's brig of war Persian, and calling together a convenient "general meeting," on the 10th day of August, 1852 (more than two years after the ratification of the convention of Washington of July 4th, 1850), formally occupied Roatan and the adjacent islands on behalf of the British crown, and declared them annexed to the superintendency of Belize, under the style of the "Colony of the Bay Islands."

This outline of the political history of these islands reveals a system of aggression on the rights and sovereignty of Honduras unparalleled for its persistency, and terminating in a series of frauds which approach the sublime of effrontery. The brutal force of Macdonald was consummated by the frauds of Wodehouse; and these splendid islands are at this day held by Great Britain in disregard of treaty obligations, and on pretexts so bald and fallacious that they serve only to render conspicuous the crimes which they were designed to conceal.

C.

(*Note to Chapter XII.*)

ABORIGINES OF HONDURAS.

IT would appear from the early records that the northwestern portions of Honduras, bordering on Guatemala, and including the valley of Sensenti, of Copan, and a part, if not all, of the River Chamelicon, were in the occupation of civilized nations. The name of *Calel* or *Kalel*, which they gave to their chiefs, and the fact that their language belongs to the same stock with the Quiché, Kachiquel, Maya, etc., proves that they pertained to the same great family of semi-civilized nations which spread over Guatemala, Chiapa, and Yucatan. But, in respect to the rest of Honduras, our information is not so clear. The chroniclers speak of a number of barbarous nations as existing in the wide region embracing the coast from the Rio Aguan (or Roman) to that of San Juan de Nicaragua (subsequently designated as the Mosquito Shore), and extending inland as far as the plains of Olancho or Ulancho. Among the tribes who inhabited this region, and who were relatively savage and barbarous, the Xicaques and Payas are constantly referred to as the principal and most powerful. These names are still retained by the Indians who occupy the country lying between the Rio Ulua and Cape Gracias á Dios. The Xicaques, greatly reduced, exist in the district lying between the Rio Ulua and Rio Tinto, and the Payas in the triangle between the Tinto, the sea, and the Rio Wanks, or Segovia. It seems probable that the Xicaques were once much more widely diffused, extending over the plains of Olancho, and into the Department of Nueva Segovia, in Nicaragua.

The question then arises, What nations inhabited the country between the Chortis of Sensenti and the Nahuals of San Salvador on the one hand, and the barbarous nations of Totogalpa and Tegucigalpa on the other? In other words, what nations occupied the present Department of San Miguel, in San Salvador, and those of Santa Barbara, Comayagua, Choluteca, and part of Tegucigalpa and Yoro, in Honduras?

No explicit answer to this inquiry can be found in the early histories, but recent investigations may serve to clear up any doubts on the subject.

That this district of country was occupied by a homogeneous people is primarily indicated by the names of places which have been retained from the period of the conquest. The present Department of San Miguel was called *Chaparristique* when it was invaded by Alvarado, and we find this termination *tique* constantly recurring in the names of places, such as Lepaterique, Llotique, Ajuterique, and Jaitique, from the Gulf of Fonseca northward to the Lake of Yojoa or Taulebé.

Within this district there are a number of towns which are wholly inhabited by Indians, who possess more or less of their original language. These towns are all situated in the mountains of Lepaterique and Guajiquero, embracing Lauterique, Guajiquero, Opotero, Cacauterique, Similiton, Yamalanguira, Yucusapa, and the large town of Intibucat. I succeeded in obtaining a short vocabulary of the dialect of Opotero from an Indian of that town whom I encountered in Comayagua. I also obtained another of the dialect of Guajiquero, which place I visited in June, 1853, and subsequently a brief one in the town of Yamalanguira, two leagues to the westward of Intibucat, and close upon the district of the ancient chiefs of Sensenti. I afterward obtained a list of the numerals used by the people of Similiton, together with a few words and phrases, from a gentleman of Tegucigalpa, who in his youth had spent some time in that town. It appears, from a comparison of these vocabularies, that they are all dialects of a single language. The Guajiqueros pronounced their language the *Lenca*, and as we find the *Lenca Indians* constantly referred to in the accounts given by the early missionaries of their expeditions in Honduras, I have adopted this name to designate both the Indians who occupied the district under consideration and their language.

Most of the missionaries who sought to penetrate the regions of the Xicaques and Payas first went to Comayagua, where they are almost always spoken of as employing Lenca Indians to assist them in their expeditions. They accompanied Verdelete when he went through Olancho, by way of the Rio Guyape, into the country of the Xicaques in 1608. This leads us to conjecture that the Xicaques may possibly have been of the same stock with the Lencas, and speaking dialects of the same language. This conjecture derives support from the expressions used by Juarros, in his account of the reduction of the province of Tegucigalpa. He says that in 1661 the Paya Indians frequently plundered the small settlements contiguous to their territories, and that the Xicaques committed depredations in the valleys of Xamastran and Olancho. This led Captain Bart. de Escoto, one of the proprietors of Olancho, to lead an expedition into the Indian country, which he did, bringing away "several Indians, whom he settled in such places as he deemed most convenient." He then, "with three Lenca Indians, went to Guatemala in search of a minister." The person recommended to him by the President was the friar "Fernando de Espino, a learned ecclesiastic, who, being a native of New Segovia, a town bordering on the lands of the Xicaques, *was well acquainted with the Lenca language.*"*

Indeed, it is not improbable that dialects of a common language were spoken by all the aboriginal tribes lying between the Bay of Honduras and the great transverse valley of the Nicaraguan lakes, excepting those who inhabited the low, or lagoon country on the Atlantic coast, now called the Mosquito Shore, and who seem to have had little affinity with the families of the interior. Thus the Indians in the district of Chontales, in Nicaragua, living on the banks of the great river Escondido, of whom Mr. Froebel obtained a short vocabulary in 1851, have a few words in common with the Lencas. These Indians are now

* The Bishop Pelaez, who, however, is very loose in his statements generally, gives an account of these circumstances, in which he speaks of the "damages caused by certain tribes of *Payas* known as *Jicaques*;" and says that it was "tres de estos infideles" (*three of these infidels*) who accompanied Escoto to Guatemala. He also speaks of the Fra Espino as reaching the *Parakas* Indians of the Lenca nation." According to Juarros, we may legitimately infer that the Xicaques and Lencas were of one family, or, at least, spoke one language; and, from the statements of the bishop, that the Xicaques and Payas are of one stock. From both we may deduce, what is probably not far from the truth, that all belonged to a single group.

called Woolwas (probably the Gaulas or Waulas of Juarros, and the *Uluas* of Pelaez). Their word for water is *wass* or *wash*, and enters into the name of one of the rivers in their territories, a branch of the Escondido, viz., *Boswash* or *Boswass*. In the Lenca, water is *güass*, *uash*, or *guash*. In the Lenca, house or hut is *taoo* or *tahü*; in the Woolwa, it is *ü* or *hü*. The word *wass* or *huas* also enters into the names of some of the rivers in the district of the Payas, as *Amacwass*, *Wass-presenia*, the designations of tributaries of the River Patuca.

The inhabitants of the Atlantic coast of Central America, at the period of the discovery, from Punta Castilla de Honduras (anciently *Punta Casinas* or *Caxinas*) to Chiriqui Lagoon (the *Abuerma* of Columbus), were completely savage. This coast, as I have already said, is for the most part low, hot, and unhealthy, and traversed by innumerable lagoons and creeks, affording conditions only favorable for tribes of hunters and fishers; and such, in fact, was the character of the Indians found there by the early voyagers, and such they have remained to this day. The same causes which deterred the semi-civilized nations of the Pacific declivity of the continent, and of the interior table-lands, from occupying this coast, operated to prevent its settlement by the Spaniards, and have retained it within the dominion of untamed nature.

As I have said in a preceding chapter, this coast was discovered by Columbus in his fourth voyage, in 1502. He coasted along it from Punta Castilla to Darien, and, from the concise but clear accounts which have been preserved of his voyage, we are able to obtain very accurate notions of the character and conditions of the inhabitants.

The first land discovered by Columbus in this voyage, after leaving Jamaica, was that of the island of *Guanaja*, the easternmost of a group lying in the Bay of Honduras, and within sight of the main land, which were long known as the *Guanajas*. He reached this island July 30, 1502. Don Bartolome Columbus was sent ashore, where he found a large canoe, "as long as a galleon," covered with an awning, and laden with commodities, such as cloths of cotton of various colors, a species of jacket without sleeves, swords made by inserting flints in the edges of pieces of wood of the proper shape, copper axes, crucibles for melting copper, and the beans of cacao, "which were used as money." Columbus dismissed the people, excepting an old man, who seemed to be "more discreet" and better informed than the others, named *Jumbe*, whom he reserved as an interpreter and guide. Being shown gold, this Indian pointed out the main land, the mountains of which were within sight, as the region where it could be found.

This Indian, it may here be observed, is called a "merchant" in the chronicles, and Herrera ventures the remark that he was returning from Yucatan when discovered by Columbus.

There can be no doubt that the inhabitants of the Guanajas constituted a single family, considerably advanced in civilization, and probably pertaining to the same stock with those occupying the main land, between Punta Castilla westward to the Gulf of Dulce. Diego de Porras, in his account of the voyage of Columbus, describes them as of "fine stature, warlike," but modest and retiring in their demeanor. The island itself is described by Peter Martyr as "so flourishing and fruitful that it might seem an earthly paradise."

Columbus reached Punta Caxinas on the fourteenth of August, and formally landed and took possession of the country on the seventeenth of the same month. This is the point which shuts in the bay, at the head of which Truxillo was afterward founded. The people found there are described as similar to those of the Guanajas. They were dressed in a like manner, in cotton cloth, and had a species of armor, like the Mexicans, made of quilted cotton, which was so thick, as we are assured by Fernando Columbus, as often to resist the strokes of the Spanish swords. There are reasons for believing that the aboriginal inhabitants of the region immediately around Truxillo were connected with those who dwelt to the westward and in the interior of the country, including the great valleys or plains of Olancho, where there were two important provinces governed by powerful chiefs, who had jurisdiction over the coast at Truxillo. Of the character and habits of the Indians here we have but little information. Herrera tells us that when Salcedo was appointed governor of *Ybueras* (Honduras), he applied himself to "know the religion, customs, and capacity of the Indians of that province." He found three principal idols worshiped in the vicinity of Truxillo; one in a temple four leagues from that town, another twenty leagues distant, and a third on an island fifteen leagues distant.* They had all the shape of women, made of a variety of green stone like marble." They had also other idols and places of worship where they offered sacrifices. The high-priests at each of the three principal temples could not marry. They wore their hair long, reaching to their waists. Salcedo farther testified that "the people were not so polite as the Mexicans," and that they "differed little from those of Hispaniola."

After leaving *Punta de Caxinas*, Columbus proceeded eastward along the coast, and a few days afterward landed at the mouth of a great river, where he again took possession of the country, calling the river, from this circumstance, *Rio de la Posession*, now Rio Tinto, or Black River. The Indians here and to the eastward "had not great foreheads like the islanders." They spoke several languages, tattooed themselves in various ways, and had, moreover, "great holes in the lobes of their ears, through which an egg might pass," whence he named this coast "*la Costa de la Oreja*," the Coast of the Ear. Fernando Columbus, in his History, distinguishes the inhabitants here and along the whole coast to the eastward from those at *Punta Caxinas*. He says: "But those to the eastward, toward Cape Gracias á Dios, are almost negroes, beastly, going naked, in all respects very rude, eating, according to the Indian Jumbe, human flesh, and fish raw, as they happen to be caught." Porras correctly describes the coast as "*tierra muy baja*," very low land, inhabited by a very savage people.

On the fourteenth of September, after great difficulties, resulting from adverse winds and currents, Columbus reached a cape whence the coast trended abruptly to the southward, which he called, in token of thankfulness, *Cabo Gracias á Dios*, Cape Thanks to God. He found here a large river entering the sea, and he sent a boat to examine it, which was upset, and some sailors lost, whence he called it *Rio del Desastre*, River of the

* The island here referred to was probably that of Guanaja, where, as we have elsewhere seen, aboriginal monuments of considerable extent are still to be found.

Disaster. He says nothing about the inhabitants whom he found here, but the inference is very distinctly conveyed by Fernando Columbus that they differed in no essential respect from those of the Costa de la Oreja. He describes the detention of the ships, and the difficulties which they encountered until the twenty-fifth of September, when they reached an island called *Quriviri*, where there was a town on the main land called *Cariai*. Here, he says, the land became higher, and "there was a better country." Columbus named the coast here, from the town on the main land, *Cariai* or *Cariay*. In his letter to the Spanish sovereigns he speaks of the inhabitants as fishers, and as "great sorcerers and very terrible." Upon landing, he found several large wooden houses, thatched with palms, which were sepulchres. In one of these was a dead body embalmed, "*embalsamado*;" in another were two bodies, all "without bad odor," carefully wrapped in cotton cloth and mats. Over these bodies were tablets of wood, carved with various figures of animals and other objects, and on some "were representations of the dead." The people had some ornaments of native gold and instruments of copper. They were tattooed. Their language was difficult, and the different towns had different dialects; "but while this was the case among the savages of the coast," Columbus thought "it otherwise among the people of the interior." Herrera distinguishes the people of Cariay from those to the northward, and describes them as like the inhabitants of Castello del Oro, which was the early designation of the country from Chiriqui Lagoon southward to the Gulf of Uraba.

From Cariay Columbus proceeded on his course until he reached *Zerabora* (now Boca del Toro), which was close to *Abuerma* (now Chiriqui Lagoon). Here the people had plates of gold like those of Cariay, and, it would seem, spoke a cognate language, since, in the words of Herrera, "they showed no fear, because the two Indians of Cariay spoke to them." These Cariay Indians are also spoken of as persuading those of Abuerma to give up their golden ornaments.

From all these facts, it appears that Honduras was anciently occupied by at least four distinct families or groups of aborigines:

I. The Chortis of Sensenti, belonging to the same great group with the Quichés, the Kachiquels, Mayas, etc., and occupying what is now the Department of Gracias.

II. The Lencas, less advanced in civilization, and, under the various names of Chontals, and perhaps Xicaques and Payas, occupying what is now the Department of San Miguel in San Salvador, of Comayagua, Choluteca, Tegucigalpa, and parts of Olancho and Yoro in Honduras, including the islands of Roatan, Guanaja, etc.

III. Various tribes intervening between the Lencas proper and the inhabitants of Cariay, or what is now called the Mosquito Shore; and,

IV. The savages who dwelt on the Mosquito Shore, from near Carataska Lagoon southward to the Rio San Juan, and who then spoke, as they still speak, a language entirely distinct from the dialects in use among the Indians of the interior, to whom they were in no respect equal.

D.

THERMOMETRICAL AND BAROMETRICAL OBSERVATIONS—1853.

Place.	Date.	6 A.M.				12 M.				3 P.M.				6 P.M.			
		Barom.	Ther.	Wind.	F.	Barom.	Ther.	Wind.	F.	Barom.	Ther.	Wind.	F.	Barom.	Ther.	Wind.	F.
Comayagua.	April 24	28.111	77.	N.	2	28.090	85.	N.	4	28.040	84.	N.	1				
"	25	28.100	77.			28.125	82.	N.	1	28.056	83.	N.	4	28.040	81.	N.	4
"	26	28.155	75.			28.138	80.5			28.059	83.5	N.	4	28.096	79.5	N.	2
"	27	28.162	76.5	N.	2	28.135	82.5	N.	4	28.069	84.5	N.	3				
"	28	28.149	75.			28.157	78.5	N.	1	28.080	84.	N.	4				
"	29	28.159	75.	N.	3	28.120	82.	N.	3	28.161	85.	N.	3				
"	30	28.122	75.	N.	2	28.061	83.	N.	3	28.019	84.						
"	May 1	28.074	75.	N.	2	28.032	84.5	N.	3	28.009	86.	N.	3				
"	7							N.	1	28.050							
"	8	28.050	74.	N.	1			N.E.	2	28.068	75.	N.E.	2	28.115	76.	N.	1
"	9	28.100	71.5	N.	1	28.095	80.5	N.E.	2	28.060	81.	N.	1				
"	10	28.140	73.5	N.		28.145	85.										
"	11	28.155	74.5	N.		28.158	80.	N.	1	28.100	81.5	N.	1				
"	12	28.160	73.	N.	1	28.165	80.5	N.	3	28.105	82.5	N.	3				
"	13	28.161	75.5	N.N.W.	2	28.159	81.	N.N.W.	2	28.085	78.5	N.N.E.	1				
"	14	28.135	75.	N.	3	28.130	80.5	N.	2								
"	16	28.080	75.														
"	17	28.100	73.			28.100	78.	N.W.	1	28.065	76.						
"	18	28.131	73.														
"	19	28.165	74.	N.	1	28.195	80.	N.	4								
"	25	28.225	70.5	N.	1	28.220	79.5	N.W.	4	28.144	81.5	N.W.	4				
"	26	28.210	73.5	N.	2												
"	27									28.151	81.	N.	2				

"		29	28.225	76.5	N.	2												
"	June	1					28.160	81.	S.E.	2	28.140	81.5	S.E.	2				
"		3					28.180	78.5	N.E.	1					28.112	79.	N.W.	3
"		4	28.200	74.5	N.N.W.	1												
"		5	28.161	74.5	N.N.W.						28.105	79.5	N.N.W.	2	28.110	78.5	N.N.W.	1
"		6	27.890	76.	N.	1	27.880	81.5	N.	4					27.825	82.	N.	3
"		7	27.900	77.	N.	4					27.860	83.5	N.	2				
"		8	27.910	74.							27.850	85.5	N.	5				
"		9	27.910	75.			27.920	77.	N.	2	27.920	77.			27.880	76.		
"		10	27.910	74.25			27.920	77.	N.	1	27.850	80.	N.	3				
"		11	27.890	75.			27.880	75.			27.880	79.75	N.	5	27.800	76.		
"		12	27.850	74.			27.825	79.							27.800	78.		
"		13	27.850	74.														
"		14	27.870	75.			27.870	77.5							27.800	78.		
"		15	27.850	73.			27.850	77.							27.800	79.		
"		16	27.850	74.			27.83	79.	S.	3					27.78	79.		
"		17	27.850	76.5	S.	4	27.850	77.	S.	4					27.850	77.		
"		18	27.900	74.	N.		27.900	79.3	S.						27.890	79.		
"		19									27.890	82.	N.					
"		20	27 860	74.5														
"		21	27.910	74.75														
"		22	27.900	73.75			27.920	78.										
"		23	27.920	76.			27.960	79.75										
"		24	27.890	76.			27.900	76.										
"		25	27.880	74.5														
"		26	27.800	74.														
"		27	27.900	74.5														
"		28	27.880	73.														
"		29	27.860	73.														
"		30	27 900	74.5			27.600	86.	N.	2								

THERMOMETRICAL AND BAROMETRICAL OBSERVATIONS—1853.—(*Continued.*)

Place.	Date.	6 A.M.		12 M.		3 P.M.		
		Barom.	Ther.	Barom.	Ther.	Barom.	Ther.	Wind.
Santa Rosa.	July 10	26.170	67.5	26.210		26.220	72.	
"	11	26.250	68.			26.250	73.	N.
"	12	26.230	68.	26.200	72.5			
"	13	26.210	67.	26.210	72.5			
"	14	26.200	70.			26.200	75.	
"	15	26.200	68.	26.200	71.5			
"	16	26.200	68.			26.150	72.5	
"	17	26.151	68.			26.150	74.	
"	18	26.200	68.					
San Salvador.	Aug. 11	27.60	70.					
"	12	27.575	71.	27.600	79.			
"	13	27.590	76.	27.600	75.	27.550	79.	
"	14	27.580	74.	27.550	78.			
"	15	27.570	73.	27.571	80.			
"	16	27.570	74.					
"	17	27.580	74.	27.550	80.			
"	18	27.570	74.					
"	19	27.590	75.					
"	20	27.580	75.			27.550	82.	
"	21	27.570	76.					
"	22	27.560	76.	27.570	81.			
"	23			27.570	78.			
"	24	27.57	74.					
"	25	27.56	76.					
"	27	27.60	76.					
"	28	27.56	76.					

E.

BIBLIOGRAPHY.

IN the Geographical Introduction to this memoir, I have referred to this Appendix for the subjoined chronological list of the books and pamphlets relating, in whole or in part, to Central America, all of which are in my possession, or have been consulted by me in the course of my investigations.

Journey over land from the Gulf of Honduras to the Great South Sea, performed by John Cockburn and five other Englishmen, etc., etc. London, 1735.

Voyage from Honduras to Merida, etc., by Lieutenant Cook. London, 1769.

Account of the British Settlements on the Mosquito Shore, vol. v. of Bryan Edwards's History of the West Indies. London, 1773.

Full Answer to the King of Spain's last Manifesto respecting the Bay of Honduras and the Mosquito Shore, its ancient Free British Settlement and Importance to Great Britain. London, 1779.

Memoir on the Mosquito Territory, by Captain John Wright, R.N. London, 1808.

An Account of the British Settlement of Honduras; being a view of its Commercial and Agricultural Resources, Soil, Climate, Natural History, etc.; to which is added, Sketches of the Manners and Customs of the Mosquito Indians, preceded by the Journal of a Voyage to the Mosquito Shore. Illustrated by a Map. By Captain George Henderson, 44th Regiment. London, 1811.

Some Account of the British Settlements on the Mosquito Shore, drawn up from the Manuscripts of the late Colonel Hodgson, etc. Edinburgh, 1822.

Sketch of the Mosquito Shore, including the Territory of Poyas, etc., by Thomas Strangeways, K.G.C. Edinburgh, 1822.

Bosquejo Politico Estadistico de Nicaragua, por Miguel Gonzales Saravia, General de Brigada. Guatemala, 1824.

Journal of Dr. Laragnino from Omoa to Guatemala, British New Monthly Magazine, No. 60, December, 1825.

Memoirs of Mr. William Veith and George Brysson, etc., edited by Dr. M'Crie. Edinburgh, 1825.

A Statistical and Commercial History of the Kingdom of Guatemala, in Spanish America, etc., etc., by Don Domingo Juarros, a native of Guatemala. Translated by John Baily, R.M. London, 1825.

On the Practicability of joining the Atlantic and Pacific Oceans by a Ship-canal across the Isthmus of America, by Robert B. Pitman. London, 1825.

Six Months' Residence and Travels in Central America through the Free States of Nicaragua, and particularly Costa Rica, giving an interesting account of that beautiful Country, etc., etc. By J. Hale. Published for the Author, and sold by W. Borrodaile, 114 Fulton Street. New York, 1826.

[A resumé of this sketch was made by Mr. Worden, and printed in French, in Paris.]

Narrative of Voyages and Excursions on the East Coast and in the Interior of Central America, etc., by Orlando W. Roberts, many years a Resident Trader. Edinburgh, 1827.

Bridges's Annals of Jamaica, chapter xiii., vol. ii. London, 1828.

Guatemala, or the United Provinces of Central America in 1827–8, etc., by Henry Dunn. New York, 1828.

An Official Visit to Guatemala, etc., by G. A. Thompson, Esq., Commissioner to Report to his Britannic Majesty's Government on the State of the Republic of Central America. With a Map. London, 1829.

Reise naar Guatemala in 1829. Central-America beschouwd uit aan geschiedkundig en statisk oogpunt. J. Haefkens. Dordrecht, 1832.

Memorias para la Historia de la Revolucion de Centro America, por un Guatemalteco (José Montufar). Jalapa (Mexico), 1832, p. 257.

Coup d'Œil sur la Republique de l'Amerique Centrale, etc., accompagné d'une Carte. Par MM. Dumartray et Rouhaud. Paris, 1832.

On the Communication between the Atlantic and Pacific Oceans, by way of Lake Nicaragua, by Caleb Phillips, R.N. Journal of the Royal Geographical Society of London, vol. iii. (1833), p. 375–280.

[Galindo, John, an Irishman, who entered the service of the old Republic of Central America about the year 1827, received the rank of colonel in the army, was governor of the Department of Peten in Guatemala, subsequently named representative of the republic to the court of St. James, but was refused recognition on the ground of being a British subject, and was finally killed in an Indian town in Honduras. He was far from being a close observer, nor was he a man of large information. He nevertheless was industrious, and gave the world many interesting facts, coupled with crude speculations, on the states of Central America and the country in general. After Juarros, he was, I believe, the first to direct public attention to the ruins of Copan. He wrote :]

Description of the Rio Usumasinta, in Guatemala, dated Flores, Lake Peten (or Itza), March 12, 1832 ; with Map. Journal of the Royal Geographical Society of London, vol. iii., p. 59–64.

Notice of the Caribs in Central America, by Colonel John Galindo, a single page (290), Transactions of the Royal Geographical Society of London, vol. iii., 1833.

Account of the Eruption of the Volcano of Coseguina, in Nicaragua, on the 17th of January, 1835, by John Galindo. Transactions of the Royal Geographical Society of London, vol. v. (1835), p. 387–392.

On Central America (containing a general Description of the Country, and an Account of Costa Rica). With a Map ; by John Galindo. Journal of the Royal Geographical Society of London, vol. vi. (1836), p. 116–136.

The Ruins of Copan, in Central America, by John Galindo, dated Copan, June 19, 1835. Transactions of the American Antiquarian Society, vol. ii., p. 543–550.

Narrative of a Journey to Guatemala, in Central America, in 1838, by G. W. Montgomery. New York, 1839.

Mémoire sur le Guatemala, et le Colonisation du Département de Vera Paz. Bruxelles, 1840.

Incidents of Travel in Central America, Chiapas, and Yucatan, by John L. Stephens, 2 vols. New York, 1841.

America Central. Reclamacion de la Intervencion del Colonel Alejandro Macdonald, Superintendente de Belize, en el Colonel Manuel Quijano, Administrador del Puerto de San Juan del Norte. Leon, 1842.

Defenza de los Derechos del Pais, en los Cuestiones promovidas por el Consul de su Majestad Britannica, etc. Leon, 1843.

Memoria sobre el Fuego de los Volcanos de Centro America, por Miguel Larreynaga. Guatemala, 1843, p. 77.

Efemerides de los Hechos Notables acaecidos en la Republica de Centro America, desde el año de 1821 hasta el de 1842, por Alejandro Marure, etc. Guatemala, 1844.

Excursion to the Lake of Nicaragua, up the Rio San Juan, by George Lawrence, Assistant Surveyor of H. M. S. Thunder, Nautical Magazine, 1840–41.

Sketches of the East Coast of Central America, from Notes of Captain Richard Owen, etc., by Captain Bird Allen, R.N., Journal of the Royal Geographical Society of London, vol. xi. (1841), p. 76–98.

Account of the Province of Vera Paz, in Guatemala, and of the Indian Settlements therein, by Padre Fr. Alonzo de Escobar, Journal of the Royal Geographical Society of London, vol. xi. (1841), p. 89–97.

Notes on Lake Nicaragua and Province of Chontales, by Chevalier Emanuel Friedricksthal, Journal of the Royal Geographical Society of London, vol. xi. (1841), p. 97–100.

On the Isthmus between Lake Granada (Nicaragua) and the Pacific Ocean. By John Baily. Journal of the Royal Geographical Society of London, vol. xiv. (1844), p. 127–128.

Notes on the Gulf of Mexico, Rio Tampico, and its Vicinity, and on the Rio Tobasco. With a Map. By Peter Masters, Seaman, of Liverpool. Journal of the Royal Geographical Society of London, vol. xv. (1845).

Bericht über die im höchsten Auftrage Seiner Königlichen Hoheit des Prinzen Carl von Preussen und Sr. Durchlaucht des Herrn Fürsten v. Schoenburg-Waldenburg bewirkte Untersuchung einger Theile des Mosquitolandes, etc. Berlin, 1845.

Canal of Nicaragua, etc., by N. L. B. (Louis Napoleon Bonaparte). London, 1846.

Narrative of a Residence on the Mosquito Shore, with an Account of Truxillo, and the adjacent islands of Roatan and Bonacca. By Thomas Young. London, 1847.

Documentos en que se funda el Derecho, que el Estado de Nicaragua tiene al Terretorio, que se disputa con la proteccion de el Gobierno Ingles. Leon, 1847.

Travels in Central America, etc., by R. G. Dunlop. London, 1847.

Memoria dirijida por el Ministerio de Estado y de Relaciones de Nicaragua, á la Asambléa Constituyente del mismo Estado, sobre los Derechos Territoriales del propio pais en la Costa del Norte, llamada Mosquitos, por Pablo Buitrago. Leon, 1847.

Documentos Interesantes sobre el Atentado Cometido por algunos Ingleses residentes en Bluefields, usurpando con mano armada el Puerto de San Juan del Norte, etc. San Salvador, 1848.

Manifesto que el Supremo Gobierno del Estado de Nicaragua hace á los Gobiernos de América, sobre el Tratado celebrado con el Comandante Ingles Sr. Granville Loch, etc. Por José Guerrero, Presidente, 1848.

Wild Life in the Interior of Central America, by George Byam. London, 1849

Coup D'Œil rapide sur la Republique de Costa Rica, par F. M. (Felipe Molina). Paris, 1849.

Panama, Nicaragua, and Tehuantepec; or, Considerations on the Question of Communication between the Atlantic and Pacific Oceans. By Captain W. B. Liot. London, 1849.

Auswanderung und Colonisation im Interesse des deutschen Handels. Der Freistaat Nicaragua und seine Wichtigkeit fur den Welthandel, etc., etc. Von A. von Bülow. Berlin, 1849.

The Gospel in Central America, etc., by Frederick Crowe. London, 1850.

A Statistical Account and Description of the Island of Roatan, by Commander R. C. Mitchell, R.N. United Service Magazine, 1850.

Central America, describing each of the states of Guatemala, Honduras, San Salvador, Nicaragua, Costa Rica, etc. By John Baily, Esq., R.M. London, 1850.

The Mosquito Question, etc., by E. G. Squier. American Whig Review (New York), February and March, 1850.

The Great Ship-canal Question, etc., by E. G. Squier. American Whig Review, November, 1850.

Volcanoes of Central America, and the Geographical and Topographical Features of Nicaragua, etc.: an address before the "American Association for the Advancement of Science," proceedings of Tenth Annual Meeting, 1850.

Tigre Island and Central America, Executive Document No. 75, First Session of Thirty-first Congress. Published by order of the House of Representatives (1850).

Extracto de una Relacion sobre el Antiguo Reyno de Guatemala, hecha por el Ingeniero Don Luis Diaz Navarro, en 1745. Guatemala, 1850.

Enquête sur la Colonie de Santo Tomas, par Blondeel van Cuelebrouk, avec Cartes. Bruxelles, 1850.

Rapport sur la Situation de la Colonie de Santo Tomas, par M. Cloquet. Bruxelles, 1850.

Souvenirs de l'Amerique Centrale, par H. de T. d'Arlach. Paris, 1850.

Canal from Lake Nicaragua, along the Rio Sapoa, to Salinas, by A. S. Oersted, of Copenhagen. Journal of the Royal Geographical Society of London, vol. xxi. (1851), p. 96–99.

Centro-Amerika, nach gegenwartigen, etc., etc., von C. F. Reichardt. Braunschweig, 1851.

Bosquejo de la Republica de Costa Rica, etc., por Felipe Molina. New York, 1851.

Dispatches of E. G. Squier, United States Chargé d'Affaires, concerning the difficulties between Great Britain and San Salvador. Published by order of the Senate of the United States, Executive Document No. 43, Second Session of Thirty-first Congress (1851).

Report of the Survey of a Route for the proposed Nicaragua Ship-canal, from San Juan del Norte on the Atlantic, to Brito on the Pacific. By O. W. Childs, C. E. New York, 1852.

Central America and the Crampton and Webster Project, by E. G. Squier. New York Democratic Review, November, 1852.

The Islands in the Bay of Honduras; their seizure and organization as a British Colony. By E. G. Squier. Democratic Review, December, 1852.

Correspondence relative to the claims of Great Britain on the Mosquito Coast, and in the Territories of Honduras or Yucatan, Executive Document No. 27, Second Session of Thirty-second Congress (1853).

Documentos Relativos á la Cuestion Mosquitos, etc., por Don Francisco Castillon. San Salvador, 1852.

Nicaragua: its People, Scenery, Monuments, and the proposed Inter-oceanic Canal, with numerous original Maps and Illustrations. By E. G. Squier, etc., etc. 2 vols. New York, 1852.

Memorias para la Historia del Antiguo Reyno de Guatemala, redactadas por el Ilmo. Señor Dr. D. Francisco de Paula Garcia Pelaez, Arzobispo, etc. 3 vols. Guatemala, 1852.

Report of Committee of Foreign Relations of the Senate of the United States on the Establishment of the Islands of Roatan, Bonacca, etc., as a British Colony, presented by the Honorable J. M. Mason. Committee Report No. 407, Second Session of Thirty-second Congress (1853).

Correspondence between Mr. Marcy, Secretary of State, and Mr. Crampton, British Minister, relative to the Treaty of Washington of July 5, 1850, Executive Document No. 13, First Session of Thirty-third Congress (1853).

Wanderbilder aus Central-Amerika, etc., von Wilhelm Heine. Leipzig, 1853.

Farther Considerations on the Great Isthmus of Central America, by Captain Robert Fitzroy, R.N. Journal of the Royal Geographical Society of London, vol. xxiii. (1853), p. 171–191.

Nicaragua, nach eigner Anschauung im Jahre, 1852, etc., von C. F. Reichardt. Braunschweig, 1854.

Waikna; or, Adventures on the Mosquito Shore, by Samuel A. Bard. New York, 1855.

INDEX.

A.

B.

C.

F.

G.

H.

www.ingramcontent.com/pod-product-compliance
Lightning Source LLC
LaVergne TN
LVHW011159110826
845150LV00006B/1260

* 9 7 8 1 4 2 5 5 4 5 6 5 9 *